Anthropological Society of Washington

Discourse and the Social Life of Meaning

Edited by Phyllis Pease Chock and
June R. Wyman

Smithsonian Institution Press
Washington, D.C., and London, 1986

The Smithsonian Institution Press pub-
lishes a series of significant volumes in anthropology edited by the Anthropological Society of Washington. The Society, the oldest continuously functioning
anthropological association in the United
States, was founded at the Smithsonian Institution in 1879. Each volume in the
series collects essays by leading scholars on
aspects of a central topic, originating in a.
program of lectures sponsored by the Society.

Library of Congress Cataloging in
Publication Data

Discourse and the social life of meaning.

(Anthropological Society of Washington
series)
Contents: Post-modern anthropology /
Stephen A. Tyler — The reconstruction of
ethnography / Paul Stoller — Of defini-
tions and boundaries / Michael Herzfeld
— [etc.]
    1. Ethnology—Congresses. 2.
Ethnophilosophy—Congresses. 3. Dis-
course analysis—Congresses.
I. Chock, Phyllis Pease, 1941-   . II.
Wyman, June R. III. Title. IV. Series.
GN302.D57 1986   306   86-42577
ISBN 0-87474-308-7

⊗ The paper used in this publication
meets the minimum requirements of the
American National Standard for
Permanence of Paper for Printed Library
Materials Z39.48–1984.

Editor, Duke Johns

Contents

Introduction: Discourse and the Social Life of Meaning

Phyllis Pease Chock and June R. Wyman
Catholic University of America

The papers in this anthology were prepared for the 1983-84 program of the Anthropological Society of Washington. The intent of that program was two-fold. The first objective was to assemble a set of papers addressing current issues in cultural analysis—and by doing so, to make these ideas available to a wider audience. Although cultural analysis is now practiced by numerous scholars in both America and Europe, the theoretical and methodological advances they are making have not been easily accessible to other anthropologists. The topics with which cultural analysis deals are of potential interest to many outside the immediate circle of those who practice its methods, and they deserve a wider hearing.

A second intention, related to the first, was to cover a diversity of topics of interest to a wide portion of the ASW membership. The two aims proved, in fact, to complement each other. The range of materials the authors published in this volume have used, and their varied approaches to these materials, allowed us to see both some effects of radical culture theories—in critiques of the ends and methods of anthropology—and some positive directions the cultural analyses growing out of these critiques have taken.

Culture Theory and Cultural Analysis

Radical culture theories[1] take meanings to shape and reproduce social forces, forms, and contradictions. Meanings, therefore, are not residues of social forces; they are truly social. They are at work in economic and productive processes, in archives of family and communal talk, in settings of communication and in what talk is about both at the center and on the periphery of society. They fuel the engines of everyday activities.

Conceptually, none of these assertions is new. Anthropological conceptions increasingly take them as grounds for what gets said, not as epiphenomena, and the papers in this volume take them as grounds without which none of their arguments could be built. What is special about this collection is the way each author takes the workings of social meanings as the object of study. The diverse routes each takes are informative in their diversity. What these authors contend is needed—and what we, the editors, urge should be emulated—are efforts to engage particular social meanings. Particular meanings, we expect, require particular engagements.

Most cultural analysis today is undertaken with ad hoc assemblages of ideas and techniques. The papers here suggest that it is best to make ad hoc engagements contingent on the event of encounters with particular social meanings. Certainly, formulaic manipulations of "data" must be jettisoned, along with other conceptual baggage that the task of rendering social meanings cannot bear. Conceits of language and reporting, Tyler and Stoller argue, impede cultural analysis. Each author in this volume proceeds cautiously on matters of language and method, devising ways of saying and showing (as Tyler puts it) that respect the particular social meanings he or she seeks to engage.

We will return to each author's particular engagements, but first we should address the issues stemming from a theoretical choice. That is, if we take discourse as our principal avenue to social meanings, we encounter two sets of conceptual and methodological problems. The first has to do with the discourse of anthropology. The "post-modern" anthropology that Tyler conjures requires that we identify and rid anthropology of the accumulated effects of speaking about an abstracted "Language" in its own discourse, and then turn our attentions to the second set of problems: how to engage social meanings in indigenous discourses.

The Discourse of Anthropology

"Language" sets many traps for anthropological projects. One of the most bothersome is representation, because, Tyler argues, representation breaks the signifier-signified bond. Language intimates—falsely—that forms exist outside content. These forms, language implies, point from appearances to something behind them—their contents, or meanings. Particular forms—signs and symbols among them—continue to be dislodged by the very anthropological practices, including "symbolic anthropology" and sundry experiments with ethnography, that are used to investigate the bond. Tyler urges a return to the act of "saying" for both object and method.

"Language" as a concept reifies speech. Tyler's paper maps the history of this reification in philosophical discourse as a veritable *mythologique* of representation. The map shows how analytic discourse is embedded in a theory of the economy of forms supplied by language. These metaphors of written discourse have insinuated themselves into anthropological thought. They replicate themselves in diverse modalities that align our thought about the world. They afford us, for instance, the subject/object distinction upon which rest both mechanistic conceptions of societies and the language used to render them.

Tyler writes that a "post-modern" anthropology would return the mutuality of speech, writing, and thought. To focus on "saying" demands that anthropology shed the ideological encumbrances it acquired with "Language." But experiments with writing do not suffice by themselves. To let ethnography simply imitate speech is to use forms to experiment with content.

Stoller, too, indicts the anthropological *episteme* for its effects on anthropological discourse. Since anthropology seeks reality behind appearances—unity behind diversity—its ends, and hence language and theory, are reductive and universalizing. This shortcoming holds true no matter what method or immediate ends an analysis fastens upon. Whether one considers Lévi-Strauss or Malinowski, Radcliffe-Brown or even theories specifically of ethnography, Stoller argues, the effects of the *episteme* are the same: anthropology as an inquiry places theory and its comparative ends above depictions of the mutuality of human conversations. This privilege is concretized in anthropological writing as a disembodied methodological voice.

The sources of Language's legitimacy are many. Another approach to legitimizing institutions, and the languages they create and justify, is proposed in Herzfeld's paper. He suggests that the cycle of mutual enhancement played out by states and languages bears inspection, and he invokes Vico to set the stage for this argument. Herzfeld argues that a state or nation creates its own ideological origins in a reduced language that purports to report only what is natural and outside itself. The illusion of literality reigns, a claim of this privileged language. Social categories in particular are made to seem "natural" and without social origins. Ideological language disguises the mutuality between form and content, words and their social grounds, meaning and context, that Herzfeld recounts from local discourses. "People," as opposed to the state, "know" that speech is not independent of their speaking ("saying," for Tyler). Their speaking is figurative, not literal; shifting, not constant; context-bound, not natural.

Perin attacks the language of anthropological debates concerning the ambiguous and the marginal on different grounds. Theoretical discussions in functional terms of "survival" and "adaptation," or cognitive and communication terms of "dissonance" and "overload," she argues, proceed as though the problems of "-isms"—like racism, sexism, ethnocentrism, ageism, and other social forces with horrifying consequences—were as flat and morally neutral as the language of utility or logic. She appeals for examination of the "mutual entailments" of meanings and neurophysiological fear, both by anthropologists and biologists. Perin offers one reading of the resulting "biology of meaning." The brain has a limited "capacity to integrate ambiguity, discrepancy, and novelty above some threshold"; it relies "wholly upon meanings." Meanings, she suggests, produce and reproduce not only social contradictions but biological fear.

Given these problems of Language, is there then an alternative or "post-modern" anthropology? Stoller proposes that we consider recent experiments in ethnographic and linguistic reporting. Haj Ross, with his example from "human" (as opposed to scientific) linguistics, provides a stream-of-thought poem as a statement on human linguistics. Yet Ross's work is not so much an experiment in itself as an ironic commentary on the conventions of social science writing.

Tyler argues against experimenting with form—for to do so is to separate form from content, the saying from the showing, what represents from what is represented. New forms of representational constraints, Tyler argues, do not address the real problem, which is representation itself—the separation of words and "things," of that which signifies from that which is signified. For an anthropology of discourse, the goal should be to reunite what is not separate in speech, what is pulled apart by the very act of writing, which introduces fragments of one discourse into another.

Is the implication that we must give up writing altogether? Maybe so, says Tyler—but perhaps there are ways of bringing writing closer to speech. One response to Tyler's query is to treat discourse as texts "written" by the culture, and the analyst as a reader or translator of these texts (cf. Marcus and Cushman 1982:43–44). Context, the unsaid, is then filled in by describing, in varying degrees of thickness, the parts of the unsaid that are taken to contribute to the meaning of the discourse-as-text.

Texts are "set up" for interpretation by abstracting them from their social context and constructing a reading of what they may have, or must have, meant to the participants. In such treatments, the anthropologist can no longer be considered the authority on his or her objects. An ambiguous and multi-vocal world demands an interpreter, a translator, a reader or chronicler to replace the realist and the monophonic voice that spoke in ethnographic realism (Clifford 1983).

Such is the approach taken by Chock and Goldstein, who single out chunks of native discourses—comments on ethnic stereotypes (Chock) and stories about magical conversions (Goldstein). Both focus on intertextuality as an interpretive device, moving back and forth between sets of texts to fill in the unsaid with accounts of what each text suggests of the others. Goldstein also fills in, in traditional realist style, with descriptions of setting and of cultural assumptions about the nature of women and group boundaries.

Like Chock, Anderson treats the genesis (Chock) or "autogenesis" (Anderson) of ethnic or national identities via their intertextualities. But he approaches it from a further remove; he gives us no chunks of discourse, but rather examines the authority of Afghan Muslims' origin stories in terms of what they connect. Herzfeld also writes at this remove, from text to intertextual context. Anderson argues that this intertextual distance is obscured by confounding the status that texts have for analysts with the status they have in their own settings, as parts of larger discourses and as commentaries on their settings.

Perin uses another form of intertextuality: in a "logic of relatives," terms contextualize themselves. Their trailing connections—their entailments—extend beyond the present instance, and frame it with the embedded collective representations she calls "predicates." Stories also figure here; Perin recounts, for example, Agassiz's telling of his experiences with black Americans. His narrative of horror was reproduced both in his public racist rhetoric and in his biological practice of taxonomic splitting.

It has not been common anthropological practice to single out monologic native discourses as texts, as Chock, Goldstein, and Perin do, but rather to embed fragments of dialogue in the ethnographer's field-notes style of narrative. Stoller's excerpt from his own work, presented in dialogical form as an exchange between ethnographer and Songhay informant, goes one step further. The result is an illustration, more like a novel than ethnography, that reminds us of Tyler's observation that writing that imitates speech is still writing: "a text masquerading as a dialogue, a mere monologue about a dialogue," as he has called it elsewhere (Tyler 1982:251). Tyler's point is that if we simply report speech in a conventional, turn-taking, dialogical model, we are still reporting only the said, not the unsaid. And if it is the said and the unsaid together that create meaning (Tyler 1978), how do we show the unsaid?

Peacock's approach to the problem of reporting ethnography is to cast the report in the frames afforded by native discourses. In the Primitive Baptist Appalachian church he has studied, events such as the emergence of factions around two elders are talked about in extempore sermons, in theological debates, and in ostensible procedures for electing officers, as elements of an elder's spiritual autobiography. "Translation" provides one such Biblical frame for human events. Peacock thus uses the conventions of native discourses as reporting devices. This novelistic style closely approximates the narrative of older works, mentioned by Stoller, that today hold the status of classics—including *We, The Tikopia* and *Argonauts of the Western Pacific*.

Still other anthropologists move further from writing, invoking visual forms to recreate the saying and the showing. Stephens exploits Sami drum pictures to locate and reproduce social meanings; meanings, she reminds us, are particularly engaged in the visual as much as in the verbal. And Tyler, heeding his own advice, turns to "thought pictures" to accomplish his own saying/showing within the limits of writing.

Tyler's challenge to ethnographic writing remains a critique of representation, and Stoller's more specific complaints remind us of the difficulties of our constructive tasks and the unspoken premises of our legitimating discourses.

Cultural Analysis

Clifford (1983: 119) observes that current experiments in ethnographic writing enlist ad hoc elements of theory into a "tool kit" (à la Deleuze and Foucault); this metaphor is also an apt description for the state of cultural analysis. Cultural analysis can more easily be characterized by what it tries not to do than by what it achieves. Gone are methods that mimic scientific inquiry and its formalist presumptions, even though these may be enlisted in the pursuit of ethnography (Tyler 1978 and infra; Stoller, infra). Neither does cultural analysis posit generic (or genetic) relationships among social meanings (Needham 1975). It treats them as empirically problematic.

Cultural analysis employs diverse means in its projects. Anderson's paper most explicitly advocates a phenomenological engagement of meanings by "assemblying" indigenous texts that reside, side by side, in particular settings, and by avoiding prejudgments of both relations among texts and among texts and social forms. But other than agreeing that native discourses—the ways people talk—afford entrée into cultural orders, the authors of these papers take widely differing tacks in analysis. Each chooses an array of means to handle particular cultural materials.

One possibility is to examine the workings of narrowly linguistic markers. Herzfeld explores the manipulations and reifications of grammar and vocabulary wrought by nationalist rhetorics. His object is to analyze the semantic and rhetorical operations of the state, neither of which the state can permit to be seen at work. In place of semantic shifters, the state constructs paradigmatic sets out of social ("ethnic") categories. The state's language implies falsely that such categories are built of one-dimensional contrasts.

Perin's cultural accounts of avoidance and stigmatization in American life begin at the points where meaning systems hinge on what they make discrepant or ambiguous. She traces their "relatives" through "chains of metaphors, implications, associations, and entailments," leading to the embedded "predicates" of social life. Signs are read assembled, not individually, in "words as spoken and deeds as done," not free of context.

Structural methods are used only pragmatically in cultural analysis, to accomplish limited analytical tasks. Since structuralisms assume formal and genetic relationships within sets of cultural phenomena—myths or elementary units of kinship, for example (Lévi-Strauss 1963)—they violate the precepts of cultural analysis by failing to engage the particularities of meanings and social forms. Cultural analysis assembles sets or classes of stories, roughly on the basis of seemingly uniform properties as a kind of "first sort," but thereafter the stories are read only within sets and between sets where their assembled similarities (their "family resemblances," which are the data of cultural analysis) are apparent (Chock, infra). Goldstein's, Anderson's, and Chock's stories and Stephens's designs are amassed and treated together as sets, on the grounds that their intertextualities are the contextualizing data previously reported as asides in ethnographic narratives.

Devices of storytelling are also used to furnish clues to stories' social import. Stories may have several projects—to reproduce social forms, to mystify, to parody, to reconstruct. The tropes that figure relationships in metaphor, metonym, or irony, for example, within and between texts accomplish these ends through their distinctive operations, whether in story or design. Identifying the pattern of operations, then, becomes a key analytical task. Is it one, for instance, of replication, decomposition, or reversal, as figured by these three tropes, respectively?

Goldstein's and Chock's stories and Peacock's autobiographical fragments from the two preachers fall under the rubric of "magical narratives" (Jameson 1981), those modern-day myths that seemingly resolve irreconcilable ideological and social contradictions. A cultural analysis must attend to characterization and to the authentication of narrators as two such devices that put stories to work on social forms. Anderson points out some ways these stories solemnize both narrating subjects and objectivated characterization by collapsing their distinctions.

The Cultural Operations of Collective Representations

Goldstein's and Chock's papers suggest that certain forms of talk about women in complex societies with power differentials draw gender, religion, and ethnicity into mutable "galaxies" (Schneider 1976) of social meanings that are convertible one into the other. In family and communal stories, women—in the Iranian Jewish case, insiders, and in the Greek-American case, outsiders—are rhetorical devices used to generate and explicate complex sets of notions about social boundaries. The two sets of notions, though, are quite different. The Iranian Jewish stories employ women characters to talk about social relationships and chasms between minority and majority groups. The stories depict the dominant group as conferring, however grudgingly, moral or religious esteem upon the minority. The Greek-American stories, on the other hand, are part of a conversation begun outside the local settings where they are told. The discourse is predominantly American, not Greek, and though ostensibly it confers honor on "Greek" practices, it ironically reduces them to markers and directs their operations toward individual identities and away from communal identities.

Peacock's paper suggests that Biblical discourse operates in the composition of the autobiographies of the two Primitive Baptist preachers and thence into the quarreling factions that grew up around them. Peacock uses these two men's autobiographies as literary devices, much as they do themselves, meeting Tyler's admonition. Assurance that one's own spiritual experiences "translate" the earthly workings of an otherwise unknowable Deity permits one to "translate" them further in setting social forces to work.

In Anderson's paper accounts of cultural genesis, the tales of Qais, first frame themselves; nothing is prior. As they unfold in retellings, they also frame social reproduction. Patrilineal units of production and reproduction—fathers, sons, and land—emerge together and in each generation replicate relations in "conversations" begun with the Qais stories. Unlike the Iranian Jewish and Greek-American stories, which convert and transform one medium into another (women to outsiders and insiders, respectively) and use discourse to constitute and operate upon unequal social boundaries, the Qais story operates in a medium of purported equivalences to reproduce ever more specific copies of itself—in the face of the tendencies of those relations to dissolve over priorities they cannot resolve.

The traditional Sami cultural operations in Stephens's analysis resemble the Afghan case. Stephens uses shamans' drum designs instead of stories to explicate the workings of social meanings in everyday Sami life. There, the systems of gender meanings create and reproduce the order of the material world and the productive order. In the traditional period the feminine gender, like the Qais stories of the Pathans, sustains and reproduces the world; the masculine gender works within this world and decomposes it into differentiated parts, which are reintegrated in turn by the tropes of feminine gender. Represented pictorially, these "cosmic maps" (Stephens, infra, Figure 2) are replicated in annual migration cycles and state an Ego's experience of the *siida*, the traditional herding unit. Social transformations are introduced historically in the pastoral period by discourses from the Scandinavian order outside Sami society. These externally originating conversations privilege masculine meanings and effect permanent social divisions and inequalities in Sami society that mirror the outside. At the same time the new masculine dominance in Sami society is an artifact of its subordination to a dominant power from the outside.

Perin reminds us that social meanings generate deep and often socially and individually painful chasms. Ideologies and cosmologies, she writes, "cause as much 'strain' as they relieve." She explores how the socially marginal is created by meanings and how meanings effect their costs—in fear and in the social penalties of stigma, avoidance, and worse—in three American cases: xenophobic readings of neighbors and strangers; racism; and stigmatization of "imperfect" people. The thresholds of both the fear and the social penalties, she suggests, are set by meaning systems, the one in the brain and the other in social processes—a constellation of thought and conduct.

Herzfeld, also considering the efficacy of forms of talk in creating social forms, describes how political dominance, this time by the state, is engendered by the mutual enhancements of the state and its chosen discourses. These transformations occur through the state's fostering the appearance that talk concerns matters outside itself that are more real than itself. The shifting, figurative local ways of talking are captured by the univocal state and the illusion of a world of flat surfaces that nourishes it.

This review of the cultural operations of collective representations in stories, designs, predicates, and statist language would not be complete without a reprise of Tyler's and Stoller's warnings about anthropology's own discourses. The stories embedded in anthropological reports—ethnographies particularly, but also, as Stoller reminds us, in journal articles—propel anthropological inquiry. They are transubstantiated into objects by a matrix of framing jargon. Together, the jargon and the stories mis-serve our aim to measure and overcome the distance between ourselves and others.

On another front, what Tyler records are some of the "just-so" stories about the basic metaphors that reproduce themselves in anthropological theory and method. These stories figure as collective representations in the discipline. Varenne has recently observed that one of these, "the individual," found also as collections of "faculties" in Tyler's Thought Picture 2 and the "corporal" *topoi* in Thought Picture 5, act as powerful operators in anthropological "conversations"

(Varenne 1984) in the United States. Ideological ideas about the priority of "the individual" have transformed many sociological texts, he argues, including texts of the radical culture theories we treat here, into reductive and quasi-psychological stories.

The Anthropology of Religion

If gender, religion, and ethnicity are mutual and mutable galaxies of social meanings in the stories of Iranian Jews (Goldstein) and Greek Americans (Chock), what of the isolation, for analysis, of bounded domains of meaning like ethnicity, politics, economics, and religion? In the stories reported by Chock and Goldstein, religion is not a separable set of symbols but part of a language for talking around, and about, social boundaries and their reflexes in individual identities. Subordinated to larger projects of explicating social meanings, representation cannot be dislodged from those broader conversations; but collective representations transcend categories of meaning bound to institutions, and so confound analytical subordination to the institutions they explicate. As Schneider (1976) points out in distinguishing cultural units from norms, their organization is of a different order of reality.

Implicit in such treatments is a radical critique of the "anthropology of religion." In older anthropological conversations, religion was usually identified functionally as the traditional repository of meaning, a cultural petri dish in which society's ultimate meanings and values were grown and operated on, in splendid isolation from less "meaning-full" cultural arenas. In other, Durkheimian discourses, religion was a shadow, a reflection or voice of the "real"—social structure and social forces. Either way, religion was atomized, whether as belief system par excellence or as mirror of the real stuff "on the ground." The same atomization bedevils a more contemporary statement that treats religion as a "cultural system" set apart from social systems in a Parsonian model of society (Geertz 1966). According to this mechanical notion, religious systems should first be understood as sets of symbols and meanings, then reconnected to social and psychological processes (Geertz 1973:125). The two systems interact, but are analytically separable.

At the bottom of all this lurks the problem of representation identified by Tyler. When pulled apart from other social discourses and treated as a separate "belief system" or "cultural system," religion must be reconnected to other parts of social life that it represents or is a representation of—something outside of itself that is of a different order. Such dualisms, however, split what are parts of the same discourse, for in the construction of social meanings religion is neither more symbolic nor less "real" than other discourses. The theoretical issue is whether they can be grasped as phenomena of the same order.

This issue is abundantly clear in the case of the Sami (Stephens, infra), whose apparent lack of an abstracted ideology has led some observers to conclude that they had no religion. But the Sami challenge us to think in new ways about how religious and other symbolic structures relate to social and material practice. In the Sami case, Stephens argues, "religion" as a category makes no sense in native terms. Ritual and the relation between humans and gods were not part of some separate domain of belief and practice, but were embedded in a "totalizing cultural logic" pivoting on the male/female dichotomy.

Representation also lies behind the particular issue from which Anderson departs: the notion of "great" and "little" traditions in Islam. This view proposes that local expressions of religion are skewed or diluted particularizations of some prior and purer (therefore more "real") scheme of interpretation. Like Herzfeld's statist ideologies, this analytic fiction reifies and concretizes a discourse that is as context-sensitive as the local "derivatives" that it supposedly generates. Anderson argues that the differences labeled "great" and "little" reflect not different discourses, but different social roles within the same community of discourse. Among Afghan Muslims, the Quranic text and formal exegeses of Islam are played out in the same settings as local traditions. Those settings pose the problematic to which the exegetical texts are responses. The analyst's task is to bring these settings into focus, to show how the production and transmission of meaning proceeds in particular settings—not to specify some discourse of a different order and award it privileged status. Our investigation of the production of social meanings, Anderson says, is not well served by specious dualisms that carve up what is the same discourse.

Anderson finds the "solid frame that encloses all thought" in the encompassing story among Afghan Muslims by arguing that nothing is prior to it. Not so in the American settings described by Chock and Peacock. Here, religion is almost peripheral, a code for talking about questions of individual identity and social boundaries, which is what is problematic in those settings. This is so even in Peacock's paper, ostensibly "about" religion in an American setting. Disputes between Primitive Baptist elders are framed as doctrinal issues that confer significance on individual autonomy and collective authority. The disputes are about consensus and dissensus, and ultimately, Peacock notes, about the relation between private and collective meanings. Among Greek Americans, Chock tells us, Greek Orthodoxy is reduced to an optional marker of individual identity—serving the church is no longer part of collective life but rather an instrument for individual achievement.

Goldstein's Iranian Jewish stories of magical conversion also subordinate religiosity to a different agenda. "Muslim" and "Jew" are categories in a discourse about social boundaries between a dominant and a minority group. Near-conversion, a religious question insofar as it concerns belief and practice, is a metaphor for the permeability of those boundaries. The stories evoke an imagined world in which crossing over remains an ever-present possibility and the challenge is to prevent it. Here, religion is coterminous with community and cannot be factored out of a discourse about community.

The papers in this volume challenge us to dispense with the notion that "religion" is some isolable cultural category or system. Indeed, Stephens suggests jettisoning the category "religion" altogether in favor of an approach that treats discourse as the unit of analysis. Religious meanings are not truly separable from other meanings—all enter the same project, the construction of social meanings, in the same way that "saying," in Tyler's words, is a unified process. Analyses are ill served by decomposing the natural semiotic of sender/receiver into another one of signifier/signified.[2] These papers reinstate that unity, which enables cultural analysis rather than the mere analysis of culture.

A Reader's Guide

As noted at the beginning of this essay, the papers in this anthology chart the directions taken by a cultural analysis that has emerged from critiques of anthropology's methods and ends. Our contributors follow three particular directions, which we summarize here to orient the reader.

In the first section of the book, Tyler and Stoller set the stage—and introduce the arguments implicit in what follows—with their reflections on history and form in ethnographic analysis. Together their papers explore the epistemological bases of anthropology, contrasting the older philosophy of ethnography with a discourse-centered approach that aims to preserve the unity of meaning and social life, of saying and doing. While Tyler makes his point with a sweeping review of the notion of representation in Western thought, Stoller fashions his critique with his own field data. Yet both converge on a fundamental challenge to the buried assumptions of ethnographic analysis. Although their prescriptions for change differ in particulars, both writers challenge us to reestablish the unity of the word and the world, the primacy of social meanings, in ethnography—to practice a truly cultural analysis.

Following up on these ideas, the two papers in the second section launch a closer examination of how the Western discourses that have shaped ethnographic analysis operate to define the "other." Perin, drawing her cases from American social thought, proposes that American ways of defining the other—expressed in hostility, disparagement, avoidance, and stigma—serve as strategies for keeping social meanings intact, and have neurophysiological bases. Looking at a different Western discourse, Herzfeld examines the language of nationalism and ethnic identity in Greek nationalist rhetoric. He argues that Western statist ideologies invest nationhood with substance, permanence, and opacity grounded in "nature"; whereas in local discourses social categories are relative, shifting, and context-dependent.

The concluding section encompasses a wide-ranging examination of local discourses on identity and change. Like Herzfeld and Perin, these authors treat the constitution of social categories, but they do so in more particular social contexts. They deal with local problems of cultural genesis: to imagine, create, replicate, transform, or abolish social forms. Peacock, Goldstein, and Anderson begin with stories that use religious talk to constitute a group identity and its permutations in American, Iranian, and Afghan settings, respectively. Their papers were conjoined in a particular local setting, the ASW's annual symposium of January 1984. Chock's paper explores an American discourse about women and Greek-American identity. Stephens examines how local discourses on identity have changed in different historical contexts among Sami Lapps.

The papers in this last section take up the challenge issued by Tyler and Stoller: to reunify the saying and the showing—meaning and social life—in analyses of socially created meanings and meaning-created social forms.

Notes

1. Radical culture theories (cf. Geertz 1973; Schneider 1976; Sahlins 1976) take meaning as prior to social and material practice. They hold that each culture must be understood in terms of its own system of meaning and action. Systems of meaning symbolically constitute and mediate both beliefs about the world and practice in the world, as well as conditions and circumstances usually seen as objective, material, or outside "culture." Radical culture theories deny the difference between subjective and objective conditions, arguing that there is no object in a world that is not symbolically constituted.

The most "radical" of these theories, developed by Schneider (1976), took culture to be an autonomous domain of meaning that could be analytically distinguished and treated apart from social context. Although today most practitioners of cultural analysis would agree that meaning does have a social life, Schneider's ideas remain, along with the others cited above, an enabling theory for those who take meaning to be the fuel, not the exhaust, of the social engine. Today radical culture theories may reject the autonomy of meaning—but they do not reject its primacy.

2. Jon Anderson furnished this concluding remark, as well as a critical reading of the text with many helpful comments and criticisms.

References Cited

Clifford, James
   1983   On Ethnographic Authority. Representations 1(2):118–146.

Geertz, Clifford
   1966   Religion as a Cultural System. In Anthropological Approaches to the Study of Religion. M. Banton, ed. pp. 1–46. London: Tavistock.
   1973   The Interpretation of Cultures. New York: Basic Books.

Jameson, Fredric
   1981   The Political Unconscious. Ithaca, N.Y.: Cornell University Press.

Lévi-Strauss, Claude
   1963   Structural Anthropology. New York: Basic Books.

Marcus, George, and Dick Cushman
   1982   Ethnographies as Texts. Annual Review of Anthropology 11:25–69.

Needham, Rodney
   1975   Polythetic Classification: Convergence and Consequence. Man 10:349–369.

Sahlins, Marshall
   1976   Culture and Practical Reason. Chicago: University of Chicago Press.

Schneider, David M.
   1976   Notes toward a Theory of Culture. In Meaning in Anthropology. K. Basso and H. Selby, eds. pp. 197–220. Albuquerque: University of New Mexico Press.

Tyler, Stephen A.
1978   The Said and the Unsaid. New York: Academic Press.
1982   Words for Deeds and the Doctrine of the Secret World: Testimony to a Chance Encounter Somewhere in the Indian Jungle. *In* Papers from the Parasession on Language and Behavior, Chicago Linguistic Society. pp. 249–274. Chicago: University of Chicago Press.

Varenne, Hervé
1984   Collective Representations in American Anthropological Conversations: Individual and Culture. Current Anthropology 25:281–291.

Post-Modern Anthropology

Stephen A. Tyler
Rice University

Post-modern anthropology is the study of man "talking."[1] Discourse is its object and its means. Discourse is at once a theoretical object and a practice, and it is this reflexivity between object and means that enables discourse, and that discourse creates. Discourse is the maker of the world, not its mirror. It represents the world only inasmuch as it is the world. The world is what we say it is, and what we speak of is the world. It is the "saying in which it comes to pass that world is made to appear" (Heidegger 1971:101).

Post-modern anthropology replaces the visual metaphor of the world as what we *see* with a verbal metaphor in which world and word are mutually implicated, neither having priority of origin nor ontic dominance (cf. Tyler 1986). Berkeley's *esse est percipi* becomes "to be is being spoken of." Post-modern anthropology rejects the priority of perception, and with it the idea that concepts are derived from "represented" sensory intuitions, that the intelligible is the sensible "re-signed." There is no movement from originary substance to derived "spirit," from thing to concept, from mind to material, or from the real to the less real. The mutuality of word, world, and mind is beyond time and space, located nowhere but found everywhere.

Seeing is always mediated by saying. Post-modern anthropology is thus the end of an illusion. It ends the separation of word and world created by writing and sustained by language-as-logos, that "univocal picture" projected in words from the standpoint of the all-seeing transcendental ego whose real message is that the world is a fable (cf. Nietzsche 1911:24; Derrida 1976:14).

In its positive aspect, post-modern anthropology returns the immanence of LANGUAGE[2] to the commonsense, plurivocal world of the speaking subject. In its negative aspect, post-modern anthropology seeks to incarnate the transcendental object called LANGUAGE, and to cast out that doxology of "signs" and "signification" which is the means of transcendence and false objectification.[3]

By returning to the immanence of language, post-modern anthropology aims to complete the revolution of consciousness begun in ancient Greece. The deconstruction of "things"—the object of perception—in the physical sciences, and the deconstruction of "selves"—the subject who perceives—in the social sciences are complete. The impudent moderns have stood Bacon on his head and left Descartes' *cogito* for dead. Their "thing" is only a trace of being in its moment of death, and their ego is a Leibnitzian infinity of perspectives on the becoming of the "thing" that never is, even in death. Their "thing" is impotent and cannot rise up as the single image of a dispersed mind.

Post-modern anthropology is both the fulfillment of that revolution and its nemesis, for it is that third, and final, stage of a revolution which destroys the means of revolution. This decomposition of things and selves was an accomplishment of textuality, that fetishization of language by writing that constituted things and selves as CONCEPTS (Nietzsche 1911:211). Both subject (self) and object (thing), knower and known, are mediated by LANGUAGE, which transcends, encompasses, and constitutes them. Thus the amaurosis of LANGUAGE, the means of that mediation, must be the final act in the decomposition of the commonsense world of words and things. It will also be the recreation of a commonsense world, for post-modern anthropology refuses that transit to absolute knowledge which establishes an identity between the subject and the object by means of LANGUAGE. It denies that:

"I speak of the world by means of language"

is identical to:

"LANGUAGE speaks of itself by means of itself,"

and declares that:

"The world is what we say it is"

does not mean:

"The world is all we say it is"

and asks:

"What sense can we make of a silent universe with no voice to speak the name of its silence?" (cf. Foucault 1965:xi)

This program is a denial of: (a) the absolute difference between signs and things, a denial that does not make an identity of signs and things; (b) the arbitrariness of the relation between signs and things that depends upon (a); and (c) the relation of speaking and thinking as an instance of (a) and (b). The consequence is yet another "no." Post-modern anthropology denies LANGUAGE and what its transcendence implies.[4] Specifically, it denies the five Platonic emanations:

(1) the transcendence of METHOD and the WILL to TRUTH;
(2) the transcendence of the SIGN in the substitution of appearances that enables REPRESENTATION and SIGNIFICATION;
(3) the transcendence of the TEXT as a transcendental OBJECT;
(4) the transcendence of the INTERPRETER as transcendental SUBJECT—the critic as oracle;
(5) the transcendence of FORM enabled by the separation of FORM and CONTENT;

and the four Plutonic mysteries:

(1) the myth of the text as cipher;
(2) the myth of appearance vs. reality;
(3) the metaphor of surface vs. depth, in which our deciphering "penetrates" the hymenal surface of the text, fathoming its underlying, real meaning, and reveling in the revelation of orgasmic mystery; and
(4) the myth of the unconscious.

Post-modern anthropology thus aims to demystify both Thoth and our chthonic connections. Only Platonic emanations one, two, and five are addressed here,[5] but first a brief account of transcendence and suppression (cf. Derrida 1972:75) follows. It is a history written after the end of history which is not a history, but an essay on metalepsis, on how the *logos* was always a *mythos* of

A Certain Picture of the World[6]

The story of this picture begins and ends in a commonsense duality that is the vehicle of metaphoric implicatures,[7] a family of founding symbols whose interconnections, maintained through time, have been the perduring problems of philosophy. Its source, if such it may be called, is the intersection of *mimesis* and *kinesis* and their metaphoric implicates:

mimesis	*kinesis*
representation	*ergon,* will
sameness, identity	difference
permanence	change
stasis	movement, activity
substance*	accidence**
real	derivatively real
noun	verb
space	time and telos
nonliving	living, *anima****
seeing	saying
writing	speech

Ens per se, the first Aristotelian category.

**Ens per accidence,* the remaining nine Aristotelian categories.

***Consisting of vegetable; animal (beings with sense, memory, and imagination); rational (beings with reason and judgment). From Aristotle, *Categoriae; De Anima.*

The persistence of these metaphors can be intuited from the metonymic substitutions that constituted different (but equivalent) understandings of mind and brain in Western speculation. Consider Thought Picture 1.

conscious, abstract	Aristotle	Reid	Peirce	McLean
	rational (reason, judgment)	rational (reason, conceptions)	cognition = triad = synechism (continuity) = symbol	neomammalian brain
	animal (imagination, memory, sense)	animal (perceptions, will)	volition = dyad = agapism (evolution, growth) = index	old mammalian brain
unconscious, concrete	vegetable	mechanical (sensations, instinct)	feeling = monad = tychism (chance) = icon	reptilian brain

Thought Picture 1 Metaphoric Equivalents of Aristotle's Categories of *Anima* (*kinesis*, action). With few exceptions, this triad has been the standard interpretation of man's essential character and, as in Peirce, the character of the macrocosm as well. These designations are largely self-explanatory. To them we could add, reading up: physical = mechanical, neural = organic, conceptual = mental. They are, in effect, the major tropic orders: metonymy, synecdochy, and metaphor (see Thought Picture 5), which chronicle the emergence of mind or spirit. They are metaphors of past, present, and future, of doing, seeing, and saying, and as such are also faculties of the emergent mind (see Thought Picture 2). (Based on Reid 1795:543–552; Peirce 1932 (Vol. 1): 148–180, (Vol. 2): 56–60, 134–173; McLean 1973.)

Anima distinctions translate directly into Peirce's *semiosis*, becoming the means of representation—iconic signs, indexical signs, and symbols. They symbolize the dominance of *mimesis* over *kinesis*, for the categories of representation become the means of *mimesis*. *Mimesis* is also achieved through sensorimotor modalities. Within each mode is movement from the sensible to the intelligible, from concrete to abstract. These modes are "saying" (thought), "seeing" (representation), and "doing" (will, work), or "words," "things," and "deeds," whose permutable combinations constitute the realm of semantics in the relations: "words and words" (sense); "words and things" (reference); and "words and deeds" (pragmatics).[8]

These are also the means of prudence (judgments based on past, present, and future) and are equivalent to the Augustinian faculties: *intellectus* (saying); *memoria* (seeing); and *voluntas* (doing). Moreover, they are the metaphoric equivalents of modern divisions of the cerebral cortex into associative, sensory, and motor areas. The three modes are, of course, metaphors of present, past, and future, respectively; of time, space, and movement as categories of intuition; of subject, object, and verb as grammatical categories of the understanding; and of *ethos, eidos,* and *pathos* as rhetorical categories. The latter suggests they also correspond to the basic divisions of *logoi*—aesthetics, science, and politics. These are realized synecdochically in poetry, philosophy, and rhetoric as forms of discourse characterized by the modes: tropic, logic, and dialectic; and the functions: evocation, description, and provocation; which have as their object: value, fact (truth), and opinion. These are the metaphoric equivalents of the sensory modes. These metaphoric connections are illustrated in Thought Picture 2.

The intersection of these two families of metaphors (*kinesis* as manner of signification and *mimesis* as mode of representation) constitute an

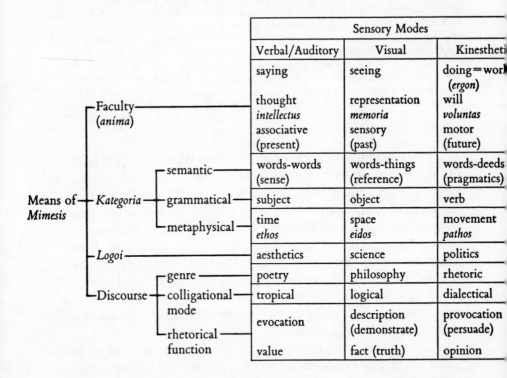

			Sensory Modes		
			Verbal/Auditory	Visual	Kinestheti
	Faculty (*anima*)		saying	seeing	doing = worl (*ergon*)
			thought *intellectus* associative (present)	representation *memoria* sensory (past)	will *voluntas* motor (future)
Means of Mimesis	*Kategoria*	semantic	words-words (sense)	words-things (reference)	words-deeds (pragmatics)
		grammatical	subject	object	verb
		metaphysical	time *ethos*	space *eidos*	movement *pathos*
	Logoi		aesthetics	science	politics
	Discourse	genre	poetry	philosophy	rhetoric
		colligational mode	tropical	logical	dialectical
		rhetorical function	evocation value	description (demonstrate) fact (truth)	provocation (persuade) opinion

Thought Picture 2 Means of *Mimesis*. These are the metaphoric implicates of the three sensory modes. Note that "seeing" has no "voice" (evocation and provocation derive from *voce,* "voice"). Its rhetorical mode is given by writing, description (< *scribere* "to write") that "shows" (*de-monstrāre* "show, loom"). *Ethos* is the essential character of a people or work of art; *eidos,* a picture, image, phantasm, representation; *pathos,* what moves to action.

interlocking episteme, a paradigm of *semiosis,* as illustrated in Thought Picture 3.

But none of these metaphors is actually "foundational," even in Western discourse—not even *mimesis* and *kinesis.* They appear "inside" and "outside" of paradigms, signifying that they are sometimes means of other metaphors and sometimes metaphoric creations. They are sometimes "defining," sometimes "defined"; both what is understood and what the understanding makes. It is not that there are no foundational concepts, but rather that there are many of them. They are constantly shifting about from steeple to foundation and back again. They form new and different figural possibilities that have not so much an origin (as seems to be suggested by beginning my tale with Aristotle), but a more-or-less predictable cycle of permutations. One after the other, each pair is the principal character on a stage. Aristotle is only the central figure in the play that ends with Descartes. We see him, through the Renaissance, receding from center stage until he fetches up in the wings, quietly waiting for his turn to come round again. All welcome the Stagirite!

"Places on the stage" suggest what comes next in this history, namely the theater of *topoi,* those locations in memory of the words and things we want to speak and think about. *Topoi* are metaphorically connected with work, duty, and fundamental character. Things are stored in memory analogically, according to their character, as in a rebus; or relatively, according to the work they signify; according, in other words, to what will best evoke them when needed for speech and thought.[9] *Topoi,* and memory itself, are vast, interlocking, figurative orderings in which things are remembered not by what they are in themselves, nor by their direct resemblance to other things, but by what they are *for* and by arbitrary analogical circumstance.

Work (doing, *ergon*) is linked with character and duty because one is what one does, and one does what one must. So spoke the ancients. Work is first a symbolic value before it is a material value, and only by being the former can it be the latter. It is not so just as a signified, but also as a signifier pointing to the mode of signification that characterizes each kind of work.

Consider the world of antiquity and most of that world we choose to call "underdeveloped." They have, like us, two kinds of work: "real" work and "phony" work. But for them, unlike us, phony work is the privilege of the few, real work the condition of the many. What do I

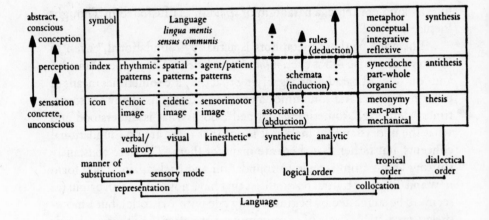

Thought Picture 3 The Intersection of *Mimesis* and *Kinesis*. This paradigm is the Cartesian product of Thought Pictures 1 and 2. It illustrates the modes of representation and collocation that define signs and sign functions. Thus, for example, perception is indexical, sensory specific, schematic, and part-whole. Schemata are analytic, "logical" means of collocation. This parallels the function of the antithesis in dialectical reason. The whole is a metaphor of the movement from sensation to perception. Language, or the *lingua mentis,* is as much outside the paradigm as in it, for it creates (re-creates?) the whole paradigm. The whole is thus a feature of language that produces language and that language produces.

*Includes kinesthesia and tactile.

**That is, how the sign substitutes its appearance for what it signifies.

mean by real and phony work? A simple distinction marks the difference: real workers "move" things, phony workers "move" no-thing except symbols. Between these two extremes lies a third kind of work, that done by those who "move" others as if they were things—the work of politicians, soldiers, and bureaucrats. In other words, workers are classified by the signs that characterize their work. Thus, real work : iconic :: phony work : symbolic :: political work : indexical. We may think of the contrast between these other worlds and ours by means of population pyramids, as in Thought Picture 4.

Beyond this realistic Aristotelian world of work are other pyramidal worlds. They are "the other of unity" (the Platonic world of oneness) and "the other of difference" (the Plutonic world of separation). The pyramids are arranged hierarchically, the Aristotelian in the

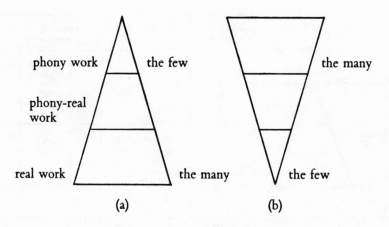

phony work — the few — the many

phony-real work

real work — the many — the few

(a)   (b)

Thought Picture 4 The Aristotelian Worlds of Work. (a) The population pyramid of the ancient world and of the underdeveloped world. (b) The population pyramid of the "developed" world. In our world most people do phony work. They manipulate symbols, not things. The underdeveloped world is the converse. The major work of phony workers is, of course, to justify the necessity of phony work and to reconcile phony-real workers and real workers with one another and to their relatively less fortunate forms of life. Each of these pyramids has a "dark twin" that is its opposite. For the underdeveloped world it is the dream of a future paradise—of which pyramid (b) is an approximation; and for the developed world it is a romanticized memory of the past—of which (a) is an approximation. The dreams and memories of these two worlds complement one another. They form a universe of interlocking fantasy as in the "star of Lakśmi":

middle, joined at its tip by the inverted tip of the Platonic and at its base by the inverted base of the Plutonic (see Thought Picture 5). Below the latter, joined to its inverted tip, is a fourth pyramid, the world of animals and dumb material. These are, of course, homologous with the four *Yugas* (periods) of the Hindu cosmic cycle, the "four ages of man" in Platonism, the "four emanations" of spirit in Zoroastrianism and the *Kabbalah,* the gyres or windings of the cosmos in Yeats, and the "fourfold" of Heidegger. They are the material, formative, creative, and archetypal worlds that provide both the stasis of myth and the movement of history generally, and of that history called evolution particularly. They are the *anima mundi,* the "world memory."

As part of the "great memory," the four worlds intersect with other *topoi*—cosmic, social, corporal, and communicational. The cosmic worlds

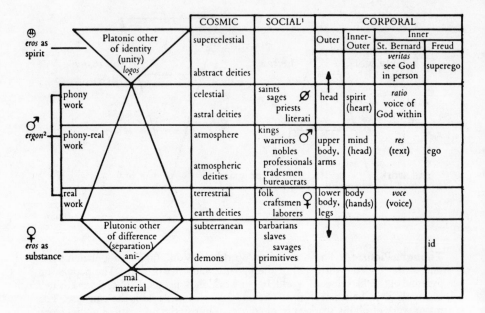

Thought Picture 5 *Topoi*. The categories of *ergon* are metaphoric implicates of iconic, indexical, and symbolic (reading up).

Notes to Thought Picture 5.

1. On these "social-cosmic-corporal" categories, see for example, the *Rig Veda*, and for Indo-European generally, Dumézil (1958).

2. Work (*ergon*) and love (*eros*), the two themes of Freud, are here the union of Marx and Freud. The world (*ergon*) is bereft of love, for it is only a place of work, war, and worship. The three levels of *ergon* are antagonistic and dialectical. The world of real work is creative, that of phony-real work destructive; that of phony work aims for atonement and reconciliation through manipulating the symbols that constitute ideology. Phony work is the neutralization of the opposition between real work and phony-real work, thus:

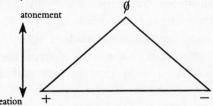

The world of *ergon* repeats in microcosm the dialectic of the macrocosm, for *eros* as substance is creative (*energeia*), in opposition to the world of *ergon*, which is destructive; while the world of *eros* as spirit is the neutralization and reconciliation of these opposing forces. This is the reversal of the Indra myth in the *Rig Veda*, where gods

Powers and Privileges of Communication					
Form of Language	Subject/Object	Form of Communication[4]	Medium of Communication	Mode of Interpretation	Mode of Evidence
	Ⓢ unity of subject and object	music Pythagorean astronomy		anagogic	monstrāre (know things as they are)
in-itself-for-itself (discourse its own object)	S O person ⟶ God	number logic grammar dialectic	written	tropological	*metaphorica* figurative
for-itself (pragmatic-insrumental)	person ⟶ PER-SON[3]	rhetoric	oral text[5] secondary orality	synecdochic	*significāre*[6] (know things as they appear)
in-itself (unselfconscious speech in the world)	person ⟶ person	poetry	oral	metonymy	*propria* literal
	S pure subjectivity as vice, desire, greed, avarice, lust, illusion	*techne*		irony	
	O pure objectivity				

Thought Picture 5 — continued

and men symbolize creation, generation, and evolution, and the demons stand for anti-growth and permanence. Gods and men are in endless battle, an irreconcilable dualism. The world picture in Thought Picture 5 not only reverses the character of these antagonists, it gives them a dialectical resolution in the world of *eros* as spirit. Only the world of *ergon* is strictly entropic, because only it is an-tropic. Note that in Kabbalistic tradition these pyramids are collapsed and interlocked, with each point of base and apex as the locus of a planet and a period of life. In Hinduism, the triangles interlock in the form of a *yantra* meant for use as a meditative vehicle to lead the mind in toward the infinite.

3. This notation with "person" capitalized signifies communication between real persons, and things or institutions as fetishized persons—or conversely between persons as if one of the persons was a thing. So persons as things and things as persons characterize the whole of politics and economy. In the realm of phony work, person ⟶ God signifies communication between real persons and concepts or abstractions as persons. In real work, communication is between real persons in face-to-face, concrete situations. Each of these represents a different sense of "dialogue." Each may be dialogue between real persons, but in the levels above real work, one of the persons is a category, stereotype, institution, concept, or fantasy. Each kind of work, then, is characterized by its own objectifying mode. Rhetoric, in the adjoining box, is predictably "agonistic" as the means of the world of war. Thus Lakoff and Johnson (1980) are able to show that "argument is war."

4. Thus, the seven liberal arts make a hierarchy, with poetry or *grammar* usually at the bottom, though the latter has tended to promote itself. Below that, of course, is mere *techne*, skilled practice.

Mode of Signification		Metaphoric Value				
Representational	Constitutive	Light	Time	Direction	Substance	
	S⁷ "mark" davar	lux pure light	future	high inner	spirit, perfect, mind, rational, form, union,	
symbol whole-part "thirdness"	S ↔ s	sol		↑	abstract, conscious, civilized, living	
index part-whole "secondness"	S → s	calor heat, shadow	present	↕		the limit of language*
icon part-part "firstness"	S ← s					
	s	energeia energy			imperfect, matter, body, content, irrational, separation, concrete,	
			past			
		pure darkness		low outer	unconscious, primitive, nonliving	

Thought Picture 5—continued

5. Oral texts are texts based on oral models of organization, as in the case of much early written poetry and the dialogues of Plato. Secondary orality is oral discourse based on texts, as in classical rhetoric and the dialogues of Plato (cf. Ong 1982:93–116, 168–169). The distinction is text based on speech and speech based on text.

6. This is the dualism between "showing" reality and showing only its appearance. Mathematics and logic arrogate to themselves the supercelestial function of *demonstrāre*. This is equivalent to St. Bernard's idea that in heaven we shall see God as he is, but elsewhere we must be content with signs of his presence (*significāre*). The world is only a place of signification, as is made clear by St. Augustine (*On Christian Doctrine*, Book II, Ch. 6, and in Book III, the discussion of "literal and figurative" meaning). So, too, in Aristotle, the sign is an inference to the nonapparent (*Rhetoric* 1.1357a, b36). In St. Augustine (*Confessions* 11:7), the word becomes only synecdochic and occurs in time; God's word is timeless, not a linear sequence of sound but whole and eternal. So, too, Wittgenstein, in the concluding parts of the *Tractatus*, tells us that what cannot be said (i.e., the mystical, which is beyond the limit of language) can be "shown" (1961). By contrast, Heidegger unites "saying" and "showing" as the "showing of saying," which he reconstructs as the original meaning of Greek *semeia* in the famous passage on signification at the beginning of Aristotle's *De Interpretatione*. This unity of "showing saying" was later broken apart

in the development of the idea of signs and signification. *Monstrāre* and *significāre* were separated (1971:114-115).

7. This is the medieval idea of the "mark," the sign that shows a thing's real character, as in the expression, "the mark of the beast (the devil)." In Leibnitz it becomes the search for a universal character (*characteristica universalis*) as a system of marks for all things on which all men agree. *Davar* is the Hebrew concept of the unity of signifier/signified. The lower case "s" at the bottom is obviously the Kantian thing-in-itself. The terms "firstness," "secondness," and "thirdness" are Peirce's. Note Derrida (1976:11), "The written signifier . . . has no constitutive meaning."

8. The "limit of language" is also the limit of the world of *ergon*. Compare Wittgenstein (1961) and Humboldt's famous distinction between *ergon* and *energeia* that identifies language as the former, not the latter (1970:27). Language is "a true world which the intellect must set between itself and objects" (ibid.:135). Compare the fourfold division here with Heidegger: "The movement at the core of the world's four regions, which makes them reach one another and holds them in the nearness of their distance, is nearness itself" (1971:105). Note too that the threefold distinction of "lust" (*eros* as substance), "work," and "love" (*eros* as spirit and the "play" of the gods) is an "externalized" metaphor of the threefold of "work," or conversely, the threefold of "work" is an "internalized" metaphor of "lust," "work," and "love." These correlative threefolds correspond to the trinitarian systems of Popper, Parsons, and Habermas in addition to those noted elsewhere (cf. Thought Picture 1). Popper distinguishes among the "first world" as the physical world, the "second world" as the world of consciousness, and the "third world" of Platonic spirit consisting of texts. These worlds emerge sequentially in the order given. Later emergents cannot be reduced to earlier ones (cf. Lakatos 1978:108). Habermas's three "domains of reality," which have corresponding "modes of communication," "validity claims," and "general functions of speech," are: "my world of internal nature," "our world of society," and "the world of external nature" (1979:65-68). In Parsons's well-known system these are the separate subsystems of personality, society, and culture (1949). Also relevant here are the three Kantian critiques—of pure reason, of practical reason, and of judgment.

(celestial, atmospheric, and terrestrial) of the *Rig Veda,* for example, correspond with the three kinds of work and are loci of gods, kings, and men, respectively (cf. Dumézil 1958; Benveniste 1969:227-260). Corresponding to the "other of unity" is the supercelestial realm, the locus of abstract supernaturals, and corresponding to the "other of difference" is the subterranean world, locus of the demons. The corresponding social categories are priests (*literati*), warriors (*nobili*), folk (*rustici, vulgari*), and barbarians and slaves. This set of *topoi* is homologized with the human body as spirit, mind, and body, a movement from inner to outer; or with the outer body as locus: head, shoulders and chest, and lower extremities. The inner man of St. Bernard is *voces* (speech), *res* (text), *ratio* (reason), *veritas* (the voice of God within), while the now better-known inner loci of Freud are id, ego, and superego.

The loci of communication give the powers and privileges of communication appropriate to each division of work. Thus, the Hegelian categories in-itself–for-itself, for-itself, and in-itself refer ultimately to forms of language appropriate to each form of work. Different possibilities of the subject-object relationship are similarly located, as in pure objectivity : animal : : pure subjectivity (desire, greed, vice, and illusion): demonic (Plutonic) : : communication among equals : real work : : communication between superiors or things fetishized as persons and persons fetishized as things : the middle class : : the communication of persons to God : the priestly class : : the union of subject and object : the supercelestial realm. Forms of communication are similarly hierarchically topologized from poetry upward through rhetoric, dialectic, grammar, logic, and number, to music in the supercelestial. Media of communication are included, too—written for priests and *literati,* oral text or secondary orality (rhetoric) for kings, and orality for workers. Modes of textual interpretation, the great problem of the Christian tradition, were hierarchized in order of ascending subtlety as: irony (saying other than you mean is a demonic and academic illusion); metonymy; synecdochy; tropology; and anagogy. So, too, did modes of evidence correspond, the most general being the distinction between *significāre* and *monstrāre.* Men know only by signification, either literal or figurative. Only in the supercelestial realm does one know things as they really are. They *show* themselves, and as St. Bernard says, we shall then *see* God as he is; for now we can only hear his voice within us as a *sign* of his presence. Modes of signification fit this pattern, although Peirce's system (already noted) is different from St. Augustine's hierarchy.[10]

Metaphoric values also follow this hierarchic system. Thus we have the metaphors of high (=good) and low (=bad); up is better than down (Lakoff and Johnson 1980). Light is better than dark; a light-heat series runs downward from *lux* (pure light), through *sol* (the sun, heat and light) and *calor* (heat) to *energeia* (the "dark," hidden power of light). Ranked metaphors also include union vs. separation; abstract vs. concrete; conscious vs. unconscious; civilized vs. primitive; future, present, and past (dark, obscured, ghostly, and demonic); living vs. nonliving; and on and on. These correspondences are illustrated in Thought Picture 5.

Such are the *topoi* that have formed the structure and content of our imagination. We do not yet know what new *topoi* will emerge from the revolution created by inverting the old pyramid of work that informed and animated this vast system of metaphors, this Brunoesque kaleidoscope in which each rank is a memory wheel inscribed with the signs of its loci, each aligned with the other in a total episteme. But standing now amid the rubble of this wondrous machine, the shattered bits and pieces of colorful metaphors glinting in the feeble, post-modern light, we know, at last, that only the [ay] peering through the other end of the shadowy tube was real. Its vision was deceived by movements caused by a hand it could think and feel but not see, and only when the wheel was turned by the hand of the other did it suspect the reality of what it saw. We know, too, at the end of this history that is not a history of a history that was not a history, that the *logos* was always a *mythos* obscured by

The Transcendence of Method and the Will to Truth

> The distinguishing feature of our . . . century is not the triumph of science, but the triumph of the scientific method over science. (Nietzsche 1913:3)

One of the constant themes of Western thought has been the search for apodictic and universal method. In our own times we see the triumph of formalism in all branches of thought. Its analogical model is, of course, mathematics. The transcendence of method derives from one simple assumption: *rules of interpretation and analysis are separate from what they interpret and analyze.* Rules are separate from what rules are for. They transcend their objects and conditions of use. They have universal and unequivocal application. They are neither contingent on, nor contained in, the content they order. This is the fetishization of logic, of reason enthroned by right (cf. Derrida 1967:59).

No one has ever demonstrated the independence of reason, of logic and mathematics, from the discourses that constitute them. They are, after all, historical emergents, and are thus not self-constituting, for their emergence depends upon two conditions: a founding written discourse, and a background of presuppositions that makes the historical quest for method reasonable. Only if reason had no history could it, by means of itself, justify its claim to universality and demonstrate that it is anything more than the means by which we justify the lies we tell.

Method, then, is immanent in a larger, founding discourse, and every application of method to a given discourse is conditioned by its immanence. Its transcendence is a condition of its immanence, and its immanence is given by the need for its transcendence. The source of this need is the "will to truth," and its means is the written text. Texts provide the ground for the emergence of method and are its original objects. From the need to interpret texts arises the will to truth and from the will to truth arises method.

Orality is momentary in its expression and depends for its duration on the durable character of the speaker as one who speaks truly, whether or not he speaks the truth.[11] In a word, truth before writing is honesty, a feature of the speaker only derivatively connected with the speaker's words. The speaker's honesty rests in some harmony between words and deeds and not in words alone, nor in any correspondence between words and things, as these are only the means of lying. Truth is always part of a fable, of something told, a thing of words alone; but honesty is both word and deed. That is why English gives truth no agentive force outside the context of telling. One may be a liar but not a "truther." Truth is born with the *logos* and dies with it (Derrida 1976:10).

Textuality is not only an historical emergent (cf. Ong 1982:78–116), but texts are always incomplete. They cannot speak at once of what they speak and tell us of their means of interpretation; if they speak of one, they can only point to the other by silence (Heidegger 1971:115). Texts, as Derrida says, always are in need of a supplement (1976:141–165). They entail a method of interpretation because they are occult. They reveal only inasmuch as they conceal, and this is the mystery that generates the will to truth, the urge to discover what the text has hidden beneath the surface of its content. But neither text nor method is absolute—their sufficiency is relative to the mutuality of their lack.

What, then, of oral discourse? Is it, too, so constrained by the will to truth that it must extrude methods to ensure its interpretation? In general, the answer is no. Writing alone creates the illusion of a higher truth beyond the momentary, particular act of speaking and indexes more than the speaker's character and intent. Paradoxically, it is writing's failure to keep its promise of truth writ large that feeds and encourages the will to truth. The less truth it delivers, the more we long for it. In the end it provides not truth immortal, but only its means, and it hopes to satisfy our lack with this changeling called method.

Oral discourse, even among literates, has no exterior method of interpretation. Its method is in it, or in its conditions, and such method as there is, is entrained not universally, to lay hold of truth, timeless and immortal, but in problematic circumstances, to solve problems arising from unclear meaning and uncertain honesty. It does not treat all discourse as universally problematic and therefore in need of universal method. Oral discourse has its hermeneutics, but it is a hermeneutics of language-in-the-world, of reflexivity and immanence, of contingent and ad hoc transcendence. Holy and mystical speech apart, it has no will to truth except in a secondary and derivative imitation of writing (Ong 1982:31–77, 139–154).

And what of logic? Is oral discourse illogical? Is it guided only by the speaker's random associations, which miraculously harmonize with those of the hearer? Or does it, too, submit to the authority of logic, without which it would be incoherent? Oral discourse has order that is emergent, shifting, changeable, impermanent, created in the negotiation of speakers and hearers seeking to understand and be understood. No text-like object or method intervenes between speaker and hearer. Order, then, lies not *in* the discourse or *in* its method of interpretation, but in the juxtaposition and reflexivity of emergent discourse and emergent "method." Method is immanent in the discourse that is immanent in the method. Each may be temporarily transcendent under proper circumstances as when we say: "But you said . . . ," invoking the discourse, or: "If you say x, then y," invoking method.

Logic, then, is not separate from oral discourse. Discourse itself is logical in a wider sense. That is to say, it is "reasonable," but not necessarily rational in any strictly logical sense. Reasonable oral discourse may include features that we would be tempted to equate with logical operations, but it uses many "nonlogical" devices that contribute far more to its reasonableness. Moreover, logical operations are themselves objects of interest only in unusual circumstances. *Ratio* is embedded in the reasonable (cf. Cole and Scribner 1973; Luria 1976). *Ratio* out of context is unreasonable. As its derivation from *logos* suggests, logic emerges as a fully separate means and object of discourse only as a product of writing, after discourse has become a visible "thing" and has taken itself as its object, as in Aristotle's *Prior Analytics.* Texts are the "kingdom of desire" out of which logic emerges. They are the means by which "the world seems logical to us, because we have made it logical" (Nietzsche 1913:27, 37).

Traditional rhetoric in the West, which we might think is not only oral, but oral method, is actually secondary orality—orality based on written discourse that, as *The Phaedrus* (Plato) makes clear, is the analogical source of its method. Secondary orality (Ong 1982:168) is the organization of oral discourse on the model of written discourse. The method of primary orality, inasmuch as we may speak of method, is not primarily oriented to the *dispositio*—the structure of argument—but to *inventio* and *memoria*, the sources of ideas in which the organization of ideas is already given in the world in the form of schemata, formulae, semantically rich key terms, fixed metaphors, and other holistic means. *Memoria* and *inventio* are not, in other words, analytic (cf. Ong 1958:114).

The absolutism of the text is founded in that *ratio* which texts themselves created. It emerges from focusing on the *dispositio* as order and arrangement, and from the backgrounding of *inventio, memoria, ethos* ("speaker"), and *pathos* ("hearer"). It marks the supremacy of *eidos*, is the condition for the separation of form and content in which *dispositio* = form (*eidos*) and *inventio memoria* = content, and enables signification, of which it is itself the paragon (cf. Ong 1958:112–116). It is the sign of

The Separation of Form and Content and the Transcendence of Form

The transcendence of method indexes the separation of form and content, for method is the expression of that separation and is also an expression of form, of the rules that order content. Form is the operation of ordering. It is independent of what it orders and it constrains and structures content. Content itself has no order; it is to be ordered by means that are external to and independent of it. For there to be a method, there must be something other than the method to which the method applies, and when method makes itself its object, that is the beginning of logic and the end of sociology. Method is the means by which "data" are created and acquire order. It imparts form to the formless content from which it is itself utterly separate and independent. Form, in the sense of "formula," is the method by which substance achieves form in the sense of "shape." Form, in other words, produces form; it is both process and structure.

What, then, is the source for the separation of form and content? All instantiations of the separation merely reflect back on one another in self-confirmation and provide no grounds for its necessity. Inasmuch as the condition for it is writing, then writing is its source. Writing is the means for a systematic separation of form and content more pervasive than that conditioned by pictorial representation, and more accessible than anything provided by hearing or touch. Writing expresses the separation of form and content visually, and promotes our consciousness of it.

Writing substitutes a dual constitution of form in a way that speech and hearing cannot. It visualizes the succession of acts (=formula), and it makes the act of visualization successive (=shape). The succession of elements in the sentence is the order of things or the visual order of action, and the succession of sentences is the order of events in narration or the order of things. Thus Albertus Magnus could rightly say that the memory image of a wolf contained the intention to flee (cf. Yates 1966:64).

The economy of written discourse—its order, arrangement, and visualization, its mode of substituting appearances—is the object, the source, and the model of theoretical discourse on order, arrangement, and signification. Theoretical discourse is discourse on discourse. It arises when the form of language takes itself as its content. Writing provides the means by which discourse takes itself as its object, and in so doing extrudes forms of discourse that emerge in ordered sequence, each as the underlying form of its predecessor—as ghosts arising from corpses. Thus rhetoric comes from the objectification of speaking, dialectic from the objectification of rhetoric, and logic from the objectification of dialectic—but as Wittgenstein saw, the objectification of logic produces only anti-logic, not meta-logic. This, perhaps more than anything else, marks the end of writing, for writing has finally closed entirely upon itself and produces nothing new. No new form of writing can grow in this nautilus. Its builder is dead and its finished chambers are let out to a new tenant. We can hear the creature's claws scrabbling on the inner walls as it crawls toward the light, and do we hear it singing?

The Transcendence of Signs

Writing, the paragon of the separation of signs and signifieds, creates only a shadow of reality and establishes the prior condition for treating the world given by normal perception and commonsense as an illusion. It shifts the locus of reality from this world to a world of form indirectly available to the knower—not through senses but through signs. Writing displaces the subject from the world. It produces as equal possibilities: (a) the transcendence of signs à la Derrida, or (b) the transcendence of signifieds as an unknowable Kantian "thing-in-itself." In either case, it sets up the universal problematic of reconnecting signs and signifieds, words and things.

In contrast, post-modern anthropology asks, "how did signs and signifieds get pulled apart?" Identifying writing as the culprit, it argues that sign and signified are mutually constituted in "saying." The sign is immanent in the signified, and the signified is immanent in the sign (cf. Heidegger 1971:115–135; Tyler 1978:459–465). The effect of this argument is to make symbols concrete rather than abstract and arbitrary. It asks not "how do signs represent?" in the fashion of contemporary semiotics derived from de Saussure and Peirce, as if one could know the origin of it all, or as if some kinds of signs constituted themselves independently of conventionality. It asks instead, "how is the signifier/ signified *constituted*?" There are three possibilities: (a) the signifier is conventionally constituted by the signified (s → S), as if in iconic representation; (b) the signified is intentionally constituted by the signifier (S → s), as if in indexical representation; (c) the signified and signifier are mutually constituted (S⟷ s), as if in symbolic representation.

Thought Picture 6 shows the dialectical relation of these possibilities. Here, "a" and "b" are inverses and "c" is their synthesis. Both "a" and "b" are "picturing" modes, but neither is necessarily representational, for "a" might be ideographic writing and "b" syllabic or phonetic

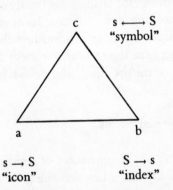

Thought Picture 6 Dialectical Relation of Constitutive Signs. s = signified, S = signifier; "a" is the inverse of "b," and "c" is the sublation of "a" and "b." The dialectic thus "rationalizes" the order of signs and encompasses logic (cf. Thought Picture 3) by means of will (intention-convention, à la St. Augustine) and person (speaker-hearer, or "interpretant," à la Peirce).

writing. "C," of course, is not "picturing" or visual in any way, for it is the *presence* of the word in the world and the world in the word. It is neither "being," nor, as we *say*, "speech."

Thought Picture 6 is amended in Thought Picture 7. Apart from their "sensory" differences, the chief difference between "c" and "a/b" is that the latter "point to" the difference between themselves and what they "picture," whereas "c" neutralizes that difference. In effect, the difference between "c" and "a/b" is also the difference between de Saussure's "signification" and St. Augustine's *significatio*. The latter, of course, restates the idea of the Trinity in the series "incarnate" (present), "excarnate" (future), "non-carnate" (past), and reflects the earlier opposition between *"significāre"* and *"monstrāre."* It also points to the tension between the "senses" of "word" in Christian hermeneutics: the word as immanent speech—"the word was in God, and God was the word"— and the word as transcendental *logos*.

The chief advantage to eliminating the idea of representation is that representation emphasizes the difference between sign and signified. There is always a constant world of things and a separate world of signs: the essential problematic is one of words and things. Representation leads us to overemphasize *mimesis*, description, and correspondence theories of truth, and tricks us into thinking of language as if it were a

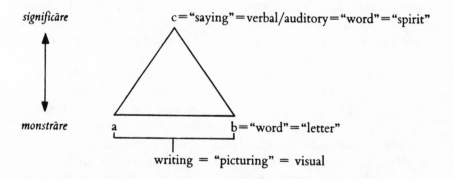

Thought Picture 7 "Saying and Showing." "A," "b," and "c" have the same values as in Thought Picture 6 except that "a" also signifies hieroglyphic or ideographic writing, and "b" signifies alphabetic writing. Note that this diagram inverts the relation of *significāre* and *monstrāre* in Thought Picture 5. Writing is thus a "showing-saying" and speech a "saying-showing." The reversal of *significāre* and *monstrāre* is the consequence of inverting the ancient pyramid of *ergon*. The reversal "demystifies" the oriental and exotic role of the hieroglyph in Western thought.

form of calculus. We abstract signs away from their representational functions and treat them as "pure forms," focusing exclusively on their modes of collocation.

The "constitutive" mode emphasizes not the separateness of signs and signifieds, but their interpenetrability and mutuality. There is no problematic relationship between word and world, for both are mutually present. It is only where there is the possibility of the *absence* of one or the other that problems arise, and it is, of course, just this possibility that writing enables. Writing either focuses on itself, absenting itself from the world, or in focusing on the world and absenting itself, tricks us into thinking that we can compare and describe as we will without being constrained by the means of composition and description. Do I "refute" Derrida? No, I merely supplement his text. He "says": "There is neither symbol nor sign but a becoming sign of the symbol" (1976:47), which is precisely what Thought Picture 6 "says." Derrida argues against the idea of signs as "substitutions of appearances" in which one appearance (first as the thing that becomes a mental image, then speech, then written sign [Aristotle, *De Interpretatione*]) precedes another as its origin and original, and is thus prior in both time and reality. The order of representation is from the earlier to the later, from the real to the unreal, from nature ("natural" signs) to culture ("conventional, arbitrary" signs).

The implication is not, as the concept of "arche-writing" might seem to suggest, that we simply reverse the order of emergence to writing → speech → mental image → thing. Rather, these are co-present possibilities within a whole, where signs are used by speakers and hearers not only to represent things, thoughts, and speech. They use signs to communicate about communicating, which is the intentional means by which signs represent conventionally and is also the convention of that intention. The participatory whole is just the possibility of the intersubstitutability and integration of the triad will, representation, and person in the pairs intention/convention, signifier/signified, and speaker/hearer, respectively. This is the fulfillment of the Peircean-Augustinian semiotic as opposed to that of de Saussure (cf. Tyler 1978:462–464).

What, then, of writing? Is it forever excluded from the participatory reality of speech, or can it somehow capture that sense of immediacy that is the mutual involvement of sign, signified, and interpretant? Two methods have been tried in the past—mystification and imitation. In mystification, the sign is taken to be both a sign and *realia,* as in the use of Sanskrit letters in *mantras* and on the lotus leaves of the Yogic *chakras*, or in Hebrew tradition where the letters of the alphabet are mystical "sign-things," or in medieval theories of the "mark" in which things bear the mark of their creation. This idea is attractive, but it tends to make writing redundant. Writing imitating speech, of course, is what we find in the written dialogues of Socrates, and the idea of dialogue is a perennial favorite of those who wish to capture in writing some sense of the mutuality of speakers and hearers. Witness the rebirth of conversational forms in recent ethnographic writing. Techniques of oral discourse have been deployed from time to time throughout history. Parabolic discourse is one such, and so too are the sermon, the method of sorites, repetitious figures, polyphony, ellipsis, and the use of enigmas and paradox, the "fragment" or "negative" dialectics of Benjamin and Adorno. Just as rhetoric is speech imitating writing, this kind of writing is writing imitating speech.

Post-modern experiments in ethnographic writing are the inverse of the modernist experiment. Where modernists sought by means of ideographic method to reveal the inner flow of thought hieroglyphically—as in Joyce or Pound, for example—post-modern writing focuses on the outer flow of speech, seeking not the thought that "underlies" speech, but the thought that *is* speech. Where modernists sought an identity between thought and language, post-modernists seek that "inner voice" which is the equivalent of thinking and speaking. Modernists sought a form of writing more in keeping with "things," emphasizing, in imitation of modern science, the descriptive function of writing— writing as a "picture of reality." This is not "realism" but "surrealism." Post-modern writing rejects this modernist *mimesis* in favor of a writing that "evokes" or "calls to mind," not by completion and similarity but by suggestion and difference. The function of the text is not to depict or reveal within itself what it says. The text is "seen through" by what it cannot say. It shows what it cannot say and says what it cannot show. When post-modern writing tries to achieve what speech does by imitating speech, it fails, as it must, for in imitating speech it merely displaces the focus of representation without changing it.

The great problem for post-modern anthropology is either to give up on writing altogether or to achieve by written means what speech creates without simply imitating speech. It may well be that some kind of naive realism is what commonsense will demand. At any rate, one may be certain that post-modern writing will not achieve its goal merely through experimentation with form. That favorite preoccupation of the modernist depends upon the independence of form and content—a presupposition that post-modern anthropology denies. Nor will it come about through some technological advance in sound and video recording, for every technological means merely imposes new forms of representational constraints without addressing the problem of representation itself. Nothing yet, as mere *techne,* is "saying-showing." These technologies are archaisms, holdovers from an era of writing whose whole *ergon* was based on the separation of saying and showing, on their difference rather than on their union, which is not an identity, but an identity within difference and a difference within identity.[12]

This is the end of the first chapter of "The Lust for the Logograph."[13] "Oh Egyptians, give us your pyramids and hieroglyphs."

Notes

1. That is, speaking and writing. This paper was given in revised form to the Rice Circle in January 1984. It incorporates remarks from a talk at the Conference on Language and Culture at Canberra, Australia, in July 1982. It is part of a series of essays that are the parerga to *The Said and the Unsaid.* Those essays grew out of my work, extending over several years, with Koya texts. Part of that work and, consequently, some of the content of those essays was made possible by a grant from the National Endowment for the Humanities, and by grants from the Ford Foundation and the National Science Foundation, to which thanks are hereby enounced. Thanks are also due to Phyllis Chock at Catholic University for inviting me to speak to the Anthropological Society of Washington and to the organizers of the Canberra Conference, especially Judith Irvine, for inviting me to attend. I am most grateful, though, to my colleagues in the Rice Circle—George Marcus, Julie Taylor, Michael Fischer, Tullio Maranhão, Gene Holland, Lane Kauffman, Ivan Karp, and others who visited us from time to time—whose comments and criticism helped me to hear better what I had thought to say. This paper is also a mediation of two strong and partly contradictory authorial voices, both speaking to me at once. I refer, of course, to Jacques Derrida and Walter Ong, whose works are cited throughout, and whose voices sing contrapuntally in my inner ears with those of Reid, Wittgenstein, Heidegger, Whorf, Laksmayya, and Kapila of the "threefold misery."

2. Capitalization here and throughout signifies concepts in the *logos* or as the *logos.*

3. Thus Derrida, "This . . . amounts to destroying the concept of 'sign' and its entire logic" (1976:7).

4. Much of this argument was already worked out in Tyler (1978).

5. The remainder are reserved for later treatment or have appeared piecemeal in other papers.

6. The allusion here is to Lyotard (1974).

7. Metaphoric implicature moves thought not by identities, but by equivalences that are unities of identity and difference. It is thus different from logical implication, which uses only identities and is thus paralyzed, goes nowhere, and cannot be the source of movement within a discourse. Metaphoric implicature moves ceaselessly through a genealogy of concepts and over a field of concepts, sometimes even coming back to what might seem to be a point of origin.

8. Here, too, belong Austin's "locutionary," "illocutionary," and "perlocutionary," though he might say "with different force" (1962) since they are "acts."

9. Yates (1966:378–388) makes the point of the relation between character and *characteristica* in her discussion of Leibnitz.

10. See the discussion below at "The Transcendence of Signs."

11. The etymology is revealing here. "Durable" and "duration" derive from Indo-European *drū ("strong, resistant, hard"), which is adjectival of *dreu- ("tree, the oak"), from which come "trust," "fidelity," and "truth." Other reflexes include "troop" (of soldiers), "to rule," "queen," "chief," and "lord" (Benveniste 1969:84–90). The association of truth and reason with nobility and power is clear, calling to mind Lyotard's "Reason and power are one and the same" (1974:13).

12. Here beginneth an essay entitled "Post-Modern Ethnography: From Document of the Occult to Occult Document" (Tyler 1986).

13. The Thought Pictures herein are culminations of hieroglyphic writing, that complete spatialization and visualization of thought that the Western tradition has always sought. They are signs of the end of alphabetic writing, the end of the narrative that is narrative.

References Cited

Aristotle
    1924 Rhetorica. *In* The Works of Aristotle, Vol. 11. W. D. Ross, ed. Oxford: Oxford University Press.
    1928 Categoriae, De Interpretatione, and Topica. *In* The Works of Aristotle, Vol. 1. W. D. Ross, ed. Oxford: Oxford University Press.
    1931 De Anima. *In* The Works of Aristotle, Vol. 3. W. D. Ross, ed. Oxford: Oxford University Press.

Augustine, St.
    1950 Confessions. New York: Dutton.
    1958 On Christian Doctrine. Indianapolis: Bobbs-Merrill.

Austin, J. L.
    1962 How to Do Things with Words. Cambridge, Mass.: Harvard University Press.

Benveniste, E.
    1969 Indo-European Language and Society. London: Faber and Faber.

Cole, M., and Sylvia Scribner
1973   Culture and Thought. New York: Wiley.

Derrida, J.
1967   L'Ecriture et la différence. Paris: Seuil.
1972   Marges de la philosophie. Paris: Minuit.
1976   Of Grammatology. Baltimore: John Hopkins University Press.

Dumézil, G.
1958   Métiers et classes fonctionelles chez divers peuples Indo-Européens. Annales, Economies, Sociétés, Civilisations, 13ᵉ année, no. 4, Oct.-Dec., pp. 716-724.

Foucault, M.
1965   Madness and Civilization. New York: Random House.

Habermas, Jürgen
1979   Communication and the Evolution of Society. Thomas McCarthy, transl. Boston: Beacon Press. (Originals: Sprachgrammatic und Philosophie and Zur Rekonstruktion des Historischen Materialismus, 1976.)

Heidegger, M.
1971   On the Way to Language. New York: Random House.

Humboldt, W. von
1970   Linguistic Variability and Intellectual Development. Miami Linguistic Series, No. 9. Coral Gables: University of Miami Press.

Lakatos, Imre
1978   Mathematics, Science and Epistemology. Philosophical Papers, Vol. 2. John Worral and Gregory Currie, eds. Cambridge, England: Cambridge University Press.

Lakoff, G., and M. Johnson
1980   Metaphors We Live By. Chicago: University of Chicago Press.

Luria, A.
1976   Cognitive Development: Its Cultural and Social Foundations. Cambridge, Mass.: Harvard University Press.

Lyotard, J. F.
1973   Dérive à partie de Marx et Freud. Paris: Union Générale d'Editions.
1974   Economie libidinale. Paris: Minuit.

McLean, P.
1973   A Triune Concept of the Brain. In The Hincks Memorial Lectures. T. Boag and D. Campbell, eds. pp. 6-66. Toronto: Toronto University Press.

Nietzsche, F.
1911   The Twilight of the Idols. In The Complete Works of F. Nietzsche, Vol. 16. O. Levy, ed. Edinburgh: Foulis.
1913   The Will to Power. In The Complete Works of F. Nietzsche, Vol. 15. O. Levy, ed. Edinburgh: Foulis.

Ong, W.
1958   Ramus: Method and the Decay of Dialogue. Cambridge, Mass.: Harvard University Press.
1982   Orality and Literacy. London: Methuen.

Parsons, Talcott
1949   The Structure of Social Action. Glencoe: The Free Press.

Peirce, C.
1932   Elements of Logic. In Collected Papers of C. S. Peirce, Vol. 2. Cambridge, Mass.: Harvard University Press.
1932   Principles of Philosophy. In Collected Papers of C. S. Peirce, Vol. 1. Cambridge, Mass.: Harvard University Press.

Reid, T.
1795   Essays on the Active Powers of Man. In Collected Works of T. Reid, Vol. 1. Edinburgh: James Thin.

Tyler, S.
1978   The Said and the Unsaid. New York: Academic Press.
1986   Post-Modern Ethnography: From Document of the Occult to Occult Document. In Writing Culture: The Poetics and Politics of Ethnography. J. Clifford and G. E. Marcus, eds. pp. 122–140. Berkeley: University of California Press.

Wittgenstein, L.
1961   Tractatus Logico Philosophicus. New York: Humanities Press.

Yates, F.
1966   The Art of Memory. Chicago: University of Chicago Press.

The Reconstruction of Ethnography

Paul Stoller
West Chester University

I na hay faabu wi i garu a ga naasu
"One kills something thin only to discover that it is fat."
—Songhay proverb

My first month of fieldwork among the Songhay of Niger was a total failure. Having previously lived among the Songhay, and having learned to speak Songhay, I had few problems adjusting to life in a rural village. Still, I did not know many people of the village of Mehanna. Following the wisdom of the literature on fieldwork, I decided to conduct a survey to get to know my neighbors. Soon after I settled in a small mud-brick house, I designed a questionnaire that would generate, or so I thought, some demographic data. But I did not want to limit my survey only to demographics, as the topic of my research concerned the use of language in local-level politics. I therefore added items to the questionnaire on the use of the various languages spoken in Songhay country, which is multilingual. These data on language use and language attitudes, I thought, might provide information on relations between the Songhay and non-Songhay groups living in Mehanna. This information on cross-ethnic relations, in turn, would reveal patterns of local-level political processes.

After I designed the twenty-item survey, I conducted a pilot test with ten respondents. None had difficulty answering the questions. Encouraged, I administered the survey to a representative sample of townspeople. As in all things one does with the Songhay, I had to make excruciatingly careful arrangements for the survey's administration. First I contacted the village chief, who approved the proposal. But before I surveyed individuals, the chief told me, I should consult with the eight neighborhood chiefs. After a series of long visits with the chiefs, I finally began my survey. Unexpectedly, each interview was so long that

I could conduct only six interviews a day. It took me thirty days to complete 180 interviews. As I collected the data I began to analyze them, and I discovered that multilingualism was greater than I had anticipated. Moreover, a cursory examination of the language attitude data suggested much cross-ethnic enmity.

Toward the end of the Mehanna survey, I interviewed a shopkeeper named Abdou Kano. Abdou told me that he spoke four languages (Songhay, Hausa, Fulani, and Tamasheq). My work with Abdou completed, I walked next door to interview Mahamane Boulla, who, like Abdou, was a shopkeeper. I asked him how many languages he spoke.

"How many languages does Abdou say he speaks?" he asked me.

"Abdou," I said, "says he speaks four languages."

"Hah! I know for a fact that Abdou speaks only two languages."

"What?" I exclaimed. "How could he lie to me?" I stood up abruptly and strutted over to Abdou's shop.

Abdou smiled and greeted me. "Ah Monsieur Paul, what would you like to buy today?"

"Abdou," I began firmly, "Mahamane has just told me that you speak only two languages. Is that true?"

Abdou shrugged his shoulders. "Yes, it is true. I speak only two languages: Hausa and Songhay."

"Why did you tell me you spoke four languages?"

Abdou patted me on the shoulder. "What difference does it make?" He glanced skyward. "Tell me, how many languages did Mahamane say he speaks?"

"Mahamane," I answered, "told me that he spoke three languages."

"He can speak Songhay and that is all," Abdou said.

"What?" I exclaimed. Turning red with anger, I strutted back to Mahamane's shop. "Abdou tells me that you speak only one language. But you just told me that you spoke three languages. What is the truth?"

Mahamane smiled at me. "Abdou is telling the truth."

"But how could you lie to me?"

Like Abdou, Mahamane shrugged his shoulders. "What is the difference?"

I spent the next week frantically consulting the other 178 people whom I had interviewed during the previous month. To my disgust, I discovered that everyone had lied to me, and that the data I had so painstakingly collected were worthless.

Any audience of fieldworkers, anthropologists or whatever, can empathize with my predicament, for I am sure that such incidents are not isolated ones. Informants routinely lie to anthropologists for any number of reasons. "What's the difference?" "We don't know you." "We know you, but we don't trust you." "Since you are too young we cannot tell you the truth (but we are too polite to tell you to go away)."

I was lucky because I discovered early in my fieldwork that people were lying to me; some of us are not so lucky. Blessed by more luck, I was fortunate to find an elder willing to advise me on learning about things Songhay.

"You will never learn about us," he told me, "if you go into people's compounds, ask personal questions, and write down the answers. Even if you remain here one year or two years and ask us questions in this manner, we would still lie to you."

"Then what am I to do?"

"You must learn to sit with people," he told me. "You must learn to sit and listen. As we say in Songhay: 'One kills something thin only to discover that it is fat.'"

During the remainder of my fieldwork and other visits to the lands of the Songhay I have followed my teacher's advice. I learned to listen to men, to women, and to children, and as a result I learned a great deal about the Songhay.

I learned to listen to one woman in particular. Fatouma had been married three times and, when I first met her, she was, as they say in Songhay, "without husband." She talked to me about her marriages: about her first husband who gave her no money, about her second husband who routinely beat her, and about her last husband who often burned her with cigarettes when she was asleep. Whenever Fatouma talked, I listened. Never did I attempt to "interview" her. She asked me questions about myself. We rarely talked about multilingualism, and we never discussed local politics.

When I returned in 1979–80 and in 1981, I went to visit this woman. On each occasion she would greet me and then recite a litany of sorrows. All the while she observed me, saying much about herself and yet revealing little. In 1982–83, I saw this woman once again in the Mehanna market. Since she had squash to sell, I bought one for my dinner. As usual, I gave her a small tip of twenty-five francs (roughly ten cents). Fatouma smiled and told me that I was a kindhearted man. Then she told me to kneel down close to her.

"Go to one of the shops and bring me a vial of perfume this afternoon, around 5 p.m."

"What for?" I asked, dumbfounded.

"Just do it. I will see you later."

Later I bought a small vial of *Bint al Hedash* and trekked up the dune to Fatouma's compound. She was seated on a straw mat next to her mud-brick house. I gave her the perfume.

"You brought the wrong kind of perfume."

"What kind of perfume was I supposed to bring?"

"You were supposed to bring *Bint al Sudan*. How can I put this in my *baata* [a sacrificial container possessed only by magician-sorcerers]?"

"You have a *baata!*" I exclaimed, quite overwhelmed.

"Of course I do."

"But you never told me . . . ."

"One never talks of these things, one acts. You see, my father was a *sorko* [a praise-singer to the spirits and a healer] and he taught me what he knew."

"I have known you for seven years, and never once did you tell me."

Fatouma nodded. "Those of us who are serious never talk about our abilities, or about our work." She stood up and led me inside her house and showed me her *baata* on her sacrificial altar. She turned to me: "I don't know if the one in the sky [a name for the spirit of lightning, *Dongo*] will accept my putting this perfume in the *baata*. But I'll do it anyway."

She opened the *baata* and placed the *Bint al Hedash* in it. It was the only one of its kind in the container. She then led me outside the hut and we sat down on the straw mat. Fatouma soon became clearly troubled. "It is not right to put the wrong perfume in the *baata*. Come, let us go and inspect the container." We went into the hut again and she picked up the *baata* and lifted off its lid. The *Bint al Hedash* I had purchased was broken into bits. "You see," she said, smiling, "the one above did not like this perfume. Go and buy some *Bint al Sudan*."

I returned to the same shop and bought the right kind of perfume. Fatouma opened the perfume briefly so I could learn its fragrance—very strong and sweet. She then closed it rapidly, walked into her hut, and put it into the *baata*. We sat down once again on the straw mat and she took out her divining cowry shells—seven of them. "If the one who is above accepts your offering, you will smell the fragrance as it wafts from the hut over to us." As she began to throw the cowries and divine my future, we both looked at one another. The sweet and strong fragrance of *Bint al Sudan* was in the air. She told me to breathe it in deeply. I did as she asked. The air around us was permeated with *Bint al Sudan*. I did not ask her how this could happen. I certainly did not know *why* this was happening. She threw the cowries once again and said: "It is time that you learn the secrets of reading cowries."

Two vignettes from the field. Two vignettes on the paradoxical nature of anthropological work. My first attempt to learn about the Songhay through a questionnaire was an unqualified failure; my respondents all lied to me. Perhaps much of the blame was mine. Perhaps my questionnaire was not well-designed. Perhaps I abandoned too rapidly an epistemology in which the goal is to produce ideal, verifiable, and replicable knowledge that we might use as a data base for comparison. But I chose a more subjective approach to fieldwork—letting the Songhay teach me about their culture and society. This approach led me over the years to meet and know people, not informants; it led me inside a *sorko*'s hut; it led me beyond an invisible threshold to a domain the Songhay call the "world of eternal war." In this "world of eternal war" much has happened that I have not been able to explain or understand. How could I explain, after all, the broken vial of *Bint al Hedash*? Sleight of hand, remembering so vividly Lévi-Strauss's (1967: 161–181) "Sorcerer and His Magic"? Perhaps the force of the spirit broke the vial? Maybe this woman, despite our long acquaintance, was, for any number of reasons, trying to deceive me?

While I prefer to be led by the Other into murky worlds where I attempt to unravel the mysteries of metaphor, illusion, humor, or symbolism, this subjective approach is not foolproof. Even when an anthropologist has gained the confidence of people after ten, twenty, or thirty years, he or she may still be the victim of misinterpretation, innuendo, and deceit. I know of Songhay who continue to deceive Jean Rouch, even though he has been a sensitive, knowledgeable, and respected participant in Songhay social life for more than forty years.

What are we to make of these fundamental problems? Are these cases representative of most anthropological work? If we transcend the limitations of the western empirical tradition, whatever they may be, what remains? Are we left with a subjectivism so laced with imperfections that it, too, is worthless? Perhaps we should be more realistic about the goals of the human sciences and take the sober advice of David Hume, who wrote that "all our reasonings concerning causes and effects are derived from nothing but custom; and that belief is more properly an act of the sensitive, than of the cogitative part of our natures" (1902, vol. 1, part 4, sec. 1).

This article follows Hume's advice by taking a realistic view of "anthropological science." Can there *be* an anthropological science? Can we discover the Truth of Human Nature? Are there underlying Laws of Culture? Do we waste our time and resources through endless theorizing, as we try to discover the Ultimate and the Absolute in our search for the Truth?

Anthropology has one strength: ethnography, the original, albeit imperfect, product of our discipline. Despite its taken-for-granted status, ethnography, rather than cultural materialism, structuralism, or any other "ism," has been and will continue to be our core contribution. It is time to appreciate ethnographers, who produce works of art that become powerful vehicles of theoretical exposition.[1]

Plato: The Episteme and the Science of Anthropology

Much of Michel Foucault's work has focused on the episteme, "that apparatus which makes possible the separation of not the true from the false, but of what may from what may not be characterized as scientific" (1980:197). In his diverse works on madness, sexuality, criminal justice, medicine, and the history of the human sciences, Foucault demonstrates how the episteme governs what we see, what we think, what we say, and what we write. He also describes how historical forces have combined in different periods of time to change a given episteme. He writes of the episteme of the Renaissance, in which words have an existence of their own. He describes the classical episteme, an age of *mathesis,* in which words are neutral, conveyors of pure representation in a mechanistic order. He discusses the modern episteme, in which scholars discover the finitude of man, a discovery that heralds the human sciences. And yet the human sciences present, as Foucault (1970:399) suggests, an epistemological paradox: "Not only are the human sciences able to do without a concept of man, they are unable to pass through it, for they always address themselves to that which constitutes his outer limits. One may say of them what Lévi-Strauss said of ethnology: that they dissolve man."

Lévi-Strauss's comment may seem wrong, unless one considers the development of the scientific epistemology that, Whitehead has suggested, "consists of a series of footnotes to Plato" (1969:153). Foucault notwithstanding, the search for Truth transcends any episteme and dissolves human *being* in the human sciences.

The Legacy of Plato

Plato emerged in Greek thinking at a time of systematic reflection, creating order from the chaos. Consider, for example, Heraclitus's attempt to characterize the perception of Being:

> Do not listen to me, the moral speaker, but be in hearkening to the Laying that gathers; first belong to this and then you hear properly; such hearing *is* when a letting-lie-together-before occurs by which the gathering letting-lie, the Laying that gathers, lies before us gathered; when a letting-lie-before occurs, the fateful comes to pass. . . . (as translated in Heidegger 1975:75)

From these philosophical fragments Plato devised the search for Truth, to paraphrase Richard Rorty (1983), in which we turn away from subjectivity (Heraclitus's oblique writing) to objectivity. Objectivity was Plato's solution to the puzzle of infinite variability in the world of appearances. And so Plato was the first thinker to distinguish appearance from reality: behind every appearance there is hidden immutable Form. These Forms are the archetypes of knowledge, distinguished from opinion, which, in Plato's view, is as unstable as the flux of appearances. Knowledge, on the other hand, is an immutable pillar of reality.

From these simple distinctions, the epistemology of western sciences was born. These metaphysical distinctions, I suggest, have not been disputed by others since Plato; rather, thinkers have disputed only how to discover the reality hidden behind appearances, how to arrive at Truth.

Saussure's Signs

Rousseau began an era in which scholars searched for Platonic Truth in the origins of things: the origin of society through an examination of pristine groups; the origin of language in comparative philology. Saussure, seeking the structure (reality) behind the variable surface of speech, argued for the synchronic study of language. In systematic linguistics, language (*langue*) contrasts with speech (*parole*). *Langue* "is not to be confused with human speech (*langage*), of which it is a definite part. It (*langue*) is both a social product of the faculty of speech and a collection of necessary conventions that have been adopted by a social body to permit individuals to exercise that faculty" (Saussure 1915:9). Saussure considered speech (*parole*) beyond his study, for it is so heterogeneous that "We cannot put it into any category of human facts, and we cannot discover its unity" (ibid.:9). Saussure further emphasized the primacy of *langue* over *parole*: "Language (*langue*). . .is a self-contained whole and a principle of classification. As soon as we give language (*langue*) first place among the facts of speech, we introduce natural order into a mass that lends itself to no other classification" (ibid.:9). In seeking the ultimate truth of language, Saussure, like Plato, sought the One, *langue,* in this case an elegantly self-contained whole, from the Many, *parole,* a heterogeneous tangle of variability.

Saussure distinguished signifier from signified, and for him the sign consisted of "the whole that results from the associating of signifier to signified" (ibid.:67). The sign, in its relationship of the signifier to the signified, is an immutable form. Although time does change linguistic signs, the fundamental relationship between signifier and signified transcends the temporary; it remains unchanged. This is tantamount to saying that the relationship of signifier to signified is an immutable form, the One underlying the Many.

The work of Saussure set the stage for two major movements in social science: structural linguistics and structuralism. The structural linguists were inspired by Saussure's notion of synchrony, as well as by his idea that linguistics is the study of *langue* rather than *parole*. The Prague School of Linguistics took up the structural analysis in phonology. In the United States, by contrast, Bloomfield extended the structural analysis of *langue* to morphology, syntax, and semantics. In both schools, units of analysis—phonemes, morphemes, syntagmemes, and so on—were all-important. For structural linguists the phoneme is a construct quite different from the phone, the sounds of which are infinitely variable. The phoneme, a minimal unit of sound that has distributive meaning, limits the infinite variability of phones. Immutable phonemes are isolated through contrastive analysis; they are units that linguists induce from phones, or, put another way, from fleeting appearances.

Lévi-Strauss's debt to structural linguistics, especially to Jakobson, a Prague School linguist, is well-known. The structural linguists taught Lévi-Strauss that language is a system of systems. And just as language is a system of systems, so culture, in Lévi-Strauss's view, is a system of systems. In culture as in language, there are hidden elementary structures, discoverable through scientific analysis, that not only link past with present, but also the Rousseauistic primitive with the modern. Following in the footsteps of Saussure, Lévi-Strauss devised a method, structuralism, in which the One, cognitive structures common to all human beings, could be delimited from the Many, individual structural relations.

In his monumental *The Elementary Structures of Kinship*, Lévi-Strauss focused on the institution of marriage. Marriage practices seem beyond explanation, as they are so alarmingly variable. But Lévi-Strauss demonstrated that what appears to be marriage is in reality the exchange of women:

> In the course of this work, we have seen the notion of exchange become complicated and diversified; it has constantly *appeared* to us in different forms. Sometimes exchange appears direct. . . .Sometimes it functions within a total system . . .and at others it instigates the formation of an unlimited number of special systems and short cycles unconnected among themselves. . . .Sometimes the exchange is explicit . . .and at other times it is implicit. . . .Sometimes the exchange is closed, while sometimes it is open. . . .But no matter what form it takes, whether direct or indirect, general or special, immediate or deferred, explicit or implicit, closed or open, concrete or symbolic, it is exchange, always exchange, that emerges as the fundamental and common basis of *all* modalities of the institution of marriage. (1969:478–479) (italics added)

To discover the meaning of a given institution, like marriage, the analyst uncovers the reality obscured by the haze of appearances. Like his intellectual ancestors from Plato on, Lévi-Strauss seeks the One among the Many:

> The ultimate goal of the human sciences is not to constitute man, but to dissolve him. The critical importance of ethnology is that it represents the first step in a process which includes others. Ethnographic analysis tries to arrive at invariants beyond the empirical diversity of societies. . . .This initial enterprise opens the way for others . . .which are incumbent on the natural sciences: the reintegration of culture into nature and generally of life into the whole of its physico-chemical conditions. . . .One can understand, therefore, why I find in ethnology the principle of all research. (quoted in Geertz 1973:346)

In my view ethnology is for Lévi-Strauss not only the principle for all research, but for the metaphysics founded by Plato more than 2,500 years ago.

Anthropological Adages

What has been good for Lévi-Strauss has been good for most anthropologists. I do not suggest that all anthropologists are latent structuralists; rather, I argue that most anthropologists are members of the community of western metaphysicians. We, like Lévi-Strauss, search for the One in the Many; we seek out the Platonic Truth, the reality lurking behind appearances.

Radcliffe-Brown (1953) did not hesitate to place anthropological science within metaphysics. In numerous articles he steadfastly suggested that anthropology, or what he called comparative sociology, was a branch of the natural sciences in which scholars would induce social structures to be compared. Through comparison, Radcliffe-Brown argued, anthropologists arrive inductively at "laws of social statics" (what Lévi-Strauss referred to as "invariants"). Plato, of course, referred to these "laws" as Forms. Like Radcliffe-Brown, Malinowski thought that general propositions can be induced from a mass of data. One first collects ethnographic facts, Malinowski tells us, and then analyzes them to see what patterns unfold.

These metaphysical patterns are present in contemporary theoretical orientations in anthropology. The ethnography of communication provides an example. Dell Hymes argues for describing society from the vantage of communication (speaking). He points, rightly, to the importance of describing cultural conceptions from the point of view of those who are being studied—the so-called emic grid. From emic data, the ethnographer of communication classifies communicative acts, events, or situations within their cultural context. Hymes warns, however, that taxonomy is not an end in itself; the object is the painstaking recording of ethnographic diversity: "The work of taxonomy is a necessary part of progress toward models (structural and generative) of sociolinguistic description, formulation of universal sets of features and relations, and explanatory theories" (Hymes 1974:35). Joining the universalists of the Platonic heritage, Hymes adds: "In sum, just as a theory of grammar must have its universal terms, so must a theory of language use" (ibid.:43). Indeed, without the universal terms natural scientists use, how can sociolinguists or social scientists compare data from highly diverse societies? How can they achieve theoretical wholes from the muddle of variable data?

The taken-for-granted Platonic distinctions, which weave themselves into so many theories, also appear in recent theories of ethnography. The New Ethnography was an attempt to produce reliable and valid ethnographic accounts. From Goodenough onward, the new ethnographers, who later became ethnoscientists and ethnosemanticists, formulated ideational theories of culture. Folk taxonomies, componential analysis, cognitive maps and rules, all of which were induced from carefully collected data, were etic reflections of the cognitive processes of a variety of peoples. As with the ethnography of communication, this research moved away from taxonomy toward a universal observation language to aid the analyst in the search for that ever-elusive reality hidden behind the mirage of data.

Agar has been particularly sensitive to the need for an ethnographic language. In one recent article he and Hobbs, a computer scientist, call for a theory of ethnography. They write that "ethnography needs theoretical guidelines for the analysis of 'informal ethnographic interviews'" (Agar and Hobbs 1983:33). They propose "Artificial Intelligence Planning" as a way of building a theory language in ethnography to make ethnographic analysis more systematic. As Agar points out, "we desperately need a language to talk about ethnography in a general way" (1982:779). Following the lead of Saussure's discussion of *parole*, and Lévi-Strauss's analysis of marriage, Agar suggests that ethnographies, even on the same people or topic, are so diverse they are difficult to compare. Agar seeks to place the "embarrassing" dissimilarities of written ethnographic accounts into a more systematic framework that he calls "knowledge representation." Here again, an innovative anthropologist looks "beneath" the phenomenon, to paraphrase Merleau-Ponty, for general principles to account for diversity: the One, an ethnographic language, from the Many.

Straw Men, Epistemes, and Discourse

The great logicians taught that the construction of straw men in argument weakens a person's contentions. My discourse on Saussure and Lévi-Strauss has been designed to demonstrate anthropology's taken-for-granted membership in the Platonic tradition (see Diamond

1974:172–174). Were I to stop here, I would be guilty not only of logical fallacy, but also of intellectual negativism. Heirs of the Platonic tradition, anthropologists are caught in institutional webs; they work within an episteme that affects the discourse, the written product of scholarship, that they produce. The search for Truth dissolves man. In contemporary anthropology, as a consequence, theorizing becomes serious business. Theoretical treatises—on ethnography, kinship, exchange, symbolism, cognition—are much more highly valued than vivid description, so published work in anthropology assesses ethnographic data from a Marxist perspective, from a cognitive perspective, from a Freudian perspective, ad infinitum.

Taken-for-granted metaphysics, Jacques Derrida (1976) warns, makes scholars lose sight of what *is* in the world. Merleau-Ponty (1964) and Suzanne Langer (1942) suggest that scientific methods, assumptions, and discourse obscure rather than illumine questions of life and consciousness. Caught in the web of metaphysics, we posit Postsocratic universal theory as an alternative to Presocratic chaos. A universal theory produces a discourse that is flat and neutral.

Writing and the Text of Texts

Flat, neutral, and "sludgy" writing is endemic in anthropological discourse. I find examples of it every time I pick up a journal, read a line or two, a page or two, rub my eyes, and put the journal down. No wonder, when I consider some typical openings, which Tedlock (1982) considers rhetorically significant.[2]

Example 1: Ethnologists and archaeologists, in general, have expressed relatively little interest in the development of a unified ecological view of aboriginal life in the Great Plains. (Osborn 1983:563)

Example 2: In anthropological theory, variations in the sexual division of labor have often been seen as causes of variations in residence patterns, marriage practices, beliefs about gender, socialization patterns, and many other aspects of human behavior and belief. (White, Burton, and Dow 1981:824)

Example 3: Interest in the way a "native" sees his or her culture has a long history in American anthropology, going back to Franz Boas, Ruth

Benedict, Robert Lowie, Ralph Linton, and many others active in the first half of the 20th century. This interest has continued with new theories and methods of description, classification, and analysis of cultural phenomena. (Kaplan and Levine 1981:869)

Example 4: Cultural understandings about ethnic identity typically entail beliefs about personality traits characteristic of particular categories of people or groups. (White and Prachuabmoh 1982:2)

Example 5: Anthropology in the English-speaking Caribbean is marked by an analytical antinomy that reflects the great historical ambiguity of Caribbean societies. (Austin 1983:223)

Example 6: Gilbert (1981) concludes that corporate cognatic descent groups exist in upper class Lima [Peru] society. (Appell 1983:302)

Example 7: This paper concerns the communication of affect, and the role therein of cultural and linguistic systems. It explores some analytical issues in cross-cultural comparison and the notion of "expressive language" and it examines modes of affective expression in a particular ethnographic case. (Irvine 1982:31)

Example 8: Keenan (1973:49) has defined the pragmatic presupposition as the "relation between the utterance of a sentence and the context in which it is uttered." (Stoller 1977:31)

This prose, including my own, reflects the alienation of the anthropological episteme. "The anthropologist who treats the indigene as an object may define himself as relatively free, but that is an illusion. For in order to objectify the other, one is, at the same time, compelled to objectify the self " (Diamond 1974:93). This objectification is expressed in anthropological discourse.

Monographs are not exempt from flat, neutral, and sludgy writing, although, given the breadth of this form, there is opportunity for eye-opening, invigorating prose. But before a reader gets to the good stuff of a monograph—if there is any to be found—he or she suffers prefaces and introductions, which tend to be longer versions of the opening lines of journal articles. One otherwise excellent book begins: "This is an ethnographic study of sound as a cultural system. . . .My intention is to show how an analysis of modes and codes of sound communication leads to an understanding of the ethos and quality of life in . . . society" (Feld 1982:3). There are many exceptions, of course, but in prefaces or introductions, contemporary authors discuss their subject and their approach via a general review of the literature. Then the data are presented to underscore the major thesis of the book. Finally, the author summarizes the data and presents the conclusions.

How many recent monographs have begun like Raymond Firth's classic *We, The Tikopia*:

> In the cool of the early morning, just before sunrise, the bow of the *Southern Cross* headed towards the eastern horizon, on which a tiny dark blue outline was faintly visible. Slowly it grew into a rugged mountain mass, standing up sheer from the ocean; then as we approached within a few miles it revealed around its base a narrow ring of low, flat land thick with vegetation. The sullen grey day, with its lowering clouds, strengthened my grim impression of a solitary peak, wild and stormy, upthrust in a waste of waters. (Firth 1936:3)

Firth's description is the stuff of great ethnography, in which the anthropologist-as-writer considers the reader-as-reader, interpreting silently a book's multilogued prose. While one may view the ideas that seep out between the lines of *We, The Tikopia* as dated, the prose of this magnificent ethnography leaves a vivid impression of the people of that island. Firth's detailed ethnography—imperfect, as are all ethnographies—becomes part of the ethnographic record, an eternal document in the history of humanity.

There are more recent examples of splendidly written ethnographies. One thinks of Michael Lambek's (1981) *Human Spirits,* especially his introduction, "Cultural Zero," in which he describes his first encounter with spirit possession on the island of Mayotte. And then there is Vincent Crapanzano's rich description of a Hamshida possession ritual (1973). And there is Jeanne Favret-Saada's highly personalized *Deadly Words*:

> Take an ethnographer; she has chosen to investigate contemporary witchcraft in the Bocage of Western France. She has already done some fieldwork; she has a basic academic training; she has published some papers on the logic of murder, violence and insurrection in an altogether different tribal society. She is now working in France to avoid having to learn yet another difficult language. . . .

...Take an ethnographer. She has spent more than 30 months in the Bocage in Mayenne, studying witchcraft. "How exciting, how thrilling, how extraordinary...!" "Tell us about witches," she is asked again and again when she gets back to the city. Just as one might say: tell us tales about ogres and wolves, about Little Red Riding Hood. Frighten us, but make it clear that it's only a story; or that they are just peasants: credulous, backward and marginal. (Favret-Saada 1981:3-4)

This kind of lush, vivid, lyrical, and personal writing lies beyond the usual parameters of appropriateness that have been established within the episteme of anthropology. Unfortunately, one does not become a distinguished ethnographer because of the quality of one's prose, or the memorability of one's descriptions.

Anthropological discourse is characterized by the search for "invariants beyond the empirical diversity of societies" (Lévi-Strauss, cited in Geertz 1973:346). The search must isolate and account for aspects of human behavior, and not the murkiness and imprecision of human existence. In a recent article on "Human Linguistics," Ross skillfully highlights the relationship between episteme and discourse. Some linguists, he writes, are concerned with answering the question: "What formal principles, both language-particular and universal, are necessary and sufficient to characterize the distribution of and relationships among linguistic elements in each of the languages of the world?" (Ross 1982:5). Human linguistics is concerned with an altogether different question: "What can the study of language tell us about human beings?" (ibid.:6).

All this sounds rather simplistic, but one's world changes drastically when one becomes a human linguist or a humanistic ethnographer. This transformation is evident in the form, content, and style of Ross's article, which is so unusual that the editor of the anthology in which it was published had to frame the piece with an editor's note: "The typographical format requested, designed, and employed by the author to make his personal statement is intended by him to reflect the style of an oral paper" (Byrnes 1982:1). I disagree. The discourse of Ross's paper reflects the form, style, and content of a human linguist. After talking about how to begin his remarks, Ross writes:

i want to show you   some of my most recent work   which
is not in   any way   to   be viewed as an extension of generative grammar   however   possibly a way can be found to

relate it to the broad and very important concerns which involve us tonight   we need soon   i think   to have a round-
table on the subject of linguistics and juggling. . . .
i will be happy to teach any of you   who would like to
learn   during the course of this conference   how to juggle
i know a way of teaching that is almost guaranteed to teach
anyone in 20 minutes   and the record time is 4 minutes
you can learn how to do the basic juggle   and it's lots of fun
one of the important things   i think   at least i've used
it as sort of a diagnostic in my own work   is if i'm not
having fun in what i'm doing   i think   there must be something seriously wrong someplace   and i start to worry
about it. (Ross 1982:1–2)

A statement on human linguistics as a poem; an editor's note. An author's direct confrontation between metaphysics and art.

Plato, Art, and Metaphysics

The birth of metaphysics, of Ultimate Forms, of the search for Truth,
set the boundaries between art and metaphysics. Plato wanted the dra-
matic artists expelled from his Republic, for the sentiments that
dramatists are capable of provoking lead people back to the heroic myths
and ignorance, rather than toward the discovery of Ultimate Forms.
Plato, quoting Socrates, writes:

> When any one of these pantomimic gentlemen, who are so clever
> that they imitate anything, come to us, and make a proposal to ex-
> hibit himself and his poetry, we will fall down and worship him as a
> sweet and holy and wonderful being, but we must also inform him
> that in our State such as he are not permitted to exist; the law will
> not allow them. (cited in Diamond 1974:187)

And why not? Because in the State, the poet or dramatist does not fit any
of the social categories prescribed by the doctrine of Ultimate Forms.
Put another way, art and metaphysics become mutually exclusive; hence
the need for the editor's note framing Ross's poetic "Human Linguistics." Hence, flat, neutral, and sludgy prefaces, pretexts, and texts in
anthropological discourse.

Yet when anthropologists are confronted with something they
cannot explain, they find that the foundation of this aged metaphysics
begins to crumble, that the discourse that worked so well in a previous
study cannot adequately represent a particular field incident.

Experience and Language

Art and science should complement one another. Indeed, if we focus upon anthropological texts not as explicit logico-deductive/inductive statements, but rather as texts that describe the texture of a society to a reader, the possibility of this complementarity stares us in the face. Merleau-Ponty's later writings focused upon the power of language, especially of what he called the "indirect language." He writes in *The Visible and the Invisible* that philosophical discourse should have the "voice" of the indirect language:

> ...words most charged with philosophy are not necessarily those that contain what they say, but rather those that most energetically open upon being, because they more closely convey the life of the whole and make our habitual evidences vibrate until they disjoin. (Merleau-Ponty 1982:102–103)

Merleau-Ponty calls upon philosophers to use language to bring readers into contact with "brute and wild being." Anthropologists need to confront language in its full being and not as a neutral mechanism of representation. Consider the words of Heidegger:

> To undergo an experience with language, then, means to let ourselves be properly concerned by the claim of language by entering into and submitting to it. If it is true that man finds the proper abode of his existence in language—whether he is aware of it or not—then an experience we undergo with language will touch the innermost nexus of our existence. We who speak language may thereupon become transformed by such experiences, from one day to the next or in the course of time. But now it could be that an experience we undergo with language is too much for us moderns, even if it strikes us only to the extent that for once it draws our attention to our *relation to language,* so that from then on we may keep this relation in mind. (Heidegger 1971:57–58)

Ross seems to have experienced the Being of language; his poem is a multilogue. It not only concerns a current debate in theoretical linguistics, but also suggests a fundamental epistemological shift toward humanism in the most positivistic of the social sciences. Favret-Saada and Contreras (1981) wrote an ethnography in the literary form of a diary, where they record Favret-Saada's experience in the Bocage of western France. This diary becomes an open window through which the reader is swept into the Bocage. Readers experience the authors' joy, doubts, fears, and disappointments. They get to know informants as people. And between the beautifully written lines of *Corps pour corps* the anthropological reader is struck by the theoretical importance of this work. But people will ask: Is Haj Ross's article really linguistics? Or: Is the work of Favret-Saada and Contreras really anthropology? These are questions asked by people who have never fully experienced the Being of language.

The Reconstruction of Ethnography

Even if one has experienced the Being of language, one is still caught in the straitjacket of the episteme, anthropological or otherwise. One cannot perceive, conceive, speak, or write in a cultural vacuum. My discourse in this paper has followed a standard form (introduction, review of the pertinent literature, argument, and conclusion). We anthropologists are all caught in an epistemological double bind: we seek Truth, the One in the Many; we covet abstract principles as we distinguish opinion from knowledge; we create categories of appearance and reality; we posit domains of metaphysics (or science) and of art; we create one discourse for metaphysics and one for art. And even if we transcend the limitations posed by all these binary oppositions—to blend science with art—our categories, as Hume (1902: vol. 1, part 4, sec. 1) wrote, are still derived from custom.

What remains in this philosophical rubble? Perhaps I can say that anthropologists can never be engineers; we must remain *bricoleurs* rummaging through the debris of deconstructed ideas for something new and meaningful. But that something new for which we search endlessly has but one fate: to be deconstructed in its own turn. For Derrida, "knowledge is not a systematic tracking down of truth that is hidden but may be found. It is rather the field 'of *freeplay,* that is to say, a field of infinite substitutions in the closure of a finite ensemble'" (Spivak 1976:xix). Derrida's critique of western philosophy offers no alternative to a world without a metaphysical foundation. Must we go to these Derridean extremes? I think not. Realistically, an anthropology formulated on positivistic or phenomenological grounds is full of imperfections. But from the debris of these imperfections, I suggest the possibility of a reconstruction of ethnography.

This reconstruction would not concern a theory to discuss ethnography in a general way (Agar 1982:779). Indeed, a theory of ethnography would only attempt to make anthropology more like "real science," to allow us to avoid the "embarrassment" of not having a theory of something—ethnography—which "is at the heart of Anthropologies that deal with living peoples" (ibid.:779). The reconstruction of ethnography is rather a call for a humanistic anthropology, a call for meaningful descriptions of what Armstrong (1971) calls "human being," a call for fine ethnographies like Fernandez's (1982).

The reconstruction of ethnography, however, implies a great deal more than a valorization of ethnographic writing; it implies a fundamental epistemological shift toward the Other and away from ethnographic realism. We need to describe others as people and give them a voice in our discourse. We need to write ethnographies as multilayered texts that communicate to a number of audiences. We need to acknowledge in the text the presence of an ethnographer who engages in dialogue with his or her subjects.

I returned to Mehanna in 1982–83 to continue my studies of the Songhay. One morning as I trudged along the paths that cut through the walled compounds of the town, I greeted Amadu, a bent-over old man well into his seventies. For more than five years, I had greeted this man as I walked by his compound: "How is your wife?" "How are your wife's people?" "How are the people in your compound?" "How is your health?" He would always respond that all was well and would ask after my health. Until that day in 1983 I knew nothing else about this man.

"I am glad to learn that you are in good health, my son," he said to me that morning. (Songhay elders often call younger men "my son.")

"That I am, Baba [father]."

"For five years you have greeted me."

"That is true."

"And you have asked nothing of me."

"True."

"For five years I have watched you, and today you shall know me. Come into my house. I like you and that is why I shall give you the story of my life."

I wondered what he would tell me. Inside his dark, thatched hut was an altar. Miniature leather sandals and small clay jugs tied to pieces of cloth hung from bundles of sticks that formed the skeleton of the hut.

"I am a *zima* [ritual priest of the possession cult], and I have been one for more than fifty years."

"I did not know, Baba."

"We Songhay do not talk of our strengths to anyone. We must know people first. I know you now, my son, and I want you to know me. Go and get your machine [tape recorder] so you can open it and learn my story."

I went to get my tape recorder and "opened" it for this great, wise man. He had been an orphan who left the island of his birth, Sinder, as a young man. He traveled about the Sahel in search of work, mostly as a farmhand. He then traveled to Aribinda, the great center of farming magic, where he apprenticed himself to a master magician. After seven years in Aribinda, he traveled to the Borgu in northern Togo, where he again apprenticed himself to a master magician. He returned to Niger and spent one year in Sangara, one of the magic cities of the Songhay. There he learned about the Songhay spirits and became a *zima*. After fifteen years of training he settled in Mehanna, where he became the priest of the local possession cult. Today he practices magic and healing and never leaves his house.

After recounting his long and detailed life history, Amadu Zima discussed with me Songhay philosophy and magic. He spoke about the spirits, recited incantations and praise-poetry, revealed the secret names of magical plants, and performed three rites that would protect me from the vicissitudes of enemies and spirits alike.

We talked for weeks and throughout our discussions Amadu Zima continued to proclaim how much he liked me. "I would never tell this to anyone," he said. "But I tell my life, my secrets, to you, Paul, because I like you. You like me. You ask questions. You want to learn my ways. You are like the son I never had."

Amadu Zima does not represent all the Songhay; his story is his own. Yet how can we ignore such a man in the name of ethnographic realism? How can we ignore what the Amadu Zimas and Fatoumas can teach us about ourselves, about life? Is it not their voices that will help us to reconstruct ethnography?

Notes

Acknowledgments. The research upon which this paper is based was made possible with the financial assistance of a number of institutions. These include the USDOE Fulbright-Hays Doctoral Dissertation Program, the Wenner-Gren Foundation for Anthropological Research, the NATO Postdoctoral Fellowship in Science Program (NSF), the American Philosophical Society, and West Chester University. I thank all these institutions for their generous support. An earlier version of this paper was read before James Fernandez's seminar on symbolic action at Princeton University; the seminar's participants provided me with much constructive commentary. Jim Fernandez, for his part, has been an ongoing source of support and guidance. Phyllis Chock was kind enough to invite me to speak before the Anthropological Society of Washington, an invitation that motivated me to complete a manuscript that had long been gathering dust on my desk. Lucille Mitchell, as always, typed the manuscript with patience, perseverance, and good humor.

1. This paper concerns the broad philosophical underpinnings of anthropology as they are reflected in anthropological discourse. A growing literature—an excellent literature—discusses ethnographies as texts. The works of Marcus (1980), Marcus and Cushman (1982), and Clifford (1980, 1981, 1983), for example, discuss indirectly the anthropological episteme. They consider such topics as ethnographic realism, the authority of ethnographic texts, the displaced authority of experimental ethnographic texts, ethnographic rhetoric, and the relationship between writers and readers of ethnography. My focus here is similar but broader. Instead of considering style, form, or ethnographic rhetoric directly, my interest lies in the epistemological constraints that govern institutional judgments of anthropological writing. More expositions, especially historical ones, are needed.

2. My "sludge list" of anthropological writing is undoubtedly skewed or unrepresentative, since I selected from the beginnings of journal articles or books. I selected these beginnings deliberately; with Edward Said (1975), I believe beginnings are rhetorically and philosophically significant. They are intentional. The "anthropological beginning" directly reflects an author's intention. Lyrical, revelatory beginnings reflect, generally, a humanistic or critical interpretation to follow. Beginnings with theoretical contentions or general assumptions, by contrast, signal a more positivistic approach. My view, of course, is preliminary.

References Cited

Agar, Michael
   1982   Toward an Ethnographic Language. American Anthropologist 84:779–796.

Agar, Michael, and Jerry Hobbs
   1983   Natural Plans: Using AI Planning in the Analysis of Ethnographic Interviews. Ethos 11:33–49.

Appell, George
   1983   Methodological Problems with the Concepts of Corporation, Corporate Social Grouping, and Cognatic Descent Group. American Ethnologist 10:302–313.

Armstrong, Robert Plant
1971   The Affecting Presence. Champaign-Urbana: University of Illinois Press.

Austin, Diane J.
1983   Culture and Ideology in the English-Speaking Caribbean. American Ethnologist· 10:223–241.

Byrnes, Heidi (ed.)
1982   Contemporary Perceptions of Language: Interdisciplinary Dimensions. Washington, D.C.: Georgetown University Press.

Clifford, James
1980   Fieldwork, Reciprocity, and the Making of Ethnographic Texts: The Example of Maurice Leenhardt. Man 15:518–532.
1981   On Ethnographic Surrealism. Comparative Studies in Society and History. 23:539–564.
1983   On Ethnographic Authority. Representations 1:118–146.

Crapanzano, Vincent
1973   Hamadsha: A Study of Moroccan Ethnopsychiatry. Berkeley: University of California Press.

Derrida, Jacques
1976   Of Grammatology. G. C. Spivak, transl. Baltimore: John Hopkins University Press.

Diamond, Stanley
1974   In Search of the Primitive. London: Transaction Books.

Favret-Saada, Jeanne
1981   Deadly Words: Witchcraft in the Bocage. London: Cambridge University Press.

Favret-Saada, Jeanne, and Jose Contreras
1981   Corps pour corps: Enquête sur la sorcellerie dans le Bocage. Paris: Gallimard.

Feld, Steven
1982   Sound and Sentiment: Birds, Weeping, Poetics, and Song in Kaluli Expression. Philadelphia: University of Pennsylvania Press.

Fernandez, James W.
1982   Bwiti. Princeton, N.J.: Princeton University Press.

Firth, Raymond
1936   We, The Tikopia. London: Allen & Unwin.

Foucault, Michel
1970   The Order of Things: An Archaeology of the Human Sciences. New York: Random House.
1980   Power/Knowledge: Selective Interviews and Other Writings. New York: Pantheon Books.

Geertz, Clifford
1973   The Interpretation of Cultures. New York: Basic Books.

Heidegger, Martin
1971   On the Way to Language. New York: Harper and Row.
1975   Early Greek Thinking. New York: Harper and Row.

Hume, David
1902 Enquiries Concerning Human Understanding. Oxford: Clarendon Press.

Hymes, Dell
1974 Foundations in Sociolinguistics. Philadelphia: University of Pennsylvania Press.

Irvine, Judith
1982 The Communication of Affect. *In* Contemporary Perceptions of Language: Interdisciplinary Dimensions. H. Byrnes, ed. pp. 31–47. Washington D.C.: Georgetown University Press.

Kaplan, Flora, and David M. Levine
1981 Cognitive Mapping of a Fold Taxonomy of Mexican Pottery: A Multivariate Approach. American Anthropologist 83:868–885.

Lambek, Michael
1981 Human Spirits: A Cultural Account of Trance in Mayotte. London: Cambridge University Press.

Langer, Suzanne
1942 Philosophy in a New Key. Cambridge: Harvard University Press.

Lévi-Strauss, Claude
1967 Structural Anthropology. Garden City, N.Y.: Doubleday.
1969 The Elementary Structures of Kinship. Boston: Beacon Press.

Marcus, George E.
1980 Rhetoric and the Ethnographic Genre in Anthropological Research. Current Anthropology 21:507–510.

Marcus, George E., and Dick Cushman
1982 Ethnographies as Texts. Annual Review of Anthropology 11:25–69.

Merleau-Ponty, Maurice
1964 L'Oeil et l'esprit. Paris: Gallimard.
1968 The Visible and the Invisible. Evanston, Ill.: Northwestern University Press.

Osborn, Alan J.
1983 Ecological Aspects of Equestrian Adaptations in Aboriginal North America. American Anthropologist 85:563–592.

Radcliffe-Brown, A. R.
1953 Structure and Function in Primitive Society. Chicago: University of Chicago Press.

Rorty, Richard
1983 Relativism. Howison Lecture, University of California-Berkeley, January 31, 1983.

Ross, Haj
1982 Human Linguistics. *In* Contemporary Perceptions of Language: Interdisciplinary Dimensions. H. Byrnes, ed. pp. 1–30. Washington D.C.: Georgetown University Press.

Russell, Bertrand
1945 A History of Western Philosophy. New York: Simon and Schuster.

Said, Edward W.
1975   Beginnings. New York: Basic Books.

Saussure, Ferdinand de
1959   [1915] Course in General Linguistics. New York: Philosophical Library.

Spivak, G. B.
1976   Introduction. To Of Grammatology (Derrida). Baltimore: Johns Hopkins University Press.

Stoller, Paul A.
1977   Ritual and Personal Insults in Songrai Sonni. Anthropology 2:33–38.

Tedlock, Dennis
1982   Anthropological Hermeneutics and the Problem of Alphabetic Literacy. In A Crack in the Mirror. J. Ruby, ed. pp. 149–161. Philadelphia: University of Pennsylvania Press.

White, Douglas, Michael Burton, and Malcolm Dow
1981   Sexual Division of Labor in African Agriculture: A Network Auto-Correlation Analysis. American Anthropologist 83:824–850.

White, Geoffrey, and Chavivun Parchuabmoh
1983   The Cognitive Organization of Ethnic Images. Ethos 11:2–33.

Whitehead, Alfred North
1969   Process and Reality. New York: Free Press.

Of Definitions and Boundaries: The Status of Culture in the Culture of the State

Michael Herzfeld
Indiana University

In the autobiography of Giambattista Vico (1977[1728]:28), we learn that the only occasion on which he was awarded any kind of academic prize was for the presentation of a treatise, "full of Greek and Latin erudition and critical treatment" (*ripiena di greca e latina erudizione e critica*), on the etymology of the term *stato*, "state." The irony is at once cruel and instructive: cruel, because Vico's followers did indeed transmute his highly flexible insight into the relationship between symbolic form and cultural identity into various types of nationalistic dogmatism,[1] and instructive because it illustrates the characteristic devotion of established academic institutions to seeking legitimacy for the parent polity.

We do not know what Vico actually wrote in his disquisition, as the text has been lost. His pursuit of etymology in the search for hidden historical truths, however, invites emulation. Thus, "playing Vico," we could highlight the fact that *stato* is used as the past perfect participle of the verb for "be" (*essere*; cf. *stare*, "stand; be in a certain state or condition"). Such an etymology represents the state as the ultimate eternal verity, that which "has [always] been," and as such an outstanding example of what we would today call "naturalization." In that case, the transmogrification of a verb particle into something having the status of a noun—*lo stato*, "*the* state"—bears witness to a process of reification that is most informative about the nature of the "cultural state"—in both senses of that phrase. We may surmise further that officialdom failed to appreciate the point. With their literalistic perception of reality, the representatives of formal culture would have taken any such etymological imaginings at face value, and assumed that they indeed validated the

75

state's claims to the standing (*status*) of an eternal verity—the political equivalent of a *statement* in language.

Vico's imaginative games with etymology were the very antithesis of that kind of literalism, however, and we can take our lead from him. The social world is suffused with "trailing clouds of etymology" (Austin 1971:99–100) that give to social experience a range of meanings both allusive and elusive. "Fact" and "fiction" come from the same root, and "invent" is derived from the Latin verb for "discover." That these two etymologies have virtually disappeared from popular awareness is a clear indication of how far the illusion of literality has triumphed over what Deely (1982:1) appropriately calls the "semiotic consciousness"—that is, the awareness that all human experience is mediated, that description must always at some level be construction.

Nor are these etymological insights the only ones to have suffered the ravages of indifferent time. Perhaps most significantly of all for my present purpose, the "nation" (*natio*), that most cultural of entities, ultimately derives its legitimacy from its foundation in "nature" (*natura*). The etymological hunt can thus also be pursued in reverse, by resurrecting a host of derivations from the "dead stretches of experience" (Ardener 1978:111)—the recorded but now largely inert history of Western academic discourse, an area usually regarded as fit only for the more abstruse and irrelevant kinds of academic burrowing. Far more than a mere punning game, the search for an etymological history of reification serves to remind us of processes that are constantly at work through language and other semiotic systems, and that principally serve the interests of those political and ideological formations that have successfully established their respective legitimacies.

In the linguistic sphere, for example, the status of the state is supported by *state*ments. The concept of the statement or constative utterance suggests, as Austin (1975:139–147) argued, a view of language that ignores the social conditions under which discourse is produced. Meaning is not a given, a datum; it is created by the interaction between an intending and an interpreting actor and by the alternation of roles between them, and the force of a performative utterance lies in the immediacy of the social situation. A *state*ment, by contrast, would be given its force by the a priori validity of its premise. All attempts to naturalize a contingent claim (for example, to the legitimacy of a new government) therefore claim to be statements, or representations of fact. By treating them as performatives, and by focusing on the constructedness of their factuality, one can challenge their legitimacy. Nationalists appeal to "tradition" because its antiquity validates their claims by rooting them in a seemingly unassailable bedrock of historical fact;[2] its constructedness is suppressed, as is the performative force of its presentation, through the solemn medium of academe. Nationalists naturalize their concerns by rendering them as self-evident truths. Ironically, however, it is the very performativity of discourse, its ability to express a fiat, that makes such a transformation possible.

Nationhood, especially as conceived by the Romantic nationalists of the early nineteenth century in Europe, was explicitly *cultural*; yet its claims to eternal validity rested on the authority of a culturalized *nature*. Thus, the concept of nation encapsulated a paradox, and in this regard it reproduced, or at least prefigured, what Alain Goldschläger (1982) has called "authoritarian discourse." This rhetorical mode has much in common with Lévi-Strauss's view of myth: mutually incompatible propositions are presented as mutually reinforcing statements, paradoxes as truisms (see Herzfeld 1985:199). The very concept of nationhood that undergirds all of Goldschläger's illustrative examples fits the pattern. The nation is conceived in the Romantic canon as a natural entity that can only reach full self-determination through the acquisition of political statehood—a quintessentially *cultural* imposition of order upon chaos. This process entails the privileging of the arbitrary; thus, it provides a classic example of semiotic illusion, or literalism, in which the *signifiant* is mistaken for the *signifié*, the natural symbols of statehood for nature itself. Here, in the abstract, is the logic of the passport office, a social institution that has the authority to "naturalize" human beings.

Nature, however, is not *necessarily* benign. In most societies, outsiders are "animals," or at least appreciably less human than ourselves. For the Greeks of today, "animal" (*zoö*) is a grave insult, suitable for Turks and antisocial individuals, but not in any sense a joking term to be used in addressing one's compatriots. Nature, then, or at least an important part of it, is here opposed to an exalted *culture*. Clearly, "nature" is employed in two quite divergent senses. On the one hand, it is a term that conjures up the supposedly bestial world of alien societies. On the other, culture is cosmologically a part of nature: it is "natural," eternal, and therefore good. The underlying opposition is thus not solely between nature and culture, but between the more inclusive categories of nature-as-evil and nature-as-good, respectively. A moral distinction thus underlies the rhetorical framing of nationhood, and it is on this distinction that the state's claim to be the arbiter of morality ultimately lies: it is the procrustean moral formation upon which all other moralities may be modeled.

The absolute finitude with which such ideas are articulated can be seen in the definite article with which official Greek rhetoric refers to the Greek people as *i Fili*, "*the* race." This is in contrast to the usage of the term in everyday discourse with either a specifier ("the *fili* of the Gypsies") or the indefinite article. The same is true of the term *yenos* (Classical *genos*, the "aristocratic conical clan" [Humphreys 1978:194] of ancient times), which has come to mean "the [national] stock." Thus, the great prophets of national independence like Koraes are often called "Teachers of the *Yenos*." The term appears in Classical Greek as an agnatic group, usually of noble status; significantly, it combines the resulting implication of aristocracy with a strong agnatic bias in its transmutation into official modern Greek: *yenos* is the term used to designate the bride's and bride's mother's respective surname groups for the purpose of completing the official registration of a marriage.

The meaning of the term has clearly bifurcated. On the one hand, there are politically insignificant *genē* whose only social meaning appears to be that of an emphasis on the androcentric ideology that belies the implications of a basically cognatic kinship system. On the other hand, the nationalist rhetoric has at one stroke absorbed the *genos*-qua-nation into the state, thereby ensuring that there should no longer exist more than one source of political unity. It has also absorbed and eradicated the very similar (and historically related) popular perception of *yeni* as "groups of people" that we encounter in, for example, certain medieval and postmedieval poems that refer to *ksantha yeni*, "blond tribes"—in other words, the Russians who were expected to come to the rescue of their enslaved Orthodox brethren, the Greeks.[3] Likewise, the popular usage of the Turks as *atimes files* ("untrustworthy races") has no grammatical equivalent in official discourse, even though the sentiment might well be acceptable there; the plural form implies a degree of political fragmentation that official rhetoric cannot accommodate. "Racial" inheritance, nobility, and the male line have all been co-opted and singularized by the discourse of the bureaucratic state. The resulting grammatical uniformity (singular noun, definite article) reproduces the conceptual reification of social and cultural experience in a unified form.

The term *yenos* has survived in the form *yenia*, usually meaning some kind of agnatic grouping.[4] Thus, doubtless aided by a separate morphological formation, it has strayed from the statist discourse just discussed and has become associated with a plurality of social groups within the local community. Even where agnation is no longer significant, as on the island of Rhodes, one may still hear that a child's character is formed by the "seven patrilines" that contribute to its ancestry (Herzfeld 1983:162–163). On Crete, the *yenia* is virtually a symbol of the local community's opposition to official norms, since it is the normative unit of blood vengeance; it is also a segmentary concept, which automatically places it in opposition to the reified concepts of social grouping necessary to any bureaucratic organization.

Underlying this is a conceptual opposition:

official *yenos*:locally operative *yenia*: :culture:nature.

Although the Greek terms for nation, state, and the like do not contain the same etymological allusions to *natura*, the *yenia* is thought by at least the villagers on whose ideas I have drawn here to be the channel for the transmission of the *fisiko*—"character," but etymologically and more specifically a person's "nature" (*fisi[s]*). The idea of a nation as a *yenos*, then, encapsulates, at least by historical allusion, the embedding of nationhood in nature, much as the Latin roots of the English terms also imply. In short, "nation" is a tropic construction; it brings together two superficially unlike entities and insists on their commonality. It is for this reason that statists must be literalists: their entire rationale rests on the premise that both the nation and the state are "real" entities, not metaphorical ones.

Nationhood thus represents both a naturalization of political centralization (in the sense of representing it as a form of logical entity) and a "culturalization" of nature (in the sense that political centralization is regarded as the finest achievement of reason). The leaders of a society control its definition of nature, and hence also that of culture. Since, however, the state's perspective is a lexicographical one—in the sense that signifiers (words, terms, legal pronouncements) are literalistically represented as invariant with regard to what they signify—the state is unable to detect the rebellious behavior of a popular discourse in which these verbal symbols are deployed in significantly different ways. Perhaps the most striking example of this divergence between the two kinds of discourse (which should nevertheless not be thought of as entirely discontinuous with each other) is in blasphemy, an unreflexive mode of ideological expression in which the doctrinally unitary figures of religious iconography are fragmented through the divisions of the social order (for example, "*your* Virgin Mary") (Herzfeld 1984).

Obviously, such usages slip through the net of definition as we ordinarily understand that concept. These usages are characterized by indefinition, or what is more commonly called indeterminacy. They correspond to the experience of everyday social life, rather than to the packaged order of the state. Definition (Latin *finis*, an earthwork boundary) provides the means whereby meaning is legislated, just as facts can be created cartographically and earthworks thrown up artificially. When one asks a Greek villager for a definition, an interesting reversal of the ethnographer's expectations can be observed. Usually, the informant responds that "X is Y," where Y is a subcategory of X:

1. "What is *filotimo*?" (This is a term commonly if too broadly glossed as "honor" in the Mediterraneanist literature.)
"*Filotimo* is a[n act of] hospitality."

2. "What is *prika*?" (This is the term generally glossed as "dowry.")
"The *prika* is:
(a) [something specific such as] money"; *or*:
(b) "when a daughter receives [a specific kind of] property at marriage."

(Herzfeld 1980b:229)

In short, an example is given in response to the request for a definition. When, on the other hand, an example is requested, the informant usually attempts to generalize (for example, with a statement about women's needs at marriage in response to a request for a definition of *prika*, the marriage portion). Examples only make sense when they are personal; and personal questions conventionally provoke evasion, itself a manifestation of the uncertainty and indeterminacy of social life in a Greek village.

The ethnographer, whose professional activity is characterized by a certain understanding of the relationship between exemplification and generalization (often under the symbolic pairing of theory/ethnography), may thus end up in the position of seeming more statist than the officials who simply take all these definitions for granted. It may well be an unexpected position for an ethnographer determined to do justice to the villagers' ideas and categories, but it is not entirely surprising when seen with the advantage of distance: any "scholar" appears to villagers as the representative of an ill-understood establishment (cf. Friedl 1962:35). For similar reasons, they present their answers to general questions in the form of a definition or an example. If, then, the ordinary sense of exemplification corresponds to a reference theory of meaning, and if reference theory better fits the requirements of statism, the fact that Greek villagers often reverse the definition-example relationship nicely illustrates the conceptual discordance between the local community and the bureaucratic state.

Morality and Identity: The Status of Eternal Verities

Nationalism treats national identity as a system of absolute values, in which the relativism of ethnic shifters has been transformed into a set of reified eternal verities: the state has "always" existed. This process of reification follows the fate of the more general class of moral-attribute shifters, but it does so within a specific and identifiable political context. Nationalism deprives the essentially moral terminology of identity of its relativity, imposing upon it a definitional fixity that sometimes creates genuine difficulties and embarrassments—as, for example, when the Greek state is forced to specify that Moslem citizens are eligible for police service because, although popularly known as "Turks," they are in fact Greek citizens. Here, popular usage is so strong that the state's claim on the loyalty of *all* citizens is implicitly called into question and has to be reinforced by a very explicit official statement.

Thus, ethnic identity is a highly relative concept that the political morality of nationalism seeks to transform into an absolute one. Identity as a "style," something that "assumes choice and allows for change" (Royce 1982:9), is transmuted into "national character"; ethnic shifters (Galaty 1982) become fixed designators. The terms for cultural identity assume a certainty hitherto denied them by the exigencies of social life. Nationalistic reification of these terms reverses the context-sensitivity appropriate and necessary to their use as terms of personal, moral evaluation; they become instead the technical vocabulary of a fixed political order.

In the final analysis, the language of national or ethnic identity is indeed a language of morality. It is an encoded discourse about inclusion and exclusion. Like all such systems, it is subject to manipulation in everyday speech. For this reason, the task of a critical semiotics of nationalism is to examine the process whereby nationalism invests certain kinds of identity with a rigidity that they do not commonly possess in everyday discourse. Such a semiotics would resist the process of literalization—the process whereby bureaucratic organizations reify the language of social interaction as a set of eternal verities. Meeker (1979:30) sums up the semiotic task appositely: "Values and ideals are interpreted in terms of their function in a particular form of discourse rather than as timeless truths which stand beyond a speaker or writer."

Statism, on the other hand, exploits the power of discourse to generate the semblance of "timeless truths" in two ways: first, by co-opting morality itself as a function of the state; and second, by inserting its own identity in the resulting canon of values. No more revealing or immediate example of this can be found than the use of *patriotis* in Greek. In everyday usage, this word simply means someone from the same local community as the speaker, and is close to Italian *paesano*; in nationalistic discourse, by contrast, it exclusively possesses (is possessed by?) the meaning with which it has entered English as a cognate: "patriot." While ethnographers have made some progress by recognizing the semantic properties of local usage as those of a set of shifters, the next task is to understand the process whereby the state's denial of those same processes becomes a means of putting discourse to the service of ideology.

If all ethnic and national terms are moral terms in the sense that they imply a qualitative differentiation between insiders and outsiders, so, too, all moral value terms are to some extent negotiable markers for the lines of social or cultural inclusion and exclusion. The close identification between moral and ethnic categories leads with inexorable logic to the state's institutionalization of moral authority—cultural rather than natural justice, as it were, but conscripted against the allegedly "unnatural" phenomena of immorality, miscegenation, and treason. (The apartheid laws of South Africa would seem to exemplify the resulting bureaucratic logic in an extreme form.) Even in the most centralized nation-states, however, it seems that everyday usage continues to reflect the relativism of ordinary discourse rather than the absolutism of the state. This situation is itself an interesting datum, since it suggests that people continue to use a theory of meaning that conflicts with the lexicographical rigidity endorsed by the state. Examples abound: consider, to begin with, how in interethnic contact situations the parties concerned make different assessments of the actual contact (see Shalinsky 1980:279–280).

What matters in such situations is not, as the literalists would have it, what group one belongs to, but what moral self-designator one can call upon in the context of a particular level of interaction. To call a Greek a *Vlakhos*, for example, is scarcely complimentary. The literalist would expect that this meant simply that the addressee was a member of the Romanian-speaking pastoral Koutsovlach community, and would assume that the distaste evinced for the term by many Greeks derives from nationalistic feelings of distrust toward a foreign group. According to this perspective, any other use of the term would be a metaphorical extension. This, however, is putting the cart before the horse: the nationalistic definition of both "Greek" and "Vlach" does not precede, semantically or chronologically, the establishment of nation-states in the Balkan region, but has merely been co-opted and subsumed by the latter process. To most Greeks, the context would be sufficiently well defined to ascertain whether the speaker meant "Koutsovlach," "Northern Greek shepherd," or simply "country bumpkin."

The meaning of an ethnic shifter depends on the relationships binding the social group in question (narrative event) to the salient social identity of the speaker (speech event). Terms of this kind conflate social identity with morality by implying that similar principles of morality apply to the discriminations made, regardless of the level at which they are made: outsiders remain inferior to insiders in any sense. Thus, in Afghanistan, Uzbeks and "Arabs" both justify their respective practices in terms of Islamic law (Shalinsky 1980:280). Each group uses the seemingly fixed conceptual abstraction of Islamic law to define boundaries and *realia* according to its own needs and perceptions. Moreover, such shifters do not have to be verbal. In the Cretan village where I did fieldwork, photographs of the late Eleftherios Venizelos, a staunchly antimonarchist liberal politician, appear in most coffeehouses, including those of conservative monarchists! Since Venizelos was Cretan, every local politician feels a certain need to claim him as a spiritual ancestor. Thus, the virtues that his portrait represents—essentially summed up in the phrase "being Cretan"—are of negotiable content. The image of Venizelos is a shifter no less than are some of the more labile terms just discussed.

The use of moral-value terms represents *social diagnoses* of where the boundaries lie. Like all diagnoses—medical ones, for example—these are open to dispute. Moreover, the criteria themselves are negotiable. Two speakers may think they share a common understanding of what is meant by "honesty," "Islam," *onore,* or "being a *Vlakhos.*" The use of the phrase "un-American activities," for which there is an equally anticommunist equivalent in Greek,[5] illustrates how even statist rhetoric may seem relativistic; in fact, it represents an attempt to fix both the term and the reality in an unchanging relationship so that the national boundaries become inflexibly coterminous with the exclusion of communists. National and ethnic terms allow for a surprising amount of semantic slippage; their appearance of semantic fixity allows actors to treat them as though they were existential absolutes rather than counters in a game.

Within state societies, the shifters that have escaped with the least damage to their semantic lability are those that signify moral values not actively endorsed by the state's own peculiar version of national morality. Thus, for example, Gilsenan's (1976:201) treatment of *makhlu'* in Lebanon deals with a concept of social identification so bound up with notions of revenge and the blood feud that it could not have served comfortably in any nationalistic canon. A young revenge killer was regarded as *makhlu'* after his release from jail, but not at the time he committed the deed. Moreover, when he was subsequently attacked by an outsider, his family's

> only concern. . .was whether one of the other families in the village had done it. Had it been so, there would have been little choice but to continue the cycle of revenge, since his being *makhlu'* defined him as socially anonymous within the defining group but not vis-à-vis outsiders, to whom he remained visible and a member of Beit Ahmad. (Gilsenan 1976:201)

Gilsenan was sensitive to the fact that attributions of *makhlu'* (and other moral properties) might well be affected by the interlocutor's outsider status, whether the latter be ethnographer or "native insider" (1976:202). The attribution is mediated by social boundaries between speaker and addressee as well as by the relationship between actor and narrator. The diagnostic signs of being *makhlu'* are rarely so self-evident as to permit absolute claims. The point to be stressed is not just that moral standing can be, and is, negotiated, but that the negotiability of the identity in question is made possible by both the seeming fixity and actual lability of the terminology.

Returning to Greek material, the concept of "barbarism" (*varvarotita*) provides a persuasive illustration of this interplay of fixity and lability, in counterpoint to the equally ambiguous status of *politismos* and of its geographical embodiment, *Evropi*. These are all terms derived from the nationalistic view of Greece as the continuation of ancient Hellas and therefore as the source of all European culture. In Classical times, barbarism characterized those whose foreign and therefore incomprehensible speech was thought to resemble the chattering (*bar-bar*) of swallows; modern Greeks similarly attribute ox-like dumbness to the Turks (Herzfeld 1980a:297), whose language seems so different from their own. In the nationalistic discourse of modern Greece, *varvarotita* is indeed treated as especially characteristic of the Turks; it sums up their supposedly inhuman (unnatural?) and rapacious cruelty, and is associated in the popular imagination with their lack of (Christian) religion.

Politismos, on the other hand, combines the meanings of "culture" (qua "high" culture) and "civilization,"[6] and is particularly associated with the ideal of European identity. For the nationalist, *Evropi* ("Europe") has a fixed semantic field, comprising geographical extent with the concept of a common heritage derived from Classical Hellenism—with the ideals, in fact, that are ordinarily understood by the term *politismos*.[7] In everyday discourse, however, this fixity melts away. *Evropi* is taken to include the Greeks in situations where a collective display of cultural patriotism is called for (notably in conversations with foreigners), but often excludes them when the Greeks have occasion, amongst themselves, to dwell on what they perceive as national failings and weaknesses—as evidence, in brief, of their erstwhile condition as the serfs of *varvari*. All this argues a measure of historical consciousness; and it is indeed the sense of history that invests all the relevant terms with their special powers of evocation (cf. Elias 1978:7). By the same token, the ambiguity of terms such as *Evropi* derives from the duality of that historical experience: tension has always subsisted between the idealized, Western-derived models of "high culture" and the often far less flattering cultural traits that Greeks associate with self-recognition.

In the same idiom, although *varvarotita* is a condition conventionally associated with the Turks and other supposedly unenlightened peoples, Greeks recognize it as a specifically Greek problem when they are talking in confidence. I well remember how residents of the island of Nisiros complained that the practice of letting off firecrackers immediately in front of people was a "barbarous custom," yet how outraged one of them was when I foolishly adopted their own rhetoric. This dual response exemplifies the lability of terms of moral evaluation. (A related example is provided by Gilsenan's analysis, at the point [1976:206–210] where he explores the way in which a "liar" can reveal "truth" by exposing another's failure to read the signs of the liar's own "lying.") Such terms do not make sense in the abstract; indeed, to attempt a decontextualized definition of them violates their semantics. Yet definition is precisely what the state (which benefits from the semiotic illusion that there exists an absolute or "correct" understanding) imposes on morality in general.

Contrastive Ethnographic Illustrations from Greece

A brief look at some contrasting ethnographic materials can make these issues stand out more clearly. The authoritative definition of moral values by the state contrasts starkly with the variety of interpretations, sometimes even indexed by grammatical pluralization, that we meet in everyday speech. In statist morality, *eghoismos* (broadly, "self-regard" and "self-interest") is a negative value. For the swashbuckling villagers of the pastoral village (here called by the pseudonym of Glendi) in the mountains of western Crete where I conducted fieldwork at various points from 1974 to 1981, however, there are forms under which it is acceptable—some of them entirely contrary to the laws of the state (notably systematic, reciprocal animal theft). But villagers sometimes speak of *an eghoismos,* to denote a particular type of this social value. The usage again points to fragmentation in the villagers' social experience, as well as to a recognition of the situational character of moral definition. It is not a usage that one would ever expect to encounter in learned or official writings.

Moral evaluations are not assessments of innate character, but rather of social inclusion. The boundaries of the state are fixed; those of the moral community of co-villagers, on the other hand, belong to a shifting and fragmentary social world and are therefore necessarily subject to continual readjustment and reevaluation. Rhodian villagers explicitly call the morally bad "those outside of here" (*i okso apodho*), and they explain that this phrase could mean equally the moral or the physical community: "here" is itself a shifter and can convey both the local community (village or district or region) and the larger community of Greek Orthodoxy. In Pefko, a Rhodian agricultural community (also here called by a pseudonym) where I worked in 1973–74, villagers justify village endogamy by using a proverb that elaborates on another adage far better known as a dictum about the folly of marrying a non-Greek.[8] All moral terminology conflates moral disapprobation with group exclusion; when the definition of "the" group is itself ambiguous or variable, the relevance of moral prescriptions opens up to negotiation in a way that directly contradicts the codified perspective of bureaucratic law.

We can summarize the Greek terminology in a few words that might help to clarify the main point. Greek villagers symbolically equate the physical exclusion of devils (through exorcism) with the social exclusion of the wicked. *Ghrousouzia,* the evil condition of flawed co-villagers, is furthermore equated with a "lack of good fortune," so that fate and not the hapless co-villager takes the brunt of the blame—an effective way, at the same time, of denying the existence of truly malign wickedness within one's own community, especially when talking to outsiders. By contrast, evil outsiders are *atimi,* "without social worth." But the latter term can, under some circumstances, be used descriptively of a co-villager—for example, in the context of an interfamilial or interpatrikin dispute. By the same token, it may not be used of any Greek at all in the context of a discussion comparing Greeks with Turks, the definitive enemy. Likewise, *ghrousouzia* is applicable to animal theft in any form in eastern Crete; in western Crete, where it is still partly endemic, the term can only be used to condemn intravillage animal theft, whereas intervillage theft is usually greeted with some approval. In short, the moral content of "outsiderhood" is not geared to any particular level or realization of that condition, although its diagnostic traits may vary somewhat from level to level. When the traits do vary, however, they themselves become shifters. A non-kin co-villager's wickedness is usually seen as very different from that of a Turk, although to both may be ascribed a subhuman lack of *filotimo,* or social worth. Women, too, are described as "illiterate" in comparison to Greek men, but they are never so described when the Greeks are collectively contrasted to the "illiterate" Turks (Herzfeld 1980a:296–297).

Thus, ethnic shifters emerge as above all evaluative terms, which nationalism reifies in much the same way as it generally assumes the control of ethical norms. The corollary is that those who regard themselves as good citizens may nevertheless, if underprivileged, talk of the national entity as an intruder; while those who see themselves as outside the law will speak of the state as the intruder. Even the most law-abiding Rhodian, for example, mindful of the recent date of the incorporation of Rhodes into the Greek state, will speak of "when Greece came here," thereby treating "Greece" as a term of ambiguous and to some extent outsider-like standing. The more rebellious Cretans with whom I worked stated the matter more succinctly: "we're the free Greece here!" Such a statement was a true challenge to the authority of the national (and ecclesiastical) law. On another occasion, confronted by an angry police official demanding respect for "the law" (to nomo), an equally angry Glendiot responded that he "had 'two shoulders' (dhio n-omous) too!" His pun poetically reinforced its own message: such wordplays challenge the authority of the official lexicon, both by introducing dialect forms[9] and by poking fun at the solemnity of official language.

In fact, the contrast between the law-abiding Rhodians of Pefko and the rebellious Cretans of Glendi illustrates more or less the extremes of semantic variation that one encounters in Greek moral terminology, as indeed in the use of national and ethnic labels as well. The Glendiots have found a way of recasting themselves as the moral center of the nation, even though they complain frequently of being at its political periphery; the milder Pefkiots, on the other hand, committed as they are to at least an outward show of lawfulness, feel unable to make the same distinction between nation and state. It is noteworthy that the Glendiots found it far easier to explicate the segmentary properties of the insider/outsider distinction than did the Pefkiots. To a Glendiot, there is nothing problematical about identifying Cretan pride with Greekness. For the Pefkiot, on the other hand, while claiming Greek "purity" in contrast to the supposed bastardization of the mainland population, the business of being Greek is itself identified with loyalty to the state.

At least as significant as self-identification, however, is the variable use of terms to designate others. The designators for out-groups are often situationally defined (for example, "Castilian" as a term for "Andalusian" [as well as for the non-Spanish ethnographer!] in relation to "Gypsy" [Brandes 1980:13, 57]). Anthropology, especially with the tools it derives from various semiotic and sociolinguistic methodologies, is beginning to come to grips with these seeming inconsistencies; they remain inconsistencies only if one adheres to the absolutist logic of the state, rather than probing the very different theoretical underpinnings of popular discourse.

Meaning and the State: The Status of Definition

The foregoing examples suggest two quite distinct semiotic orientations on the part of informants. On the one hand, the relativism of informant usage argues a "use" or "action" theory of meaning as the organizing conceptual framework. The official representatives of the state, by contrast, maintain a much more lexicographical perspective on meaning. That this is so becomes abundantly clear when one considers legal terminology: Pefkiots, for example, use the terminology of inheritance in senses directly opposed to the meanings given in codified law, and their uses of the terminology are consistent only if one takes every definition in combination with the context of utterance (Herzfeld 1980b). This lability, moreover, is consistent with their own concept of "meaning" (*simasia*), which corresponds most closely to an action theory.

It is perhaps a truism that the nature-culture distinction is not given in nature, but culturally created and constantly recreated. What happens when a statist ideology supervenes, is not merely that nature becomes "culturalized," but that culture itself becomes more sharply defined, with a concomitant rigidification of the "meanings"—now said to be discovered rather than invented—in nature: context gives way to eternal verity. This does not mean, however, that everyone accepts the new definition of things—a definition that foists the rather loftily applied term of "minority" upon those who happen to differ in one of the newly regimented diagnostic traits. On the contrary, the suppression of the outward display of ideas about meaning that conflict with those of the state—or of any other hypostatized entity of similar structural characteristics—may mask alternative perspectives. This is what happened with the legal terminology of inheritance in Pefko: lexemic consistency masked radical semantic divergence.

Thus, the process I have described here is not simply that whereby the state arrogates to itself the moral privileges that hitherto belonged to competing social groups, as Blok (1981) has suggested for "honor," although that is certainly an important part of it. It is also the process whereby the fundamental concepts of morality are homogenized in a uniform and unitary image of the state. By recognizing the essential connection between morality and social or ethnic identity as two aspects of a single phenomenon, we can perceive how difficult it would be for the state to tolerate a "use theory" view of morality—in all senses, not merely those relating to patriotism and the like. Reference theory, on the other hand, provides a prescriptive idiom of definition that serves the conceptual needs of territorial, political, and moral finitude all at once.

The unity of the state thus generates unitary definitions. Since they are unitary, they are also absolute; and, being absolute, they acquire the culturally attributed characteristics of the natural. The naturalization of culture reproduces the conceptual absolutism of statist ideology. Even in popular discourse, people increasingly identify "nation" with "culture," and thereby surrender the right of cultural definition to the agencies of state control: folklore gives way to folklorism.

At the same time, however, the growth of both an anthropology concerned with the negotiation of social values, and a semiotics capable of undermining the bluff claims of rhetoric, have raised the possibility of an alternative, critical perspective. The latter, however, should not be simply an exercise in the deconstruction of social texts. Clearly, people do not think, act, or speak exactly as the schematized ideologies of statism would prefer. Nevertheless, they do continue to serve their national entities with great loyalty, and to move within the legal and political frameworks that the latter provide. By questioning the naturalization of culture in statist ideologies, as well as the concomitant reification of nature, we can perhaps begin to understand how sensitive actors can negotiate the tensions of social identity and daily life within the turbulent context of the modern nation-state. This perspective, rather than either total regress or statist reification, restores Vico's original vision of the human capacity for symbolic invention to an anthropology no longer restricted, one hopes, to the merely exotic.

Notes

1. For example, that of Cuoco, Monti, and Manzoni in Italy, and Zambelios in Greece.

2. For a useful analysis of this issue from a semiotic perspective, see Handler and Linnekin 1984.

3. See *Istoria tis Vlakhias,* line 2333, in Legrand 1881:314.

4. I have adopted the neologism "patrigroup" for this term, as "lineage" begs too many technical questions about the definition of corporateness. On Crete, the segmentary *yenia* is an electorally effective political unit; see Herzfeld 1983.

5. *Anthellinas,* "anti-Greek," is a term much favored by extreme nationalists for those who criticize the Greek claim to a Classical heritage, or who in other ways attack the nationalist position. It was extensively used by the military regime of 1967–74 to describe its enemies—a clear case of a government's identification of itself with polity and nation.

6. *Politismos* is derived from *polis,* "city-state"; cf. the derivation of "civilization" from *civis,* "inhabitant of a *civitas.*"

7. *Koultoura* is a term sometimes used by, especially, left-wing social commentators. An ironic derivative of this term is the newly coined *koultouriaris,* "one who makes a profession out of knowing about culture, a member of the intellectual establishment."

8. "A shoe from your own place, even if it is patched,/but where you know the craftsman who made it!" The panhellenic variant uses only the first line; the second would not necessarily make much sense in the wider context, although "knowledge" is a formal definition of the insider (*dhikos mas*) at *all* levels of social differentiation (including the mass national and religious ones).

9. The pun depends on a common transference of the terminal prevocalic *n* of the masculine accusative definite article to the succeeding noun. *Omos* is the usual term for "shoulder," *nomos* for "law." Such transferences have generated well-known forms, especially in toponymy (for example, *Nidhra* from *Idhra* [Hydra]).

References Cited

Ardener, Edwin
   1978   Some Outstanding Problems in the Analysis of Events. The Yearbook of Symbolic Anthropology 1:103–121.

Austin, J. L.
   1971   [1956–57] A Plea for Excuses. *In* Philosophy and Linguistics. Colin Lyas, ed. pp. 79–101. London: Macmillan.
   1975   [1962] How to Do Things with Words. J. O. Urmson and Marina Sbisà, eds. Cambridge, Mass.: Harvard University Press.

Blok, Anton
   1981   Rams and Billy-Goats: A Key to the Mediterranean Code of Honour. Man, n.s., 16:427–440.

Brandes, Stanley E.
   1980   Metaphors of Masculinity: Sex and Status in Andalusian Folklore. Publications of the American Folklore Society, n.s., Vol. 1. Philadelphia: University of Pennsylvania Press.

Deely, John
1982 Introducing Semiotic: Its History and Doctrine. Bloomington: Indiana University Press.

Elias, Norbert
1971 The History of Manners. The Civilizing Process, Vol. 1. Edmund Jephcott, transl. New York: Pantheon.

Friedl, Ernestine
1962 Vasilika: A Village in Modern Greece. New York: Holt, Rinehart & Winston.

Galaty, John G.
1982 Being "Maasai"; Being "People-of-Cattle": Ethnic Shifters in East Africa. American Ethnologist 9:1–20.

Gilsenan, Michael
1976 Lying, Honor, and Contradiction. In Transaction and Meaning: Directions in the Anthropology of Exchange and Symbolic Behavior. ASA Essays, Vol. 1, pp. 191–219. Philadelphia: Institute for the Study of Human Issues.

Goldschläger, Alain
1982 Towards a Semiotics of Authoritarian Discourse. Poetics Today 3:11–20.

Handler, Richard, and Jocelyn Linnekin
1984 Tradition, Genuine or Spurious. Journal of American Folklore 97:273–290.

Herzfeld, Michael
1980a On the Ethnography of "Prejudice" in an Exclusive Community. Ethnic Groups 2:283–305.
1980b The Dowry in Greece: Terminological Usage and Historical Reconstruction. Ethnohistory 27:225–241.
1983 Interpreting Kinship Terminology: The Problem of Patriliny in Rural Greece. Anthropological Quarterly 56:157–166.
1984 The Significance of the Insignificant: Blasphemy as Ideology. Man, n.s., 19:653–664.
1985 Lévi-Strauss in the Nation-State. Journal of American Folklore 98:191–208.

Humphreys, S. C.
1978 Anthropology and the Greeks. London, Henley, and Boston: Routledge & Kegan Paul.

Legrand, Emile
1881 Bibliothèque grecque vulgaire. Vol. 2. Paris: Maisonneuve.

Meeker, Michael E.
1979 Literature and Violence in North Arabia. Cambridge, England: Cambridge University Press.

Royce, Anya Peterson
1982 Ethnic Identity: Strategies of Diversity. Bloomington: Indiana University Press.

Shalinsky, Audrey C.
   1980   Group Prestige in Northern Afghanistan: The Case of an Interethnic
          Wedding. Ethnic Groups 2:269–282.

Vico, Giambattista
   1977   [1728] Autobiografia. NUE, n.s., 37. Torino: Einaudi.

A Biology of Meaning and Conduct

Constance Perin
Massachusetts Institute of Technology
© Constance Perin 1985

Shared meanings are resources as important as every other within a group's ecological niche. Meaning is essential to conduct, and the ability to act and react in predictable ways is essential to life. To survive, human beings fear and avoid whatever they believe to call into question the meanings they live by—new ideas, incompatible or discrepant ideologies and cosmologies, ambiguous events and experiences. The fear is not fear of such challenges for their content alone, but for their import: they are signs that embedded meaning systems could become unreliable. Like complexly articulated spines, meaning systems are backbones to acting: slipping a single disc shifts the distribution of supports to meanings, weakening the ability to act. How people create, hold onto, and act on meaning is a key to social order—ours and every other.

This paper explores the proposition that the autonomic responses we call fear and anxiety *are* helplessness, and in avoiding it and in preserving their capacity to act and to predict the actions of others, people use various strategies for keeping intact the meanings by which they have been living. Although these can also be creative and generative, the strategies I examine in cases drawn from American social thought and practice are by and large inimical to others. That its collective representations lead each group to define every other beyond its pale of meaning is a constant paradox and tension of social orders. I am proposing that the hostility, disparagement, avoidance, and stigma expressed in social thought, social patterns, and social structure signify strategies for keeping meanings intact.

Constitution in its several senses is the bridge among the cultural, biological, and social systems I examine: the constitution of meaning—how we construe ourselves in our world; the human constitution—our species' biological dispositions; and, in the cases I discuss, the U.S. Constitution, its social principles explicitly setting this nation apart from all others, shadowed by our tacit constitution, those silent understandings and meanings no less American, no less coercive.

This synthesis of cosmology, ecology, and biology is no different from that by which we understand kinship systems and the social patterns they define as fundaments of social order. No less potent than the kinship concepts and conduct that connect and nurture is this darker side of social order: institutionalized stigma, social disparagement, and social disdain that divide and harm. Until now, we have been calling this darker side "liminality" when expressed by ritual and cultural "pollution" and "racism, sexism . . ." when expressed in social stratification, exploitation, and hierarchy.[1]

The neurophysiological responses of fear and anxiety manifest themselves as freezing, flight, and fighting in all mammals; uniquely, humans socialize these responses as distancing and hostility in various forms. In our own social order, Americans who are seen as signs threatening to privileged yet inexplicit meanings experience less social respect and fewer civil rights; these include people who are black not white, women not men, newcomers not old-timers, children not adults, old not young, renters not owners, homely not beautiful, handicapped not able-bodied. Their dishonor and denigration depends not on facts about any of these groups, but on the very ideas constituting American social order. The cases I examine here are offered as evidence for the mutual entailment of the constitution of meaning and the human biological constitution.

I must not be misunderstood: far from suggesting that our biological commonalities have explanatory precedence over humankind's myriad cultural differences, this synthesis is intended to inspire curiosity within and outside of anthropology about how biology and culture are, case by unsettling, wayward case, implicated in each other. That social hostilities and condemnations have biological sources is, moreover, a proposition not to be elaborated only in the terms of behavioral biology. Its neutral, functional constructs of "survival," "adaptation," and "reproductive fitness" are irrelevant to tragedies of history and the little murders of everyday life that horrify ordinary reason and devastate simple justice. Speaking as I am of human choice and action, the ethical, moral, and cultural perspectives of philosophic and Constitutional discourse remain indispensable.

This biology of meaning and conduct represents an attempt to advance Boas's concern with "'the psychological origin of the implicit belief in the authority of tradition' [and] Boas' interest in the universal role of irrational factors in human behavior and in the interrelationship of human consciousness and social tradition" (Stocking 1968:160). Here, my interest is not in irrationality but in the part biology may play in social evaluation, a connection that John Dewey insisted on in his *Theory of Valuation* in the same terms of physiological equilibration as I will be developing here—"in situations as a whole where disequilibrium and equilibrium, respectively, are exhibited, from the point of view of organic behavior *need* and *satisfaction*" (Thayer 1968:395). Here my concerns with "valuation" are not with its positives, however, but with its negatives.

An anatomy of fear is essential to the exposition of this theory of meaning. That "fear is entirely normal in the experience of humans and other animals both in the biological senses (adaptive and physiologically inevitable) and the psychological senses (ubiquitous and universal) of the word 'normal'" is asserted by biological anthropologists (Konner 1982:228). Yet the structure of fear remains opaque in discussions of the social consequences of "ambiguity," "anomaly," "cognitive dissonance," "uncertainty," and "threat" (Douglas 1966; Leach 1964; Pettigrew 1982 [1980]). Even more to my point, as "normal" as fear is, it has not been adequately acknowledged for the immensity of its social consequences: fear and anxiety are as significant in ordering human affairs as are sex and subsistence. Folk models of fear do not penetrate its processes as deeply as modern neurophysiology and behavioral biology now allow. As tentative and provisional as those understandings may be, they still are sufficiently grounded to provide important hypotheses about cultural sources of threat and the behaviors these can set in motion.

My discontent with circular explanations of the consequences of "nonmeaning"—those events, roles, and symbolic constructions anthropologists have seen to be or to be representing that which is called interstitial, marginal, or anomalous—has led me to seek more satisfactory accounts of the "anxiety" these interpretations have also associated with them. I read in the established scientific literature, from Hebb's classic "On the Nature of Fear" (1946) to Gray's two synthetic works (1971, 1982) in which, based on experimental evidence, he suggests neuropsychological models of human fear and anxiety. Their biology of fear and anxiety has been indispensable to the biology of meaning and conduct I am proposing here. Yet works from those perspectives do no more than intimate what I am claiming: that differences in meanings, in the sense I will be giving that term, are as much implicated in precipitating anxiety and fear as are other events and experiences at odds with expectations.

A Biology of Meaning

Challenging our abilities to make meaning is every experience of novelty, discrepancy, and ambiguity. Until we do, we are unsure how to act and what to expect of others. Until we are sure, we experience unease, tension, anxiety, fear, and sometimes panic. Human beings' ability to tolerate ambiguity is singularly limited, yet so is our capacity to make meanings. Only in the realm of the arts, as we reflect on facets carved with deliberate ambiguity, have we become accustomed to welcome it—and even there, it takes continual practice and the special assistance of teachers, critics, docents, and catalogs. So strong is the human bent for sharp, positive definition that Keats called the tolerance for ambiguity our "negative capability"—"when man is capable of being in uncertainties, Mysteries, doubts without any irritable reaching after fact and reason." Irritability is the least of the visceral feelings that ambiguity, uncertainty, and the confusions of novelty prompt. More than feelings: we go to great lengths to vanquish these ambiguities, as though they were a plague.

A "literal-minded" vocabulary, the one we use in talking about the natural world, is inadequate in speaking of the constitution of meaning (Fernandez 1983). It requires another vocabulary, and especially so to establish the connection with human biology. The one I choose is semiotic. To cultural scientists, underlying systems of ideas, beliefs, and values generate our lived-in worlds and what we make of matter and materials: that is the semiotic premise. Not essences, nor classes, but filaments—those *connections* out of which webs of meanings are spun are the subjects of cultural inquiry. Its search for signs starts by plowing semantic fields in which each term bears a relationship to every other, each a "fragment of a system," through which the complete system can be "envisaged":

> Where ordinary logic talks of classes the logic of relatives talks of systems. A system is a set of objects comprising all that stand to one another in a group of connected relations. Induction according to ordinary logic rises from the contemplation of a sample of a class to that of the whole class; but according to the logic of relatives it rises from the contemplation of a fragment of a system to the envisagement of the complete system. (Peirce 4.5 in Singer 1978:210)

The position of one fragment puts us in mind of its connections to others; by contrast, other logics send us searching for a closed class in which to include it. First to identify the threads there are, then to propose what ideas run along them—harder still, cultural inquiry must also suggest how these webs have come to be constituted as they are, instance by instance, place by place.

We require not types but schemata for interpreting the metaphors and gestalts by which meaning is constituted; the logic of classes is not the only logic by which we diminish ambiguities. This "logic of relatives" allows meanings to be the foundation of acting; its principle of relations draws us out of Aristotelian categories, taxonomies, and names into semantic fields of experience where the search for signs and what they stand for to the members of any given group can be a strictly "observational science like any other positive science" (Charles S. Peirce, cited in Buchler 1955 [1940]:99). Relying on no prior formal theory, this naturalistic perspective makes it possible to see a wider range of human actions and events not screened by one or another school of thought about social structure and culture. And to see them in context— words as spoken and deeds as done (linguistics in the semiotic perspective remains the science of language, not a model for explicating culture). Semiotics allows for analyses of experience reproducing the original unity of thought, action, and context sustaining its meanings (Colby, Fernandez, and Kronenfeld 1981:438; Ellen and Reason 1979:14,17; Tyler 1978:205).

The "connected relations" of a system of meaning I call *predicates*. These are the concepts, most often silent, on which we predicate choice and conduct; these are what novelty, ambiguity, and discrepancy threaten to unhinge. Smiling and frowning, for example: our system of facial expressions uses these physical signs to express our predicates Approval and Disapproval. American conventions allow that a smile stands for Approval or Understanding; a frown for Disapproval or Doubt. Each facial sign is again a fragment embedded in a still larger semantic field, so that we may not know what a person's smile means and know thereby how to respond, unless we have also seen his or her smirk, which members of this culture are likely to read as a sign of Conceit; or a grin, as Triumph; simper, Self-Indulgence; sneer, Ridicule; leer, Lust. If any one sign is ambiguous, we are confused about our appropriate response. (These predicates—Approval, Conceit, Triumph—themselves connect the fragments of other semantic fields; *meaning* is labyrinth.) By such systems of conceptual relationships humans constitute the meanings we live by; accounting for the constitution of each predicate is work for archeologists of knowledge and belief.[2]

Consider one more familiar system of predicates organizing the conduct of our personal relationships with neighbors and with strangers. These are but two relationships out of the total system of personal relationships: those with relatives, lovers, friends, acquaintances, workmates, newcomers, and enemies. How neighbors are endowed with meaning in this system is especially revealing; of all the relationships we have, those with neighbors are likely to be the most ambiguous, and how Americans act toward their neighbors varies greatly. To give meaning to "neighbor" at any given time, we distinguish it from other relationships and contexts, each taking shape from its felt differences from every other—"My neighbor is more an acquaintance than a friend"; "My neighbor is a better friend than any relative." A system is at work; our ideas and feelings about any one relationship are hinged to those about every other, each taking its meanings by way of its predicates' differences and similarities: "He's my cousin, but I wouldn't call him a friend."

Because each person next door or around the corner can be experienced also as friend, relative, acquaintance, enemy, and stranger, the "neighbor" relationship does not tell the whole story. In not settling once and for all the difference between neighbors and all other relationships, "neighbor" carries no predictable meaning. We decide in each instance how we will act on "neighbor," running through the choices American predicates allow. Systems of meanings are moral systems that guide our choice of actions. We may think in categories, but we act on and live by meanings.

The variety of concepts it can draw on accounts for the natural ambiguity of the neighbor relationship. Some are compatible, others not. When they contradict one another, our choices become confused, and our ability to act is impaired. Spatially, "neighbor" is, by definition, Near, which in turn connotes Coming First, Potency, and Influence (Lakoff and Johnson 1980). Experiencing our relationship with a particular neighbor as stranger or acquaintance contradicts those concepts of Near, First, and Influential: the neighbor as stranger employs the wholly contradictory concepts of Far and Distant; the Spatially Close neighbor who remains acquaintance or stranger also upends those concepts. The Commandment to "love thy neighbor" furthers the confusion—one should show Love, but not the Sexual Love reserved for spouse, according to that same law.

These ideas most often go without saying, of course; they are the core concepts of our society—*"what is essential goes without saying because it comes without saying*: the tradition is silent, not least about itself as a tradition" (Bourdieu 1977 [1972]:167). These silent predicates are Intimacy, Trust, Obligation, Choice, Reciprocity, and Love, among others, and all their shadings of intensity in our feelings and the weightings we give them in practice. We receive each concept as a convention embedded in an invisible social history, and throughout life we elaborate on it through a personal history formed out of experiences in every domain. Nothing in our individual and common life fails to draw on these core concepts. The smallest gestures are signs of them, as shaking right hands signals Trust and holding left and right hands, Intimacy.

When Nearest is not Dearest, it is especially confusing. For Close and Love, paired with the predicates Blood and Intimacy, endow relatives with the deepest intensity and heaviest weight of all American personal relations (Schneider 1979, 1980). When neighbors are friends and we fine-tune Close in our actions toward them, we reserve some of that same moral space of Intimacy and Love for each relative by blood and marriage. What each of them in turn means is modulated by religious, ethnic, and personal emphases on the kind and degree of Obligation, Reciprocity, Trust with which we choose to act toward children, grandparents, aunts, second cousins, fathers-in-law, and ex-wives.

Systems of meaning are such systems of predicates, tunneling by the thousands beneath the surface of everyday life. Making our actions possible, they make our world meaningful. Until we can envisage the connections between fragments—of action, event, person, or idea—within a familiar structure of predicates, we will be puzzled about how to act and react. We will be thrown off balance. So it is that novelty, ambiguity, and discrepancy bring us to the issues central to this biology of meaning, for whatever contrasts sharply with received meaning systems arouses responses of immobility, avoidance, or resistance.

The brain's strategy appears to try to keep clear what is already clear. It accommodates best to what is only somewhat novel, discrepant, or ambiguous, not markedly at variance with what is already known. The brain awards first priority to the undisrupted equilibrium experienced neurophysiologically as comfort and coherence and second priority to those pleasurable experiences arousing "just enough" laughter, curiosity, attention, and exploration. These responses, according to experiments with mammals, seem to be founded on the avoidance of pain. Whatever it perceives to be "too" novel, discrepant, and strange the brain responds to as to stimuli of pain, frustration, and fear (states now thought to be functionally and physiologically equivalent) (Gray 1971:141; 1982:290).

My reading of modern neurophysiology suggests that biologically we are constituted to learn and not to learn, to assimilate new experience and to resist doing so, simultaneously. The brain seems to be inherently limited in its capacity to integrate ambiguity, discrepancy, and novelty above some threshold. Encountering novelty—by definition, what is unexpected—clouds foresight of reward or punishment. Frustration ensues, culminating in a physiological reaction similar to receiving mild punishment. The brain's responses depend wholly upon meanings: above some threshold it is unable to relink the chains of implications, metaphors, and entailments that novelty, ambiguity, and discrepancy break into (Gray 1971, 1982; Hebb 1946, 1955; O'Keefe and Nadel 1978). Its physiology sets the limits: equilibrium is its ideal state (some call it a basic "drive"). Mammals' main responses to frustration and pain are the motor behaviors of avoidance and immobility (Hebb 1946:270–271; Brehm and Cohen 1962:224–225). These behaviors I read as being strategies for maintaining equilibrium: to allow for the continuation of conduct based upon *what already has meaning,* the brain's primary autonomic responses are freezing and flight. Only when unable to flee will mammals tend to fight.

The most important fact about fear is that its arousal depends not on what is unknown, but on what is already known. The brain's preference for equilibrium *is* its tenacious preservation of the known. Fear is "learned" in the sense that other things have been learned first, as in human infants' "stranger fear," which does not begin at birth but only after the brain develops its "match-mismatch" capacity (thought to occur after the myelination of the fornix) (Hebb 1946:244; Konner 1982:223). Moreover, the number of meaning systems ("belief systems," "world views," "mind sets," "tapes") the brain keeps in working memory seems to be limited, leaving much else to be perceived as novel. Learning reduces novelty and its uncertainties, of course. But fear of novelty diminishes as humans mature for another reason: we become adept at reading cues of *potentially* unfamiliar, frustrating, and disrupting experiences, the better to avoid them in the first place (Hebb 1955:256). The responses of disequilibration come under the control, then, not of what is new and unknown, but of an existing commitment to a course of action, to a set of beliefs, to those perceptual configurations we call "classical," and to the meaning systems of a group. These constitute the equilibrium humans experience as comfort and coherence.

The brain monitors the degrees of discrepancy by comparing actual with expected stimuli, in the hippocampus, it is thought, the region where fear and anxiety, curiosity, and exploratory behavior also appear to lie. A simple distinction between novel and familiar stimuli is a first-level monitoring operation for this brain system (which also has circuits to the amygdala and hypothalamus, structures that may be involved in rage and attack). More complex comparisons follow at a second level, where, it is proposed, the hippocampus generates and tests hypotheses (Gray 1982:295). This "trouble-shooting" function "is mobilized when the animal's normal routine ... is interrupted by one of several adverse conditions, notably, novelty, non-reward, error, or punishment. Its task is then to work out what has gone wrong so that existing plans can be applied again or new ones substituted" (ibid.:262). In humans, experimental evidence has been found·of "both novelty neurons and comparator neurons by recording directly from individual nerve-cells during the repeated presentation of originally novel stimuli. . . .Novelty neurons were found in the visual cortex, the reticular formation and the caudate nucleus, but the most important concentration of them was in the hippocampus" (Gray 1971:204).[3] ("Novelty" and "comparator" neurons are standard terms in the discourse of neuropsychologists.)

That threshold between what is known and what is novel is crucial, of course, because losing equilibrium to some ambiguity and novelty is a source of autonomic pleasure as well, as when, by experiencing mild fear and mild frustration and the nuances of wit juxtaposing the expected and the surprising, we are pleasurably aroused (Hebb 1946:231). These are the same pleasures of graduated learning, playing games, and viewing art and hearing music not too "far out" from a golden, conventionalized mean.[4]

The final element of this biology of meaning and conduct is the transference or projection of the arousal to the stimulus of it. At the high side of the threshold, when there is "too much" discrepancy, humans translate the discomfort socially as resistance, avoidance, hostility, disparagement, and stigmatization. At the low end, when arousal and attention are stimulated by "just enough" novelty, the stimulus is credited with furnishing the pleasures of delight and inspiration.

American Meanings and Conduct

Case 1: Racism

This case illustrates how fear and pain experienced outside of protected environments may transform neurophysiological responses into patterns socialized and institutionalized as racism. The self-recorded experience of Louis Agassiz (1807–1873) after seeing black people for the first time led both to his abandoning scientific evidence of a single human species and to his becoming a lifelong, active proponent of racism. A professor at Harvard, founder in 1859 of its Museum of Comparative Zoology and its director until his death, Agassiz was a Swiss naturalist and specialist in fossil fishes who arrived in the United States in 1846 as a "devout creationist" who believed all human beings to be of one species (Gould 1981:43). In 1845 he wrote of "'the superiority of the human genre and its greater independence in nature. Whereas the animals are distinct species in the different zoological provinces to which they appertain, man, despite the diversity of his races, constitutes one and the same species over all the surface of the globe'" (ibid.:44).

Agassiz had never seen a black person in Europe. Until 1846, when he first observed blacks as servants at his Philadelphia hotel, he believed in "the doctrine of human unity," "the confraternity of the human type." This experience precipitated an "immediate visceral judgment" leading him to "instantly" abandon "the Biblical orthodoxy of a single Adam" and to advocate the racist line that each of the human races is a single species, ordered by "'the relative rank [and] the relative value of the characters peculiar to each. . .'" (ibid.:44,46).

Agassiz's experience of a "pronounced visceral revulsion" at first encountering blacks is recounted in his own hand. It provides a specimen case of the process I have been outlining, documenting the relationship of novelty to fear and the manifestations of fear as stereotyping (a human version, I suggest, of freezing); of fear as stigmatizing, our way of taking flight or distancing; and of disparagement and abuse, as a social mode of attack.[5] Agassiz's political and institutional relationships also illustrate how these transformations of freezing, flight, and fighting (resonating with collective representations and experiences) come to be socialized and institutionalized.

Agassiz described the details of his experience in a letter to his mother in 1846, telling "truth before all." Gould found this "unexpurgated" passage among the Agassiz letters at the Houghton Library at Harvard, and "translated it verbatim, for the first time so far as I know" in The Mismeasure of Man:

It was in Philadelphia that I first found myself in prolonged contact with negroes; all the domestics in my hotel were men of color. I can scarcely express to you the painful impression that I received, especially since the feeling that they inspired in me is contrary to all our ideas about the confraternity of the human type [genre] and the unique origin of our species. But truth before all. Nevertheless, I experienced pity on the sight of this degraded and degenerate race, and their lot inspired compassion in me in thinking that they are really men. Nonetheless, it is impossible for me to repress the feeling that they are not of the same blood as us. In seeing their black faces with their thick lips and grimacing teeth, the wool on their head, their bent knees, their elongated hands, their large curved nails, and especially the livid color of the palm of their hands, I could not take my eyes off their face [sic] in order to tell them to stay far away. When they advanced that hideous hand towards my plate in order to serve me, I wished I were able to depart in order to eat a piece of bread elsewhere, rather than dine with such service. What unhappiness for the white race—to have tied their existence so closely with that of negroes in certain countries! God preserve us from such a contact! (Gould 1981:45).

Agassiz's testament of his experience follows the biological and social path I postulate. His experience begins from the embedded system of predicates with which he encountered this new experience, the unarticulated concepts through which, to a Swiss Christian and natural scientist, humans are "really men," a fragment of the semantic field of living beings. *Discrepancy*: "I first found myself in prolonged contact with . . . their lot inspired compassion in me in thinking that they are really men . . . it is impossible for me to repress the feeling that they are not of the same blood as us . . . especially the livid color of the palm of their hands. . . ." *Pain*: "I can scarcely express to you the painful impression. . . ." *Freezing*: "I could not take my eyes off their face in order to tell them to stay far away. . . ." *Flight*: "I wished I were able to depart. . . ." *Avoidance*, as *Stigmatizing* and *Distancing*: "degraded and degenerate. . . . What unhappiness for the white race—to have their existence so closely. . . . God preserve us from such a contact!" *Socialization*: "His conversion," Gould reports, "followed an immediate visceral judgment and some persistent persuasion by friends. His later support rested on nothing deeper in the realm of biological knowledge" (ibid.:44).

Next, the penultimate steps, *Denigration* and *Stereotyping*. Writing in 1863, Agassiz said: "'Social equality I deem at all times impracticable [he supported legal equality]. It is a natural impossibility flowing from the very character of the negro race' . . . for blacks are 'indolent, playful, sensuous, imitative, subservient, good natured, versatile, unsteady in their purpose, devoted, affectionate, in everything unlike other races, they may but be compared to children, grown in the stature of adults while retaining a childlike mind. . . . No man has a right to what he is unfit to use. . . . Let us beware of granting too much to the negro race in the beginning, lest it become necessary to recall violently some of the privileges which they may use to our detriment and their own injury. . .'" (ibid.:48). He also rated Indians and Mongolians: "'The indominable, courageous, proud Indian—in how very different a light he stands by the side of the submissive, obsequious, imitative negro, or by the side of the tricky, cunning, and cowardly Mongolian!. . .'" (ibid.:46).

By whatever system of meaning Agassiz apprehended the white

race, black people were a sign of discrepancy to it. From his biography and from his racist assertions, perhaps some predicates of this system can be plausibly reconstructed. Hierarchy seems a major predicate to this Swiss Christian and "devout creationist who lived long enough to become the only major scientific opponent of evolution" (ibid.:43). An ordered human world is a ranked world, lowest to highest in all respects, physically and morally:

> There are upon earth different races of men, inhabiting different parts of its surface, which have different physical characters; and this fact. . .presses upon us the obligation to settle the relative rank among these races, the relative value of the characters peculiar to each. . . . (Agassiz, quoted in Gould 1981:46)

John Block Friedman proposes in his study, *The Monstrous Races in Medieval Art and Thought,* that, from earliest recorded history, color differences have been "easily interchanged with moral polarities, and the blackness of immorality contrasted with the whiteness of salvation. The black Ethiopian was associated with sin and with the diabolical by homiletic writers . . . who explained that they were burned black not by the sun but by vices and sin. . . . [In] one very popular school text in the Middle Ages, the innocuous word 'Ethyopum' is interpreted allegorically: 'Ethiopians, that is sinners. Indeed, sinners can rightly be compared to Ethiopians, who are black men presenting a terrifying appearance to those beholding them'" (Friedman 1981:65).

A map dated A.D. 926 labels "Ethiopia" (variously Africa and India) as a region "where there are men of diverse appearance and monstrous, terrifying, and perverse races as far as the borders of Egypt" (ibid.:48). The "edge" position assigned them is one sign of the cosmologies such maps of the period inscribe in space and in time, for their remoteness was taken as a sign of the justice of their exile:

> Some texts proposed that God had exiled the races because He saw that they were dangerous to humanity. Consequently their physical and social abnormalities were not at all evidence of the plenitude of the Creation and the "playfulness" of the Creator, but rather of God's protective care of His children, and of His power to pass on His curse from generation to generation. Writers [in the Middle Ages] who held such views regarded the races with awe and horror as theological warnings. (ibid.:90)

Does Hierarchy in the service of Salvation form the central predicate of this orthodox Christian's view of who can be judged to be "really men"? By this system of meaning, then, does his proximity to all signs of Sin threaten his own place among the Elect?

Agassiz's behavior demonstrates human beings' neuro-physiological responses of distress to threats to the meaning systems they live by: flight transformed to disparagement and fear displaced onto those arousing it—as prejudice, stereotyping, and that irrational shrinking from others we call stigma. What Gould calls Agassiz's "immediate visceral judgment" seems not mere metaphor, but physiological fact.

The fact that Agassiz was "an extreme splitter in his taxonomic practice" seems to be a facet of the hierarchical predicate. "Taxonomists tend to fall into two camps—'lumpers,' who concentrate on similarities and amalgamate groups with small differences into single species, and 'splitters,' who focus on minute distinctions and establish species on the smallest peculiarities of design. Agassiz was a splitter among splitters. He once named three genera of fossil fishes from isolated teeth that a later paleontologist found in the variable dentition of a single individual. He named invalid species of freshwater fish by the hundreds, basing them upon peculiar individuals within single, variable species. . ." (Gould 1981:44).

As important as Agassiz's classificatory turn of mind may have been in reinforcing his cosmology, his social position was critical. It enabled him to bring about the ultimate step of this process, *Institutionalization*. "Agassiz was a charmer; he was lionized in social and intellectual circles from Boston to Charlestown. He spoke for science with boundless enthusiasm and raised money with equal zeal to support his buildings, collections, and publications. No man did more to establish and enhance the prestige of American biology during the nineteenth century" (ibid.:43). Moving in circles of wealth and power, identified with the nation's then most prestigious university, and an eminent authority, Agassiz was able to become "the leading spokesman for polygeny in America" (ibid.:43). Although, finally, Agassiz's "students rebelled" and his "supporters defected," he "remained a hero to the public" (ibid.:50). Without this forum for articulating and elaborating to laypeople his "painful impression," the history and tenacity of American racism among elites might have been quite different (see Solomon 1956).

That Agassiz changed a long-standing intellectual position after his Philadelphia hotel experience is a remarkable testimony to the superior force of neurophysiology. Agassiz may have had intellectual predispositions toward the racist position, Gould speculates: he mentions Agassiz's fears about miscegenation and a theory of the spatial distribution of the races. Yet until first encountering blacks, he had weighted the logic of contrary evidence more.

Case 2: American Stigmas

People falling short of Western predicates of physical perfection are treated as discrepancies to the meaning systems those predicates sustain, and they become targets for that peculiarly human translation of freezing and flight—stigma. In the great chain of being, humans are mammals among many—about 15,000 species of mammals. We are different, yet not wholly so, and from an ambiguity Western civilization finds worrisome, it constitutes less-than-perfect human beings as signs that those few differences are being obliterated: they are perceived as resembling animals the more. These meaning systems are predicated on Western civilization's considered ideas of Evolution, Instinct, Beauty, Rationality, Intention, Control, Foresight. . . . Children and handicapped people, as well as those who are disfigured, not white, and not male, upset the ballast of civilization. Mistaken for the distress they arouse, they are allowed the least favorable positions in the social order.

Imperfect people ask us to consider what humans' unambiguous differences from animals are. So concerned are Americans to keep intact the systems of meaning by which they know themselves to be least like animals, however, that they distance themselves even from factual knowledge. A national sample of 3,107 people eighteen and over responded to a questionnaire in a study for the U.S. Fish and Wildlife Service: "Americans appeared to possess an extremely limited understanding of animals. For example, on four endangered species questions, no more than one-third of the public gave the correct answer—e.g., only 26% knew the manatee is not an insect, and 25% correctly answered the questions, 'timber wolves, bald eagles and coyotes are all endangered species of animals'. . . . Additionally, just 13% knew raptors are not small rodents and one-half of the national sample incorrectly answered the question, 'spiders have ten legs.' A better but still limited

54% knew veal does not come from lamb, and only 57% correctly answered the question, 'most insects have backbones.'" (Kellert and Berry 1980:7, 11).

Children born prematurely, mentally retarded, with low birth weight, or with congenital defects are more likely than are normal children to suffer abuse at their parents' hands. For example, histories of "extensive physical abuse or neglect" were found in 45 percent of a group of only mildly retarded children (Zigler 1980:183). Why this should be so is not known with any certainty; researchers suggest only that these parents may experience stress and anxiety at higher levels than parents of normal children. Frustration over slower learning, perhaps, would be natural, but why should it be expressed so harshly? Perhaps the fact that retarded children are doubly discrepant has something to do with parental distress: not only are the children imperfect specimens but, in accordance with the way Americans position children in this semantic field, they are imperfect adults as well. These parents' humane instincts may run aground on the ice floe of stigma to which the family as a whole is likely to be consigned.

"By definition, of course, we believe the person with a stigma is not quite human," Goffman observes. "On this assumption we exercise varieties of discrimination, through which we effectively, if often unthinkingly, reduce his life chances. We construct a stigma theory, an ideology to explain his inferiority and account for the danger he represents. . . . We tend to impute a wide range of imperfections on the basis of the original one and at the same time to impute some desirable but undesired attributes, often of a supernatural cast, such as 'sixth sense,' or 'understanding'" (Goffman 1963:15–16). This "danger" is the doubt these human beings cast on inexplicitly embedded meanings.

Moreover, imperfect humans prompt the fear that systems of meaning and conduct will not suffice in dealing with them, "less than human" as they are seen to be. How people act toward the disabled is evidence for the tenacity of familiar systems of meaning in the face of discrepancy and novelty. Unmistakably, "normal" people do not *know* how to behave under the most ordinary circumstances, retreating to familiar albeit utterly inappropriate systems of meaning and conduct. Paralyzed by the ambiguity of imperfect people, "normal" people behave awkwardly and ineptly. Or their ignorance (helplessness) takes the form of hostility and embarrassment and the awkward "fear of saying or doing the wrong thing":

Too often the disabled are presumed to be unhappy and are pitied, avoided, treated as children, spoken for as if they are not there and not "seen" as whole persons beyond the disability. . . . The personal discomfort of the able-bodied often stands in the way of their establishing rewarding human relationships with the disabled. Fear of saying or doing the wrong thing, a desire not to be reminded of the fragility of the body and a lack of experience contribute to painfully awkward social relationships or downright avoidance of the disabled. (Brody 1981)

Disabled people are treated like children because children are imperfect adults: the same predicates constitute their meanings—Dependent, Unpredictable, Uncontrolled, and Immature, at the least. "Normal" people distance themselves from discrepancy by freezing the disabled in a familiar system of meaning and conduct predicated on Immaturity and Dependency, in order to continue to act—inappropriately, in the eyes of the handicapped.[6]

The Jerry Lewis Muscular Dystrophy Association Telethon, "with its pity approach to fund-raising," is objectionable, writes Evan J. Kemp, Jr., executive director of the Disability Rights Center and himself disabled with a neuromuscular disease:

The very human desire for cures for these diseases can never justify a television show that reinforces a stigma against disabled people. . . . With its emphasis on "poster children" and "Jerry's kids," the telethon focuses primarily on children. The innocence of children makes them ideal for use in a pity appeal. But by celebrating disabled children and ignoring disabled adults, it seems to proclaim that the only socially acceptable status for disabled people is their early childhood. . . . The telethon emphasizes the desperate helplessness of the most severely disabled. In doing so, it reinforces the public's tendency to equate handicap with total hopelessness. When a telethon makes disabling conditions seem overwhelmingly destructive, it intensifies the awkward embarrassment that the able-bodied feel around disabled people. By arousing the public's fear of the handicap itself, the telethon makes viewers more afraid of handicapped people. Playing to pity may raise money, but it also raises walls of fear between the public and us . . . barriers to employment, transportation, housing and recreation can be more devastating and wasteful of our lives than the diseases from which we suffer. (Kemp 1981)

Visible differences are "almost always [believed] to be linked with deeper lying traits than is in fact the case" (Allport 1958). People tend to see things of like quality as belonging together and as causally related, according to this theory of cognitive balance. That includes the tendency for one negative to evoke another (shouting at a blind person, for instance), just as one positive does another: physically attractive people are believed also to be kind, vivacious, and poised (Berscheid and Graziano 1979). "Normal" people tend to "talk down to a physically handicapped person as if he were mentally retarded and sometimes even as if he were deaf or blind, and they tend to be surprised at discovering that the disabled person may be quite intelligent and competent" (Katz 1981:20). Searching for cognitive balance, the brain fixes on a congruence having nothing to do with the "sender" of the stimulus (attractive; disabled) and everything to do with the "receiver's" search for its own equilibrium.

But when frightened by the novel and disequilibrating predicates imperfect people signify—Degeneration of the Species, God's Curse, Alien Strain—"normal" people can also attack. Among "all types of visible disabilities, facial disfigurements seemed to provoke the greatest amount of anxiety and aversion in children and adults." People "marked with facial anomalies provoke stronger aversion than do blind people, even though blindness is the most feared disability and the one considered to be most severe" (ibid.:20). The mother of a thirteen-year-old "with several handicaps, including a cranial facial anomaly" speaks of his experience in a public school: "Athelantis is a special, exotic kind of child—he doesn't look like other children. . . . It was very difficult for him in the mainstream. If the teachers had been calm about it, the other children would have accepted him. But the teachers were physically repulsed—they freaked—and so the children thought they could say whatever they liked" (Dullea 1982).

Just before surgery on a seventeen-year-old American girl for wholly disfiguring facial tumors ("Elephant Man" disease), her doctor said: "Her face just won't allow people to react normally to her." A newspaper article reported that "people . . . somehow feel compelled to ridicule her in public," that insults "have followed her to crowded shopping centers, to the campus of her university, even to the quiet woodlands where she goes walking near her home," that "men and women, who have never seen her before and do not know anything about her, have abused her before their children. . . . Lisa is clearly tired of being told that the most important things are her mind and her personality. 'I don't want anybody to tell me that beauty isn't important, that just what I have inside is important,' she said. 'I know that I am not going to look like Farrah Fawcett-Majors. I don't want to look like Farrah Fawcett-Majors. But I can't take this abuse all of my life and you'll never make me believe that most people will ever accept me for what I am'" (Severo 1981).

The weight of Western civilization—burden, not heritage—kept Lisa from being accepted "for what she is." Not only is a "beautiful face" a sign of God's grace, the human face itself carries the prime signs of our difference from all other living creatures—language and imagination. Masking these symbols, facial disfigurement casts doubt on the differences. Masking the conventional signs we expect to read clearly in others' faces, we confront ambiguities and experience frustrations. Rather than ask for clarification, the autonomic response is to flee enigma through stigma.[7]

These examples are but a few of the social forms that resistance to novelty and unfamiliarity takes. In the particulars of the resistance will be found the meaning systems at issue (Freud's methodological discovery seems likely to be the biological universal). In a world of options and alternatives, the tenacity of meaning systems (Boas's "shackles of tradition") in individuals, families, ethnic and religious groups, political movements, professions, and sciences is the key to their hearts.

Living within few and intensely entailed meaning systems, when realigning one realigns all, accounts for the "intolerance for ambiguity" of "narrow-minded people" and of those we call "provincial," whose store of predicates is small. People "freeze" into meaning systems, allowing in nothing new or different to avoid confusion and to retain equilibrium. From this perspective, then, human "identity" consists of some few familiar meaning and acting systems that we tend to "freeze" into for the social survival they guarantee. They allow us to know, without having to think twice, the sanctions and rewards of salient relationships. Otherwise, we may expect rewards but receive punishments instead. Only among "our own kind," as we put it, do we so readily understand what acting one way or another "means," with the least chance for misinterpretation or misstep and the most opportunity for spontaneity, recognition, and esteem. Not only are the predicates governing the relationships of this life salient but, for most of the world's peoples, those of a next as well.

Meanings as Social Order

Meaning systems regulate themselves affectively, cognitively, and experientially with a threshold of arousal, a law of avoidance, a rule of distance, a principle of immobility, an axiom of aggression. Biologically, we are constituted to learn and not to learn, to adapt and not to adapt, simultaneously. Meaning systems are lodes of conservative energies, mined to provide the visceral comforts of equilibrium. They accept change, exogenous or indigenous, only gradually, only when changes are more attention- than fear-arousing, more certain to be rewarding than not. Meaning systems are nongenetic yet biologically sustained mechanisms through which sociocultural systems both persist and change.

That people continually seek and are rewarded by stimuli that are novel, unfamiliar, surprising, complex, and varied is undoubted; that there are limitations on tolerable levels is just as clear. Why any single stimulus should act at one or the other end of this continuum is above all a cultural question, a question of its meaning. This meaning determines the perceived degree of discrepancy and novelty of every stimulus, and that perception determines the experiences of dissonance, fear, and anxiety, and of retreat toward felt coherence and equilibrium. Human neurophysiology in itself is a potent incentive to keep meaning systems intact.

Through norms, our species socializes its drive to equilibrium. By definition, norms afford us the comforts of social consensus, predictability, and belonging. They orient us in a confusion of alternative ways of acting. They resist change for that very reason. Americans whose behavior is discrepant to shared norms can be another kind of sign—some give us realistic reasons to fear them. We would be foolhardy not to do all we can to avoid neighbors and strangers who carry handguns, people who are high on drugs, drunk drivers, thieves, and cheaters.

But social deviants and cultural discrepants are not the same. Ageism, ethnocentrism, classism, racism, and sexism blame and condemn groups that are, each for its own reasons, signs of discrepancy to silent American predicates. These signs are wholly byproducts of concepts through which important systems of meaning are constituted and from which norms are derived. That each social order and each group's identity is a hierarchy of homeostasis constituted from the relationship between cosmology and biology is a proposition with which to reexamine ethnographic materials.

Making meanings and keeping them intact are both self-preservative and all too often other-destructive. Maintaining equilibrium underlies endogamy and sets the limits of exogamy; group membership and its comforts is a major issue, if not *the* major issue, of any social order. Yet the comforts of belonging are likely to be purchased at others' expense, with the currency of invidious beliefs that those living by other lights are innately inferior or degraded or degenerate or dangerous and should be so treated. Taken as signs of inferiority, degradation, or danger, all kinds of "strangers" and "others" suffer the consequences of the drive to equilibrium. At the least we take refuge in prejudice; at the worst we permit holocausts; and in between we foment social strife, wholesale injustice, and lives of pain.

So clear is this evidence from behavioral biology that one biological anthropologist throws caution to the winds in discussing the social implications of fear: "Let it suffice to remark that no reasonable analysis of human behavior can fail to grant that the situations that most seriously jeopardize human survival and human dignity, past, present, and future, owe much more to irrational fear than to irrational rage" (Konner 1982:234). Fears are often *not* "irrational," however—they are "biosemantic" fears with the same credulity as those we view as "realistic" (of tornadoes, of armed bandits), only experienced outside of protected environments. For the discrepancies, discontinuities, incompatibilities, and disorientations of meanings humans experience outside of intentionally educational institutions, we are left largely to our own devices. "Politics" and "religion" are the most likely social repositories for such experiences. Yet ideologies and cosmologies generate as much social "strain" as they relieve: when they assert the locations of equilibrium (truth, beauty, faith), they also create their discrepancies and the candidates for transferred distress. What people believe is meaningful determines what they will fear; that is the dilemma of our species as makers of meanings.[8]

Anthropology seems also not to escape this dilemma. Other peoples, surprisingly enough, can evoke disequilibrium and distress that fieldworkers have dealt with by placing them in times remote from our own, when they are in fact entirely contemporaneous with the anthropologists living among them. Fabian (1983) provides a fine ethnography (he thinks it is a polemic) of distancing within anthropology; I see his work as providing evidence of a strategy by which fieldworkers cope with their distresses at living within their own meaning systems while confronting peoples living through entirely unfamiliar systems of meaning and conduct. He documents one way in which "normal" science seems to have institutionalized the biological fact that human beings' ability to do what Fabian asks—*simultaneously* to acknowledge incongruent meanings—is cerebrally limited. Human neurophysiology avoids what he wants students of other peoples to do: to encounter the other in "dialectical terms of confrontation, challenge, and contradiction" rather than as an "object of knowledge . . . separate, distinct, and preferably distant from the knower" (Fabian 1983:136, 121). "We do not 'find' the savagery of the savage, or the primitivity of the primitive, we posit them, and we have seen in some detail how anthropology has managed to maintain distance, mostly by manipulating temporal coexistence through the denial of coevalness" (ibid.:121).

But as deeply as anthropologists have been able to immerse themselves and to keep up their end of the dialogue, they *do* go home again: to take their children to baseball games, to sit on committees, to comfort the bereaved, to live within those meaning systems that are their life, their equilibrium. What Fabian sees as another form of imperialism may signify the quest for familiarity, a strategy to comprehend others by making them more like ourselves. To bring Western "progress, development, modernity" to peoples who are (we also posit) "stagnating, underdeveloped, and traditional" is to make them less strange, less distressing to that homeostasis underlying human ways of seeing everything. What he interprets as "illness" and "a festering epistemological sore" in anthropology may be its own coming to terms with these human constraints. While our professional credo is that "nothing human is foreign to us," Terence did not also promise that it would leave us unaffected.

Nor does it leave the general public unaffected, not only in its proclivity to ethnocentrism. My own experience confirms with "exasperating predictability" that a well-read public *relies* on anthropology to help it keep its distance: "I am surely not the only anthropologist who, when he identifies himself as such to his neighbor, barber, or physician, conjures up visions of a distant past. When popular opinion identifies all anthropologists as handlers of bones and stones it is not in error: it grasps the essential role of anthropology as a provider of temporal distance" (ibid.:30).

Education, which is our way of making the new or discrepant less ambiguous and threatening, continues to offer the single appealing nostrum. But it is oh so slow; the history of "social change" can be read just as well as the documentation of cultural persistence.[9] And there is still another barrier: even as practice may change, symbols carrying the previous nexus of affect and association remain evocative because through them people are accustomed to locate the balance in their lives. Important symbols may also be deliberately refueled by those out to keep political and economic power; elites may be cynical and manipulative, of course, but they may also be caught up in systems of meaning so wholly taken for granted as never to be taken apart, least of all by themselves.

Nor is that the end of it. The entailment of symbols keeps denigration and stigma emotionally available, for all signs of lesser social respect are perceptual reminders that newcomers, renters, women, widows, children, and the disabled are constituted (each for their own reasons, as these few examples explore) as discrepancies to the received meaning systems forming the backbone of social order. The more each is believed to be "minor" to an imputed "major," the more they are oblique to "the center." The more they do not *appear* to be valued and to belong, the less chance of belonging they have. Even as "tokens" may help to diminish the degree of unfamiliarity of a group, they can also draw more fire than they put out, being so clearly discrepant. The human brain relies more on visual than any other sensory stimuli; that fact accounts for the wisdom of the American folk principle that justice, Constitutionally decreed, must be *seen* to be done.

Our biological constitution requires meanings just as it requires equilibrium. There is nothing "superorganic" or transcendent about culture; it is the unique biological endowment of our species. On the one hand, keeping our neurophysiological balance is as autonomous as sleeping and seeing; on the other, we lose it only because our predicates, constituted as they are, themselves define what is ambiguous and discrepant. In considering how to break out of this circularity, we might contemplate either biological or cultural changes—the one a profound ethical question only now on our agenda, and the other, as history reveals, taking more time than we may have.

Philosophers point to another way by continuing to state the relationship between natural rights and the social contract. In the American case, our Constitution bridges these biological and social systems: as a matter of empathy and ordinary justice, we have already understood, even without knowing why we make them, that it is Constitutionally intolerable to draw "invidious distinctions" depriving citizens of social rights. Giving voice to more of our silent predicates in "the universe of the discussed" may help philosophers, the judiciary, and ourselves toward ever more enlightenment (Bourdieu 1977 [1972]).

To be able to act, then, we take—we *have* to take—our conventions and the predicates they represent entirely for granted. For their credibility and legitimacy, conventions rely on the weight of history; for their tenacity and persistence, they rely on humans' omnipresent need to act in this collective enterprise of life. These necessities lull us into forgetting that the concepts they signal are received and arbitrary, built up from a philological stratigraphy of still other concepts and conventions and the experiences they govern.

Despite the many questions we might raise about it, however, culture—ours and every other—resists interrogation. Its resilience, set at equilibrium, makes it friend to few new concepts and enemy to many more. But its tenacity is a rationale for existential despair only from the perspective that, like an immovable mountain, culture is all essence and immanence. Seeing it anew as filaments of constituted meanings and constructed metaphors allows us to come into our species' own, using intelligence, feeling, and imagination in understanding its "nature" as question-able and arbitrary.

This digging for conceptual treasure should not be forced only into critical or demystifying molds. Powerless and empowered, we are all without any choice but to communicate through and to live by constituted meanings, collectively constructed and collectively reinforced. Anthropology in this semiotic vein should be seen also as an expedition for edification, seeking in this culture and in our experiences themselves the means to create alternatives.

Notes

1. Cultural anthropologists, psychologists, and social psychologists most concerned with such social patterns have been explaining them as matters of logic, not of meaning. Social "categories" are created on the logical principles of exclusion and

inclusion, such that they have lines and boundaries that ambiguity "transgresses," evoking social "condemnation." These principles of set theory may then be combined with the "overload" notions of communication theory (Douglas 1966:48–53). For example, Douglas suggests that ambiguity is socially reduced by re-labeling to conform with existing categories; it can be physically controlled by killing "deformities"; it can be avoided altogether; it can be "labelled dangerous"; or it can be made use of in its own right, as in poetry (ibid.:52–53). These nominalistic and functional explanations do not pursue the question of why any one of these responses to ambiguity should exist in the first place—for example, "a rule of avoiding anomalous things affirms and strengthens the definitions to which they do not conform. . . . Attributing danger is one way of putting a subject above dispute. It also helps to enforce conformity. . . . In general [reflecting on our main classifications and on experiences which do not exactly fit them] confirms our confidence in the main classifications" (ibid.:51–53). Equally preoccupied with the logic of classification and the efficacy of naming is Edmund Leach's (1964) "general theory of taboo."

Later work on categorizing has cast doubt, furthermore, on the precision attributed to these logical processes. Categories are more likely to be continuous than separate and clear-cut (Rosch 1977). Nor does the seasoned literature on the political, economic, and institutional sources of war, nationalism, racism, genocide, ethnocentrism, prejudice, and xenophobia move beyond the principles of inclusion and exclusion and communications theory in explaining the psychological etiology of prejudice and stereotyping (see Allport 1958; Klineberg 1968; LeVine and Campbell 1972; Pettigrew 1980; Tajfel 1969, 1981). Furthermore, these analyses declare the "intrinsic" characteristics of each group's beliefs and customs, genes and history, resources and powers to be the only relevant stimuli. That a more general symbolic process overarches such particularities is one contribution of this biology of meaning: what one group signifies in the meaning systems of any other will determine the kind and degree of social response and interaction.

2. A few cautions are due in light of semiotics' new imperialism. Social conventions are likely to be called "rules," a technical borrowing from linguistics that is incompatible, I think, with the challenges of cultural analysis, whose principal mission is to finger in context the concepts spinning the filaments. Social "rules" follow from those predicates; they are not, like the rules of mathematical, algebraic, linguistic, or logical systems, prior, constant, and unarbitrary. Predicates are human constructions and, like the Articles of the U.S. Constitution, we can preserve, amend, or repeal them.

"Codes" is another jargon to beware, especially for its connotation of a deliberate secrecy or misrepresentation. (The term itself, devised by scholars, is a sign of the Mystery that culture has been allowed to remain. "Semioticians hold that all intelligibility depends upon codes. Whenever we 'make sense' of an event it is because we possess a *system of thought,* a code that enables us to do so" [Scholes 1982:143, italics mine]). Culture is not deliberately withheld from us; our conventions and usages and their institutionalizations, fateful to be sure, are under no one's control but our own. We remain largely unaware of these systems of thought, however, so much do we take them as givens in the nature of things, revolutionaries as well as conservatives among us, for we would all be incapable of living without them. Pointing up their power to enshrine the status quo, whether of politics or literature, Barthes calls conventions "myths"; speaking of them as "durably installed," Bourdieu terms them a "*habitus. . .*a system of lasting, transposable dispositions which, integrating past experiences, functions at every moment as a *matrix of perception, appreciation, and actions* and makes possible the achievement of infinitely diversified tasks" (Barthes 1972

[1951]; Bourdieu 1977 [1972]:82–83, emphasis in original). American predicates and the meaning systems they sustain I liken to a shadow Constitution in hopes of spiriting them out of the "universe of the undiscussed (undisputed)," never reaching a court of appeals, never reinterpreted to accommodate contemporary facts (Bourdieu 1977 [1972]:168).

3. This septo-hippocampal system is part of the limbic system believed to control feeling states and their expression; it is a "substrate" shared by nearly all living creatures. In a major theoretical statement on the unity of the physiology and psychology of fear, Gray synthesizes many experiments on the production and diminution of anxiety in humans, fish, birds, mice, cats, dogs, pigs, monkeys, and rats, finding that "in spite of this diversity of experimental subjects, there is virtually no need to qualify any of the conclusions reached with respect to species" (Gray 1982:48).

4. Restating the history of art as a history of intentional "discontinuities" or, in the terms of this paper's biology of meaning, discrepancies from what was once familiar and meaningful, Peckham suggests that human beings actively seek out discontinuities as "rehearsal" for the jolts to expectations that life inexorably presents. "Art is rehearsal for those real situations in which it is vital for our survival to endure cognitive tension. . . . [A]rt is the reinforcement of the capacity to endure disorientation so that a real and significant problem may emerge. Art is the exposure to the tensions and problems of a false world so that man may endure exposing himself to the tensions and problems of the real world" (Peckham 1965:314). That people seem more likely to experience the discontinuities of art than to be receptive to fundamental social and cultural change testifies to that observation.

So also Meyer observes (but does not account for) that music's "variations" and "deviations" from familiar "style systems" explain its impact (Meyer 1956:54, 289). In music, the "customary or expected progression of sounds can be considered as a norm, which from a stylistic point of view it is; and alteration in the expected progression can be considered as a deviation. Hence deviations can be regarded as emotional or affective stimuli" (ibid.:32). This biology of meaning may explain this well-observed sequence of events and, as well, the tiny audiences for modern music.

5. Both animals and humans respond to novelty with "startle," "arrest," or "alerting" (O'Keefe and Nadel 1978:243; Kagan 1974). Freezing is a posture of tense and silent immobility; animals sit "rigidly motionless, or slightly trembling, in a hunched or prone position, with eyes open" (Berlyne 1960:125). If an animal already in motion confronts a dangerous, novel, conflictful, or frustrating situation, its response is flight; if already still, then it will freeze.

In human beings, when a discrepancy exceeds a certain threshold, confusion and complexity "may be handled by distorted perceptions, ignoring or muffling anomalous features . . . like those [perceptions] that characterize people with a high 'intolerance of ambiguity'" (Berlyne 1960:169). This "muffling" and resistance are, I suggest, human homologies of freezing: avoiding the pain of uncertainty, the brain's drive toward homeostasis gives priority to familiar and predictable meaning systems.

6. These experiences parallel those we call "culture shock," when a new environment frustrates our customary expectations. The metaphor is correct: the pain of the frustration may be as great as, if not greater than, the reaction brought on by mild punishments. When animals are unsure of either reward or punishment, they will simply avoid all stimuli (Gray 1971:141). To experience "culture shock" is to lack

appropriate systems of meaning with which to act and to shape expectations of what will follow. When culturally confused, people tend to become more aware of previously automatic behaviors, such that the confusion may not only limit the ability to act, but may elaborate into even more limitation (Mandler 1983:100–101). Travel can be narrowing, that is, by making us exceptionally aware of now useless predicates, now more than ever silent, and by reason of that helplessness, vulnerable to distress and fear.

7. These are issues common throughout Western civilization. A German child with Down's syndrome had plastic surgery to change her facial appearance, and, freed from stigma, was then "treated normally by other children and adults and . . . made enormous strides in social development." She was one of the more than 250 people in Frankfurt between three and twenty-four to have their lives thus changed since 1977. Israeli psychologists who saw this work initiated a pilot study of eleven children; one of the surgeons said, "I became convinced. There is practically no risk. It's very cheap. There is no significant trauma. And it gives the children an opportunity to be seen as individuals, rather than just members of a strange and inferior group" (Pines 1982).

8. Although this biology of meaning shares Piaget's ideas of self-regulation and equilibration, the structural parallel is superficial and misleading. Systems of meaning and conduct are far from affectless, unlike the conflict-free, wholly cognitive processes Piaget founded his theory on (Piaget 1967).

9. That thousands of cultures and their "subcultures" persist is more to be explained than that they change in light of obvious economic incentives, increased literacy, transistor radios, and battery-operated television. Cultures change, I suggest, by "selecting" (as evolutionists put it) from arrays of innovations those regarded as not being above some threshold of discrepancy to central systems of meaning and acting. The plough or steel axe is not the choice they make, but what its incorporation signifies in existing systems. Cultures resist innovations discrepant to the meanings they live by, especially those believed to foreclose expected rewards.

References Cited

Allport, Gordon
 1958   The Nature of Prejudice. New York: Anchor Books.
Barthes, Roland
 1972   [1951] Mythologies. New York: Hill and Wang.
Berlyne, Daniel E.
 1960   Conflict, Arousal, and Curiosity. New York: McGraw-Hill.
Berscheid, Ellen, and William Graziano
 1979   The Initiation of Social Relationships and Interpersonal Attraction. In Social Exchange in Developing Relationships. Robert L. Burgess and Ted L. Huston, eds. pp. 31–60. New York: Academic Press.
Bourdieu, Pierre
 1977   [1972] Outline of a Theory of Practice. Cambridge, England: Cambridge University Press.

Brehm, Jack W., and Arthur R. Cohen
1962   Explorations in Cognitive Dissonance. New York: John Wiley.

Brody, Jane E.
1981   Removing Barriers in Relationships with the Disabled. New York Times, December 2, p. C13.

Bruner, Jerome S.
1957   Going Beyond the Information Given. In Contemporary Approaches to Cognition: A Symposium Held at the University of Colorado. pp. 41–69. Cambridge, Mass.: Harvard University Press.

Bruner, Jerome S., J. Goodnow, and G. A. Austin
1956   A Study of Thinking. New York: John Wiley.

Buchler, Justus (ed.)
1955   [1940] Philosophical Writings of Peirce. New York: Dover Publications.

Colby, Benjamin N., James W. Fernandez, and David B. Kronenfeld
1981   Toward a Convergence of Cognitive and Symbolic Anthropology. American Ethnologist 8:422–450.

Douglas, Mary
1966   Purity and Danger: An Analysis of Concepts of Pollution and Taboo. London: Penguin.

Dullea, Georgia
1982   Handicapped Pupils Join the Mainstream. New York Times, September 13, p. B8.

Eco, Umberto
1976   A Theory of Semiotics. Bloomington: Indiana University Press.

Ellen, Roy F., and David Reason (eds.)
1979   Classifications in Their Social Context. New York: Academic Press.

Fabian, Johannes
1983   Time and the Other: How Anthropology Makes Its Object. New York: Columbia University Press.

Fernandez, James
1983   Afterword: At the Center of the Human Condition. Semiotica 46:323–330.

Friedman, John Block
1981   The Monstrous Races in Medieval Art and Thought. Cambridge, Mass.: Harvard University Press.

Goffman, Erving
1968   [1963] Stigma: Notes on the Management of Spoiled Identity. Baltimore: Penguin Books.

Gould, Stephen Jay
1981   The Mismeasure of Man. New York: W. W. Norton.

Gray, Jeffrey A.
1971 The Psychology of Fear and Stress. New York: McGraw-Hill.
1982 The Neuropsychology of Anxiety: An Inquiry into the Functions of the Septo-Hippocampal System. New York: Oxford University Press.

Hebb, Donald O.
1946 On the Nature of Fear. Psychology Reviews 53:259–276.
1955 Drives and the C.N.S. [Conceptual Nervous System]. Psychological Reviews 62:243–254.

Kagan, Jerome
1971 Change and Continuity in Infancy. New York: John Wiley.
1974 Discrepancy, Temperament, and Infant Distress. In The Origins of Fear. Michael Lewis and Leonard A. Rosenblum, eds. pp. 229–248. New York: John Wiley.

Katz, Irwin
1981 Stigma: A Social Psychological Analysis. Hillsdale, N.J.: Erlbaum.

Kellert, Stephen R., and Joyce K. Berry
1980 American Attitudes, Knowledge and Behaviors toward Wildlife and Natural Habitats, Phase III: Knowledge, Affection and Basic Attitudes toward Animals in American Society. New Haven, Conn.: Yale University, School of Forestry and Environmental Studies.

Kemp, Evan J., Jr.
1981 Aiding the Disabled: No Pity, Please. New York Times, September 3, p. A19.

Klineberg, Otto
1968 Prejudice: I. The Concept. In International Encyclopedia of the Social Sciences, Vol. 12. pp. 439–448. New York: Macmillan and Free Press.

Konner, Melvin
1982 The Tangled Wing: Biological Constraints on the Human Spirit. New York: Holt, Rinehart, & Winston

Lakoff, George, and Mark Johnson
1980 Metaphors We Live By. Chicago: University of Chicago Press.

Leach, Edmund
1964 Anthropological Aspects of Language: Animal Categories and Verbal Abuse. In New Directions in the Study of Language. Eric H. Lenneberg, ed. pp. 23–63. Cambridge, Mass.: MIT Press.

Levine, Donald N.
1979 Simmel at a Distance: On the History and Systematics of the Sociology of the Stranger. In Strangers in African Societies. William A. Shack and Elliott P. Skinner, eds. pp. 21–36. Berkeley: University of California Press.

LeVine, Robert A., and Donald T. Campbell
1972 Ethnocentrism: Theories of Conflict, Ethnic Attitudes, and Group Behavior. New York: John Wiley.

Mandler, George
1975   Mind and Emotion. New York: John Wiley.
1983   Stress and Thought Processes. *In* Handbook of Stress: Theoretical and Clinical Aspects. Leo Goldberger and Shlomo Breznitz, eds. pp. 88–104. New York: Free Press.

Meyer, Leonard B.
1956   Emotion and Meaning in Music. Chicago: University of Chicago Press.

O'Keefe, John, and Lynn Nadel
1978   The Hippocampus as a Cognitive Map. Oxford: Clarendon Press.

Peckham, Morse
1965   Man's Rage for Chaos: Biology, Behavior, and the Arts. New York: Schocken Books.

Perin, Constance
1986   Belonging in America: Reading between the Lines. Manuscript.

Pettigrew, Thomas F.
1982   [1980] Prejudice. *In* Dimensions of Ethnicity: A Series of Selections from the Harvard Encyclopedia of American Ethnic Groups. Stephan Thernstrom, ed. pp. 1–29. Cambridge, Mass.: Belknap Press of Harvard University Press.

Piaget, Jean
1967   Six Psychological Studies. New York: Random House.

Pines, Maya
1982   Down's Syndrome Masked by Surgery. New York Times, August 31, p. C2.

Rosch, Eleanor
1977   Human Categorization. *In* Advances in Cross-Cultural Psychology. N. Warren, ed. pp. 1–49. London: Academic Press.

Sahlins, Marshall
1965   On the Sociology of Primitive Exchange. *In* The Relevance of Models for Social Anthropology. Michael Banton, ed. pp. 139–236. London: Tavistock.

Schneider, David M.
1979   Kinship, Community, and Locality in American Culture. *In* Kin and Communities: Families in America. A. J. Lichtman and J. R. Challinor, eds. pp. 155–174. Washington, D.C.: Smithsonian Institution Press.
1980   American Kinship: A Cultural Account. 2nd edition. Chicago: University of Chicago Press.

Scholes, Robert
1982   Semiotics and Interpretation. New Haven, Conn.: Yale University Press.

Severo, Richard
1981   Woman with Elephant Man's Disease Chooses Bold Surgery. New York Times, December 8, p. C1.

Singer, Milton
1978   For a Semiotic Anthropology. *In* Sight, Sound, and Sense. Thomas Sebeok, ed. pp. 202–231. Bloomington: Indiana University Press.

Solomon, Barbara Miller
1956 Ancestors and Immigrants: A Changing New England Tradition. Cambridge, Mass.: Harvard University Press.

Stocking, George W., Jr.
1968 Race, Culture, and Evolution: Essays in the History of Anthropology. New York: Free Press.

Tajfel, Henri
1969 Cognitive Aspects of Prejudice. Journal of Biosocial Science, Supplement 1.
1981 Human Groups and Social Categories: Studies in Social Psychology. Cambridge, England: Cambridge University Press.

Thayer, H. S.
1968 Meaning and Action: A Critical History of Pragmatism. New York: Bobbs-Merrill.

Tyler, Stephen A.
1978 The Said and the Unsaid: Mind, Meaning, and Culture. New York: Academic Press.

Zigler, Edward
1980 Controlling Child Abuse: Do We Have the Knowledge and/or the Will? In Child Abuse: An Agenda for Action. George Gerbner, Catherine J. Ross, and Edward Zigler, eds. pp. 3–34. New York: Oxford University Press.

Barchester Towers in Appalachia: Negotiated Meaning

James L. Peacock
University of North Carolina at Chapel Hill

"We multiply by dividing." Thus did a Primitive Baptist elder summarize the social history of his denomination. He was right. Primitive Baptist associations in the United States have indeed multiplied through division and reorganization. Such splits entail politics as instructive as ecclesiastical maneuvering in higher places, and issues and principles as fundamental as any in Anthony Trollope's novel (*Barchester Towers*) of ecclesiastical politics in England.[1]

Primitive Baptists, sometimes known as Hardshelled Baptists, resemble Great Britain's Strict and Particular Baptists, with whom they share roots in the Baptist separatist movement among the Puritans of Cromwell's England. In America their history began when Roger Williams founded a Baptist Church in 1638 in Rhode Island, shortly after establishing that colony. The oldest surviving Primitive Baptist Church is the Welsh Tract Church in Delaware, established in 1701. The particular association with which this paper deals, which I term the Highlands Association,[2] was founded in 1798. It spans a North Carolina county and a Virginia county in the Blue Ridge Mountains.

Theologically, the Primitive Baptists are staunchly Calvinistic, more firmly so, perhaps, than any other American denomination. They believe that God decided, before the foundation of the world, who would be saved and who damned, and that no human effort can change one's eternal fate. Save for those known as Absoluters, however, they do not believe that God predestined all action on earth—only that ultimate state, the condition of one's eternal existence. Espousing this "hard" doctrine, the Primitive Baptists split with those who became Freewilled

Baptists in 1832, refusing to support missionary activities, Sunday schools, musical instruments, or other agencies for influencing the "fleshly emotions" in a vain hope of gaining salvation. Salvation, they believe, lies entirely in God's hands.

Most Primitive Baptists in the Highlands Association are farmers, artisans, housewives, or wage-earning women. They tend to be old (Primitive Baptists seem to live long; some are more than 100 years old), and their education is often limited to elementary school. Despite their limited formal schooling (or perhaps because of it), their eloquence and learning are remarkable. The best preachers, the "elders,"[3] have virtually memorized the King James Bible, and their sermons, which must be delivered straight from the stand without notes or preparation, are in the King James language. These mountain men, who refer to themselves ironically as "hillbillies," have also studied such eighteenth-century British theological writings as those of Gill, Spurgeon, and Philpott, and they boast a superior knowledge of church history. In fact, their intense intellectuality finds expression in doctrinal dispute, which accentuates schism. The conflict discussed here, however, turns less around differences of doctrine than of cultural value.

In narrating this case, I have tried to reflect the Biblical and Calvinistic rhetoric and world view framing the events and their interpretation by participants. Such a frame was apparent in the imagery of sermons and other accounts, in the way scenes were set and rituals enacted, and in the way the Primitive Baptists constructed the motives and forces that shaped their lives.[4]

The incident[5] that started this conflict took place at the Low Valley Church in the Blue Ridge area of Virginia to the northwest of the Highlands Association. Established in 1775, this church has an image polarized by legend. It is traditionally romanticized as once a Beulah Land, a happy house of God, full of joyful people, attracting even the young, and giving liberty to preachers, who recall being "blessed" when taking the stand there. More recently it is described by some as a hotbed of intrigue, destroyed by pride and a family quarrel.

Today, three brothers, the Cahooneys, dominate the Low Valley Church. Sons of a deceased and respected elder, they are themselves elders, and are said by some to have assumed too much authority. The majority of the congregation are said to be their kinfolk.

One member of the congregation, a deacon, Redd, was employed by the Virginia highway department. After an accident, he retired, supported by disability payments, though some allege that his accident was a fraud. In any case, one of the Cahooney brothers spotted him at work on his roof (some say on the roof, others say merely holding a ladder for someone else), and brought the matter before the congregation. The Cahooneys moved, and the congregation voted, to exclude Redd; "exclude" is the Primitive Baptist term for "excommunicate," and it means that the individual is cast out of the congregation and rendered unfit for other Primitive Baptist churches as well. After Redd was excluded, the Cahooneys moved to exclude, one by one, everyone guilty by association with him—those who had sat with him in a pew or rode with him in a car—until finally they had excluded thirty-seven members of their church, a large portion of the congregation.

The Low Valley Church affair does not itself concern us, except that it became an affair of the Highlands Association. The excluded members sent a "Macedonian call" for help, and a delegation from a neighboring association, Pivot, went to Low Valley. They attended church, only to be reviled by the Cahooney brothers, who, they report, called them "fools and wolves," scriptural terms of abuse. They report that the first brother opened the abuse during his pastoral prayer, and the second continued it during his sermon. The delegation did not wait to shake hands in the fellowship ritual that ends the service, but walked out and returned home.

Several months later, in February, a second delegation went to Low Valley. It included two men who had gone the first time and several from neighboring associations in West Virginia, Georgia, and Virginia. Notably, it included—in fact, in some sense was led by—the moderator of the Highlands Association, Elder Jones. Jones sent letters by registered mail to the Cahooney brothers inviting them to meet and discuss the quarrel. Receiving no reply, he and the delegation met at the home of a female member of the church. After hours of deliberation, dutifully recorded in minutes circulated to members of the delegation and some of their home churches, the delegation declared the excluded members to be the "orderly element" in the Low Valley Church, implying that those who had excluded them, the Cahooneys, were out of order. The "orderly element" then established an independent congregation.

When news of these developments reached the Highlands Association, some considered the action of the second delegation premature if not entirely unjustified. This faction—represented by the Highlands clerk, Thomas—held that the Low Valley Church was simply having a family quarrel and was best left alone to settle its differences. In any event, a church is autonomous and cannot be dominated by an association, so what right had the Highlands Association to override decisions of the Low Valley Church? Thomas further objected that Moderator Jones had gone without authorization from the Association. Yet no one disagreed that the Cahooneys' actions had been, at best, abrupt and ill-considered.

During July and August, as these opinions were being expressed, several incidents occurred. The wedding of the daughter of Reed, assistant moderator of the Highlands Association and the pastor of Downwind Church in Virginia, one of the Highlands churches, was held at Downwind. After the wedding, clerk Thomas invited the Cahooneys to his house for supper, together with some elders, Thomas's son, and those of us engaged in this ethnographic study. At the Downwind church service that night, Thomas audibly proposed to Pastor Reed that the Cahooneys be invited to come from the back pew where they had been sitting in exile (from not only the elders' bench but even from the members' benches) and join with the elders in a hand of fellowship. Pastor Reed did so, and also asked one of the Cahooneys to give the prayer of dismissal. Pastor Reed and clerk Thomas later confirmed that this action signaled that the Downwind and Low Valley Churches were in good fellowship, despite the Cahooney incident. The relationship cemented was church to church, elder to elder. It overrode and opposed the rift between the Highlands Association and the Low Valley Church created by the prior actions of Moderator Jones.

A few days later Jones approached clerk Thomas to discuss the issue with him. Thomas told Jones that he disagreed with his actions, but, advised by his wife and the wife of a deacon not to meet privately with Jones at his house, he declined Jones's invitation. Instead, Thomas planned to introduce the matter at a meeting to settle another affair, and it was said that his son had a proposal to resolve the dispute. The matter, however, was not discussed at this meeting.

Now the prospect loomed of debating the matter at the annual meeting of the Highlands Association, slated for early September. The immediate issue was the disagreement between Moderator Jones and clerk Thomas and a faction allied with Thomas. The dispute could result not only in the replacement of Moderator Jones, but in more serious consequences as well.

The Two Factions

The Highlands Association is composed of nine churches, four on the North Carolina side of the state line and five on the Virginia side. Considering the contrasting stereotypes of the two states (in North Carolina, the small farmer and businessman of little historic renown; in Virginia, the aristocratic planter with family ties to the nation's founders), it is remarkable how little distinction the Primitive Baptists draw between the two. This egalitarianism could be explained by two factors. First, the mountain region as a whole does not display the state identities found in the lowlands: "First an Appalachian, then a North Carolinian," one elder put it. Similar statements could be heard from Virginians. Primitive Baptist allegiance comes before all. Second, the Association has endured almost 200 years.

Despite this underlying unity, attendance among the churches does tend to divide along state lines. With one exception, each church meets only one weekend per month; hence, a member who wants to attend every week must attend several churches. Each week, one or more Virginia churches meet and one North Carolina church meets. Accordingly, a Virginia member can, if he or she chooses, circulate solely among the Virginia churches; likewise, a North Carolina member can circulate solely among the North Carolina churches. Attendance does, in fact, follow this pattern. The Highlands Association, formally unified, is thus divided into two practicing clusters, separated along the state line by the New River, across which a bridge was not built at this point until 1927.

Moderator Jones is associated with the North Carolina cluster, which includes his home church and other churches he pastors, while clerk Thomas is associated with the Virginia cluster, where his home church is located.

Thomas's home church and the cluster of churches pastored by Jones also differ in settlement patterns. Thomas's church sits in his hometown of Shady Grove, a village of small frame houses with yards and gardens. Jones's three churches are distributed at distances of two to six miles from his home church, which, like his other churches, is isolated among fields and hills. Thomas's milieu, then, is communal while the settlement pattern of the North Carolina churches is dispersed.

This observation holds generally for the entire Virginia faction in this dispute, which includes all the officers of the Highlands Association except Jones: Thomas, assistant moderator Reed, and Thomas's son, the assistant clerk of the Association. All are linked with the village of Shady Grove and its church, Downwind. The leadership of the Association, which includes nine churches, is thus concentrated at one church. The Downwind Church is further buttressed by communal and kinship ties among members as well as by its own bureaucratic layer—the clerk, the deacons, and an organization man, Pastor Reed. Even the music reflects Downwind's bureaucratization, for Downwind has moved closer to mainstream Protestantism by adopting major keys and abandoning the pentatonic modes and minor keys of the older, isolated Primitive Baptist churches of the frontier.

Jones's churches in North Carolina contrast with this pattern. Dispersed, not highly organized (their deacons tend to be old and their clerks old, unassertive, or, in one case, retarded), they express in their songs the distinctive Primitive Baptist sense of tragic yet stoic individualism. They oppose bureaucracy, since the doctrine of predestination deems the feeble organizations of humankind folly compared to the power of God: "Guide me, O Thou Great Jehovah,/We are weak and Thou art strong. . . ." What lends moral force to these North Carolina churches, seemingly feeble against the concentration of clerks at Downwind, is the character of Jones, a charismatic preacher. He is, as a Primitive Baptist hymn puts it, one of those "old professors tall as cedars," towering over the bureaucratic enclave at Downwind.

Clerk Thomas and Moderator Jones share many traits. Both are old (Thomas is seventy, Jones nearly seventy-four), and both are mountain men, born and raised in that "country," as they say, referring to the Blue Ridge area. Both have spent their lives doing manual labor; both are retired. Most important, both are devout Primitive Baptists.

In appearance and demeanor, however, they contrast. Thomas is short, squat, and powerfully built, with thick hands. Jones is taller, also very strong, but slender of hand for one who has spent his life at hard labor. Thomas speaks deliberately and slowly in a resonant voice of constant timbre. Jones speaks rapidly, with striking fluency and variation in timbre, facial expression, and gesture. Thomas spent his life working for the state, rising to supervisor after years of running heavy machinery, and then retiring with a pension. Jones has never had a corporate job but worked at many independent pursuits: stone mason, farm worker, plowing, and dairying. Thomas has one son, who serves with him as a deacon at Downwind and assistant clerk of the Association. Jones has many daughters and two sons.

Jones's spiritual autobiography is a rich history of experience, action, and interpretation. One experience he terms "translation." Explaining this in a sermon, he first notes that translation, as in translation of the Bible from Hebrew to English, includes two elements: words, the passive element, and a translator, the active element. "Words don't translate themselves," he says. Second, he refers to the biblical event of Elijah "translated" from earth to heaven; here, too, are passive and active elements, the passive Elijah and the active God: God took Elijah up, not the prophet himself. Finally, Jones recounts his own experience on a certain mountaintop fifty years ago. Overcome by his feelings of sinfulness to the point of despair, he vowed to pray to God until he wrested an answer; he struggled to do this near a certain ridge but failed. In a wretched, hopeless state, he went on to the top, and in this state of receptivity he was "translated" by God to a state of spiritual ecstasy.

During the Cahooney controversy, "translation" was on Jones's mind. He discussed it privately, he preached it, and he alluded to it in his opening remarks at the Association meeting at which he risked being deposed as moderator. Among other themes, "translation" alludes to his own impending death.

Jones's life story includes a series of critical spriritual experiences, lending themselves to doctrinal analysis. He was first a Union Baptist but then, following a remarkable vision featuring the she-bears of the scripture, he risked persecution to preach the doctrine of predestination, left the Union Baptists, joined the Primitive Baptists, was baptized in icy November mountain waters, and then ordained to preach. A gifted preacher, he has been in demand from Texas to Pennsylvania, though some of the Virginia faction allege that misconduct has caused his talent to wane.

Clerk Thomas reports no exhilarating spiritual experiences but one remarkable fact that attests to his sturdy integrity: he attended the Downwind Church weekly for thirty years before finally consenting to join. He explains simply that he did not consider himself worthy. Thomas does not preach and will not even pray publicly. He confines himself to clerical work for the Association.

This contrast in temperament between the two men is illustrated in a story told by Thomas about Jones. Once Jones and other elders were preaching a communion sermon at Downwind and staying at Thomas's home. Among the elders was the old Cahooney, father of the quarrelsome brothers at Low Valley. As is frequently reported by laymen about elders, Jones and Cahooney launched into a heated discussion about theology. Thomas told them at ten o'clock that it was time to go to bed. They asked for a few minutes more. He notified them again at eleven, at midnight, and at one, encountering the same resistance. Finally, at two, he laid down the law and commanded them to retire. As they went upstairs, Cahooney asked Thomas: "Where's my gritchel [grip, satchel]?" He got it and then asked, "Where's old Jones sleeping?" Told where, he went on into Jones's room, and they got the discussion going again. At four o'clock Thomas, on his way to milk a cow, stole softly downstairs. He found Cahooney awake, chewing tobacco in an old car in front of the house. Cahooney told him, "Two winks came in that room last night, and Jones got both of them."

The Fall of an Elder

Old Elder Adenauer, long moderator of the neighboring Pivot Association until his replacement in 1985 by young Ford, told of a dream he had in his youth while in conflict with a revered moderator, Reynolds. Adenauer dreamt of peering at a beautiful pool of calm, clear water, when suddenly a black snake came out of the bank. Drawing his gun, he shot it, whereupon it turned into Elder Reynolds, who, he says, "crippled away," followed by many baby snakes.

Soon after, at an Association meeting, Elder Adenauer was "blessed" in preaching against the position of Reynolds and he defeated the moderator, breaking his authority. Reynolds had been like a father to Adenauer, and before the meeting, when asked what side he would take, Adenauer had replied, "I will side with the old Elder." His conscience had forced him, however, to go with the scripture against Reynolds. On his deathbed Reynolds later forgave him and said he was right. Yet shortly after the meeting, Adenauer told his dream to a fellow Primitive Baptist who replied, "You certainly did shoot Reynolds."

Adenauer recounted this experience while discussing the forthcoming Highlands Association meeting and the Low Valley controversy. He must have had in mind the parallel between his unseating of Reynolds and the impending possibility of his close friend Jones losing his authority over the Low Valley issue. Certainly this possibility was in the minds of many as the meeting approached. Jones was still widely acknowledged to have been given the "gift." He possessed a remarkable memory, poetic power, analytic acuity, and eloquence. And he had once been physically vigorous, working at hard labor twelve hours daily while preaching and traveling constantly.

Yet now he was almost seventy-four and afflicted with emphysema, which had diminished his once powerful voice. Though kind and engaging, he had always been more preacher than pastor, and his health now restricted organizational activity. One of his three churches had shrunk to less than a dozen members, and his allies appeared neither strong nor numerous.

As the day for the Association meeting approached, the prospects for the fall of Elder Jones were strong; if not this year, then soon he would be replaced as moderator, as had his friend Adenauer the year before. As we rode with him revisiting the familiar places of his life—the cabin where he was born, the house where he preached his first sermon, the church where he enacted a vision clarifying for him the Primitive Baptist doctrine, the stone buildings he had erected—he was alternately cheered by memories and gloomy about what would come, at least in this world.

Gloomier still was our expectation that charismatic leaders like Jones would give way to prudent pragmatists like Thomas, ushering in a rule of strong clerks instead of strong elders.

The Association Meeting

Friday morning, September 2, was rainy as trucks and cars pulled up at ten o'clock to Plum Valley Church to open the 185th annual meeting of the Highlands Association. Clerk Thomas led the singing, with Reed beside him in the front row.

A visiting elder from Georgia, McNemar, a member of the delegation that had visited Low Valley Church, walked down the aisle—a large, square, deep-voiced man in a dark suit and cowboy boots. He sat down in the second-row corner of the members' bench, accompanied by a smaller, compact, bespectacled man, Ransom, also from Georgia, who had not been there before. Following them came a faithful cripple, a sufferer from a muscular disease that caused his limbs to splay and his mouth to remain in an exaggerated grin. After he had struggled to a seat in the front row of the women's section, his mother smoothed his hair and took her seat one row back.

Jones came in, dressed in a dark suit and wearing a somber expression. When he caught sight of the two Georgians, friends from far off, he cocked his head humorously, and McNemar broke into a broad grin, his pleasure at seeing Jones too much to contain. Jones took his seat on the elders' bench in front of McNemar and Ransom.

The singing continued, dreary as the weather, in a minor key: "Tell me no more of this world's vain store. The time for such pleasure with me now is o'er." Then, "I am a stranger here below, and what I am 'tis hard to know. . ." and, finally, Isaac Watts's hymn: "Hark, from the tomb a doleful sound. . . ."

Moderator Jones took the stand, stating that this was the 185th meeting of the Highlands Association. "Someone said, it makes no difference whether or not it exists. It makes all the difference in the world to me." He called for the singing of the introductory hymn, itself a "doleful sound," about how man approaches God with nothing. He then professed that he was "deeply moved" and began his opening remarks. He stated that his "primary subject is translation," and he introduced some of the themes he had mentioned in the sermon noted above. Translation had been on his mind for several months, he said, no doubt because he saw his own life coming to an end.

Then he slipped into another mode of personal reflections. He said he was not trying to disturb the peace, but that he could not "hold still" on matters close to him: "If I cease to be a member of the Old Baptist church, there is nowhere else for me to go." He said he had a strange feeling about this Association and that his life was marked by periods. His voice trailed off. At other times, he had mentioned that twenty-one years to a day had passed between his joining the Union Baptist and leaving it for the Primitive Baptist, and that twenty-one years had now passed since that second joining; he had implied that a third "translation" was due.

But on this occasion, Jones shifted from the theme of translation, not finishing his argument as in his previous sermons. Instead, he concluded that "this 185th annual session *does mean* something to me." Then he dismissed everyone for dinner on the grounds, asking them to return at the sound of singing.

Dinner was an unusually joyless time, as people hurriedly ate outside in the drizzle. Back in the church, around one o'clock, Jones opened the meeting and then announced the election of the officers.

Thomas asked leave to speak and made a firm statement. He had been clerk seventeen years (his voice broke as he recalled those early times), but now, he said, he must step down. His hand was crippled, and he could not write. He suggested a younger man, the merchant Selby, who only a month before had been elected deacon at Downwind. Thomas's son spoke also, saying he could continue as assistant clerk but could not take over as clerk (as normally might have been expected) because of travel commitments.

A third man, also associated with the Downwind Church, stood and moved that the elections for clerk, assistant clerk, moderator, and assistant moderator be decided by secret ballot. Every messenger representing a church of the Association should write on a slip of paper whomever he preferred for each job.

Jones accepted the suggestion. In contrast to recent times, when nominated officers were elected by affirmation, a ballot vote was held. A certain tension among those waiting while the ballots were counted was signaled as men opened windows at the church's four corners. The results were that Jones was returned as moderator, Reed as assistant moderator, and Thomas's son as assistant clerk. The only new officer was the merchant Selby as clerk, replacing Thomas.

Jones then remarked that he appreciated the Association's confidence and that he had been a poor moderator, while Reed (his heretofore unannounced opponent from the Virginia faction) would have made a better one. He would do his best for the year, he said, although "that's as far as [he] can go."

After remarks by the other officers and a brief anecdote by Thomas about Selby, who now took his seat, Thomas moved that the moderator make the appointments to committees. Jones did so, with some hesitation and difficulty in remembering names. He gave most positions to people from his own churches, although he did put Thomas on the arrangements committee, joking that "If Joe ain't gonna clerk, get him right there." Then he announced that Ransom, from Georgia, would preach.

So Jones was returned as moderator for another year.

From the remainder of that weekend, the following events or remarks bear on the conflict. On Friday evening, Thomas did not go to services, as did none of the Virginia faction save for assistant moderator

Reed. Appointments to preaching omitted Reed, while placing Reed's archenemy Ford at the penultimate position on the last day.[6] Ford preached on sin. Reed walked out. The final sermon, delivered by an elder who was trusted by both the Thomas and Jones factions, was on the subject of "hands." This led to Jones's final remarks. Jones said this might be his last time to preach, and he emphasized that the hand of fellowship is central in the faith. He called for the hand of fellowship before they closed, and everyone shook hands with everyone else. (The last word, however, came from clerk Thomas, who shouted to everybody to pick up copies of the minutes.)

Themes

Among the many themes exemplified by these events, I shall focus here on ritual—those repetitive and sacralized forms that have only crept into the edges of this narrative.

As stern Calvinists of separatist Puritan background, the Primitive Baptists are in many respects antiritualistic. They oppose any fusion of church and state or ritual and community (as exemplified by Durkheimian theory, and instances varying from medieval Catholicism to Falwell's moral majority). To wed ritual to community is to lose the transcendence of the sacred.

Over and against both ritual and community, the Primitive Baptists set the Spirit. Mistrusting form, they affirm meaning, as given by the Spirit. No musical instruments, no robes, no stained-glass windows, and no pictures or crucifixes are permitted in the church. (What is a cross, thundered Elder Ford, but a timber on which criminals were hanged? What matters is not the cross but Christ.) Also condemned is destruction of meaning for form, as in speaking in tongues or the "shout," where words lack clear meaning.

Against routine, the Primitive Baptists affirm the word, as given by the Spirit. A person cannot routinely prepare to join the church but must receive a spiritual "impression," for which he or she may wait a lifetime, only then to come forward. An elder must be called, and his gift can also be taken away. An elder cannot prepare a sermon but instead must mount the stand hoping to be blessed by the Spirit. Seeking the Spirit's guidance, the Primitive Baptist prays and meditates in the hollows and low places, occasionally to be lifted to the mountaintop. Such a quest is accompanied by intense solitary study of scripture and theology.

Yet out of these personal quests for meaning—framed by local history and theology—have been constructed public ritual patterns. This ritualization revolves around three familiar, overlapping oppositions: sacred vs. profane, public vs. private, and male vs. female.

The degree of ritualization of the church's administrative and political process is striking. Following the Saturday service a church is declared "in conference," and the pastor moderates a brief business meeting. Each meeting follows rules of decorum printed in the minutes, as well as Robert's Rules of Order; it appears that most matters are worked through from start to finish in this context rather than reflecting any prior deliberations. Business is thus conducted in the sacral context of space and time—right in the church, in the context of the service—and publicly. Business is ritualized.

With this background, one can understand Thomas's objection to Jones's holding the meeting about the Cahooneys "in the house of a sister," rather than "in the church." Said Thomas: "What is started in a church should be finished in a church."

"In the house of a sister" was the other side of Thomas's objection. Business meetings are dominated by men, although women are present. Not only may women not preach—they should not speak at business meetings, which are led by the pastor and the deacons. Business, then, is not only sacral and public, it is masculine. "What do the women do?" I asked an elder. His wife, a mathematics teacher, stuck her head out of the kitchen door and laughed, "They cook." The major church-related function of women is indeed to prepare dinners after communion and foot-washing services. Although cooking can spill into sacral spheres, as when the deacon's wife prepares the bread and wine for communion, Primitive Baptist women are, practically speaking, consigned to the profane and private spheres.

Into this opposition Jones injected a reversal. "You sisters who listen in silent reverence," he preached, "are a type." "You," he would say, turning to the men's pews, "are not a type." By this, he explained, he meant that women are symbolically the bride of Christ, and hence are symbols of the church itself.[7]

Discussing Jones's argument with him, I proposed the kind of interpretation suggested by Needham (1980:63–105) of an opposition between an explicit, instrumental power (that of the men, who publicly dominate church ritual and business) and a mystical power (associated with the women) that resides not in what one does or controls but in what one is, what one symbolizes and manifests. Jones neither accepted nor rejected this interpretation but instead shifted the ground to scripture, justifying his own argument by exegesis of the Song of Solomon.

Jones's argument bestowed on women meanings and powers outside the church's administrative and ritual routine. Such a symbolization explains how Jones and his colleagues could accept the sister's house as a suitably liminal place in which to assemble the excluded members of Low Valley and reconstitute them as a new congregation: women, at this mystical level, *are* the church. Thomas, less mystical and more bureaucratic, simply rejected this "betwixt and between" category represented by the sister's house. Business should be public, formal, and sacral; what starts in the church should be finished in the church.

The difference between Jones's and Thomas's attitudes about the role of women reflects their personal experience. Jones's wife, who has never joined the Primitive Baptist church, plays no role even in the profane sphere of cooking and hospitality, while Thomas's wife is active in this respect. Thomas's wife also informally influences church affairs, while Jones grumbles about such "women who run the church through the telephone." Thomas the bureaucrat permits women to slide into the sacral pragmatically, while Jones the preacher restricts their role to the symbolic.

Now to the outcome of the Association meeting: what did the vote mean? Jones was reelected moderator and Thomas resigned as clerk. Jones then cemented his position through the two means at his disposal: appointments to committees and appointments to preach. In both positions he placed his own men, largely excluding those of the other faction. Charisma beat bureaucracy; North Carolina won out over Virginia; Jones prevailed over Thomas.

But such a bare-bones assessment of logistics fails to capture the ritual context of these actions. Jones's conduct during the Association meeting was not that of a political strategist so much as that of a man of sorrows, acquainted with grief. He remained absorbed in reflections on his own life, his coming death, and the history and fellowship of the Association as it was bound with these. His mournful remarks and somber countenance were in evidence throughout.

One could, of course, interpret this spiritual posture as itself a political weapon. What guilt would be laid on him who would dare, at this point in Jones's life, to "crucify" him? Such a cynical interpretation would distort the ritual frame in which Primitive Baptist business is conducted. The spiritual and the tactical are not as sharply differentiated as a pragmatic outsider might assume. Accepting that the two spheres fuse, that church politics are ritualized, one might interpret the case more accurately in the following vein.

At one level, political maneuvering of a deliberate and rational type was indeed being practiced, by both Jones and Thomas and by their factions. Awareness of this was revealed in various comments and actions, though it was largely tacit. At another level, the accustomed forms were followed; the conflict was worked through as part of a sacral fellowship and rite. And at a deeper level, Jones's reelection was a drama embodying a profound set of isomorphic symbolizations. These symbols included Jones's life story, his gift, and his coming death; the biblical archetypes of death, from Elijah's "translation" to Christ's crucifixion; and the collective history of the Primitive Baptist Association, with its struggles and schisms. The resonances of such symbols were made surprisingly explicit by Jones's mournful utterances and demeanor, which set a heavy mood at the meeting.

Behind all this lies the question of ritual in a reformist sect. Growing out of a "purifying" movement, such a sect must remain skeptical of communal ritual. Strictly individualistic, its members seek meaning not in the public rite as much as in private experience—yet those experiences and understandings can be "translated" by gifted, charismatic spokesmen like Jones into public statements, and such utterances then become part of a desperate grasping for the ritual and sense of community that was virtually lost through Puritanism. For such Puritans, forms and fellowship are deeply felt, perhaps more intensely than by those of other denominations who take communal ritual for granted. Ritual in such a Puritan group must be constructed and negotiated. It represents the product of a creative struggle to wrest meaning from disorder and dispersion. It may be crystallized somewhat obsessively, but always with awareness of ultimate destiny—the looming destruction of such forms, together with all that is mortal.

To cast this example within the frame of social anthropological interpretation, we might refer to Gluckman's concept of "ritual of social relationship" (1962). According to Gluckman, such a ritual can occur only in groups where social relationships are "multiplex," that is, entailing many strands, as when persons are kinfolk, neighbors, co-workers, and many other things to each other simultaneously. Such a collectivity is found, Gluckman argues, in traditional tribal and village communities. In a multiplex community, conflict ramifies widely and deeply, spilling over into natural and supernatural spheres; given conflict, crops fail, people fall sick, the spirits grow restless. To restore order, a ritual of social relationships must correct the disturbed relationships, casting them in harmonious and sacralized form. The ritual antidote must be as powerful as the social poison that penetrated the social body in the first place; the ritually enacted harmony is then perceived as restoring order to all those disturbed spheres.

Within the Highlands Primitive Baptist Association, relationships do tend toward this kind of multiplexity. Jones, Thomas, and the Cahooneys are entangled in a network within which they have spent their lives and which stretches back even before they were born, as in Jones's relationship to the Cahooneys' father. Disturbance did ramify through this network, in the fashion posited by Gluckman.

But the situation differs in a crucial respect from his model: the Highlands Association cannot permit itself to be defined as primarily social; it must always be framed by a transcendental vision. Social relationships can be only pawns in this game; the stakes are not of this world but of the next—whether one will be saved or damned.

Calvinism is essentially suspicious of any social relationship, suspecting idolatry and the glorifying of the merely human. The act of fellowship, which certainly gains resonance and poignancy from the multiplexity of human relationships, is thus as tragic as it is charismatic, for it is recognized only as a passing vanity of the world and a limited manifestation of the sacral.

Within this tortured frame, then, the ritual that unfolds in Association meetings—here to combat the threat of schism and its destruction of fellowship—must again be negotiated. It cannot unfold mechanistically or automatically, as Gluckman's traditionalist model would suggest. And even to the extent that it could do so, it would be challenged and reinterpreted by those who seek constantly for the truest way in which to manifest God's will.

In interpreting such a situation, we are thus suspended between traditionalist social anthropology and the more ephemeral interpretive perspectives of cultural analysis—in a word, between the heirs of Durkheim and of Weber. Durkheim instructed us about public ritual, Weber about private consciousness. The case described here involves the dialectical relations between the two, and reminds us that we still lack adequate theories to explicate that relationship.

Meanwhile, Jones and Thomas struggle, in their separate ways, to construct and sustain a form of worship and community that embody both the public meanings and the private quests of those who feel guided by the Spirit.

Notes

1. Fieldwork and discussion concerning this case were carried out in conjunction with Ruel Tyson of the Department of Religion at the University of North Carolina at Chapel Hill. I am much indebted to him for his company and ideas. "We" in the text refers, unless otherwise indicated, to Tyson and me. I am also grateful to the National Endowment for the Humanities and the Wenner-Gren Foundation for Anthropological Research for funding the fieldwork during which these incidents were observed. Deepest gratitude must of course be expressed for the generosity of the Primitive Baptists in permitting us to participate in their activities.

2. All the names of organizations and local persons and communities are pseudonyms, to help preserve their anonymity.

3. Primitive Baptists do not pay salaries for preachers, so elders must support themselves.

4. It should not be thought, however, that Primitive Baptists always speak in the meter of the King James Bible. Sometimes they do, as when Jones preached or mused about this life and the future, but conversational accounts of the case were usually matter-of-fact.

5. This narrative account of what might be termed the "Low Valley affair" is a summary of myriad sources. I first heard about what had happened while having breakfast with Elder Jones in May 1983, when he briefed me on the news of the previous winter. (I had not seen him since fieldwork in summer 1982, and the Low Valley incident had erupted in the intervening months.) During June, July, and August 1983 my fellow fieldworkers and I lived in the locale of the Mountain District Association, as we had in summer 1982, and from time to time we heard versions of the affair from others, including Thomas and Reed. We also met the Cahooneys and, at their invitation, visited them and attended the Low Valley Church; but they would not discuss the case with us, as they were under litigation. We were also shown minutes and correspondence describing the first and second visits of the Mountain and Pivot delegates to Low Valley; this occurred in the context of a conversation with one of the delegates, who offered his own comments on the affair. We were present at some of the significant events, such as the welcoming of the Cahooneys to Downwind Church and Jones's reelection at the September 1983 meeting of the Association.

6. A female-linked issue played into the conflict between Jones and the Virginia faction allied with Thomas, though it has seemingly not been emphasized by Thomas himself. This involved the question of an elder having two wives. Elder Reed is, Jones says, a fanatic in asserting, based on a passage in the book of Titus, that no elder can have two living wives through divorce. Jones claims that a more contextual reading of the whole Bible permits an exception when the divorce is due to a wife's adultery.

The issue has come to a head around the person of Tom Ford, a powerfully built man in his early thirties whose demeanor reflects his physique and physiognomy (his face is of a ruddy English cast, but with the extremely prominent jaw sometimes seen in the mountains). Orphaned, he lived in an abandoned automobile for a time, was the "front man" in a Vietnam combat squad, and now works in a pipe factory as well as at other laboring and construction jobs from dawn to dark. This incessant labor has enabled him to acquire a decent house and a streamlined, large-tire truck, which he drives at high speed on mountain roads. His main recreation is hunting deer with a bow.

Ford converted to the Primitive Baptist faith after returning from the war, and he became a protégé of Elder Jones. He himself became an elder, preaching in a forceful style with a resonant chanting voice, and he has become moderator of the neighboring Pivot Association as well as pastor of a church in the Highlands Association.

Ford's first wife reportedly left with another man for Maryland. Ford, accompanied by a friend who is another young elder, pursued them and caught them together. He sued for divorce on the grounds of adultery, having been instructed by Jones that only in that case could he legitimately serve as an elder after a divorce and remarriage. He was later remarried.

Because of the remarriage, Elder Reed considers Ford an illegitimate elder, and he refuses to invite him to the stand in any church he pastors. Reed also condemns Jones for supporting Ford. Because Ford was instrumental in the visit to Low Valley, and because Ford and Jones were tainted by the two-wives question, Reed connected the two controversies in building his opposition to Ford and Jones.

7. An intriguing comparison could be made between the Primitive Baptists and another mountain sect, the Sons of God. Whereas the Primitive Baptists speak of the positive female symbolism of the church (the bride of Christ), the Sons tend to speak of it negatively (the whore of Babylon). Yet where the Primitive Baptists forbid women to preach, the Sons have female preachers who, however, are said to represent the fleshly aspect of the established church, from which all should escape in order to become entirely spiritual (see Wise 1977).

References Cited

Gluckman, Max
    1962   Les Rites de passage. In Essays on the Ritual of Social Relations. Max Gluckman, ed. pp. 1–52. Manchester, England: Manchester University Press.

Needham, Rodney
    1980   Reconnaissance. Toronto: University of Toronto Press.

Wise, James E.
1977   The Sons of God Message in the North Carolina Meetings: An Exercise in
       Thick Description. M.A. thesis, Curriculum in Folklore, University of
       North Carolina at Chapel Hill.

Iranian Jewish Women's Magical Narratives

Judith L. Goldstein
Vassar College

This paper presents a set of stories, which I call "tales of magical causation," told by Iranian Jewish women about attempts to convert Jewish women to Islam.[1] The women relating these stories fear that individuals, often against their wills, can be detached from the groups into which they have been born and around which their lives revolve. I examine the construction of these narratives—their form and performance and the way they relate individuals to groups—and the ways in which the narratives are embedded in general group concerns about history and identity in a dominated, remnant community.

Iranian Jewish women's tales of magical causation are built around practical objects gone awry—puzzling episodes whose strangeness calls for interpretation. It is the storyteller's task to provide explanations for events that the ordinary onlooker would not "see" at all, let alone perceive as problematic. The symbolic vehicles of the stories are mortars and pestles, sugar cones, rugs, and clothing. By using objects with which they are intimately associated in daily life, the women call to mind Benjamin's comment —"An orientation toward practical interests is characteristic of many born storytellers" (Benjamin 1969:85)—while the interpretation implied in constructing this particular series of near-conversion stories reminds one of Ginzburg's (1980) efforts to locate narrative ability in the reading or "diagnosis" of concrete signs.

The concrete interpretation of signs that makes it possible to see stories in odd events is embedded in community concerns. The construction of magical narratives illustrates the permeable boundary between the particular events of an individual's life and the public reading of those events. The stories are often told about particular named women, but they can also be told as general truths that show the consequences of competition between religious groups for members. The first type of story tells of "my mother-in-law, Shirin"; the second refers to "a woman." This double construction enables the listener to understand that these stories are true because they happen to certain individuals, and that they also happen to certain individuals because they are true.

The two types of stories—those with individualized characters and those without them—reinforce each other. Each type of story has a message, but it is the relation between the two types of story, the choice that a telling implies, that is most meaningful. In saying so, I differ with Jameson, who has taken an evolutionary approach to the appearance of the individual in narrative. He calls the kind of stories Claude Lévi-Strauss collected "pre-individualistic narratives," arguing that "they emerge from a social world in which the psychological subject has not yet been constituted as such" (Jameson 1981:124). In this analysis, the pre-individualistic phase is followed by the individualistic phase characteristic of bourgeois society. Jameson looks forward to a post-individualistic period, because "only the emergence of a post-individualistic social world, only the reinvention of the collective and the associative, can concretely achieve the 'decentering' of the individual subject" (ibid.:125).

The dialectic I describe between individualized stories and anonymized stories characterizes a particular kind of collectivity. In their social context, the relevant issues are best understood not in an evolutionary framework such as Jameson's, but in a frame such as Dumont's (1970), where individuality or collectivity can be differentially stressed at different times within the same society.

In Iran the relation between individual and group is complex; it changes, and has changed, over time. It does not reflect simply a "now you see it, now you don't" pattern of emerging and receding individualism. The stories recounted here, when placed in their social contexts, offer another way of thinking about community.

These arguments about narrative, magic, history, and group identity are presented in three sections. The first, "A Story in Three Aspects," presents several tales of magical causation. The second, "The Social Context of Conversion: The Stories as Myth," considers what it is about the cultural construction of women that makes them prime candidates for conversion stories. The last, "Narrative as a Socially Significant Act: The Stories as History," returns to the issue of the community: how these narratives allow Iranian Jewish women to share each other's stories, and thus to construct a history appropriate to a remnant community.

The Setting

Yazd is a traditional, still largely preindustrial desert city in the province of Fars in central Iran. Shi'i Muslims are the majority of the inhabitants; Jews, Zoroastrians, Baha'is, and a small number of Christians are also included in the population, which in 1975 numbered 120,000.

Famous for its manufacture of silk, Yazd was once one of Iran's most prosperous cities. Even through times of economic trouble for the rest of the nation, it maintained its manufacturing base of silk, carpets, and cloth of cotton, felt, and wool. Although its fortunes declined in the nineteenth century, its strong merchant families continued to trade in dried fruits, cocoons, silk, and cotton on the world market (Issawi 1971:46). Some merchants were able to amass considerable capital, and a traveler in the 1850s observed that Iranian merchants "play the same part as European credit institutions" (ibid.:36). In fact, some traditional merchants did become modern bankers. Beginning with Reza Shah's reign in the 1930s, the capital of the mercantile economy was increasingly applied to new areas of industry, particularly textile mills (Bonine 1981:208). These new investments weakened the bazaar as Yazd's economic center. However, this process has been reversed under the Islamic Republic, partly because of the traditional alliance between the bazaar merchants and the *ulama*. The breakdown of the banking system has also stimulated the return of the bazaar's former functions of moneylending and currency exchange (ibid.:207).

Jews were not permitted as merchants in the bazaar until the time of the Pahlavis, and neither Jews nor Zoroastrians, while participating in the bazaar's economic functions, enter into its political and religious functions. Poor Yazdis, both Jews and Muslims, are commonly weavers, silk-spinners, and, more recently, factory workers; the poorest Jews are peddlers.

Yazdis of different religions are quite aware of each other, but they do not socialize to any significant extent. Interaction across denominational lines generally takes place only in the bazaar and in civil institutions such as schools and government offices. Social contacts tend to occur within the bureaucratic class—whose members generally are not from Yazd—and among the lower classes, who live together in changing neighborhoods whose more recent inhabitants come from the villages surrounding Yazd. Rules of ritual purity also separate Yazdis of different religions. Each public bath, for example, is used only by members of one religion, with the exception of the Baha'i bath, which Jews and Zoroastrians can also use. Jews cannot use Muslim barbers, but do cut Zoroastrian hair. The rules of purity also mean that Yazdis of different religions do not eat together. Jews and other non-Muslims are not involved in food distribution—they do not own restaurants or groceries or work in bakeries, unless these serve only members of their own religion. Jews instead sell dry goods, which usually are not thought to carry "pollution" as food and water do.

Jews and Muslims do share a cultural repertoire. For both groups, religious life remains central both to the organization and to the definition of the community. Both Jews and Muslims have adjusted to radical changes in ideology: the modern state, led by the shah, defined them as citizens as well as subjects, and secular schools replaced religious training while new opportunities opened up outside Yazd. The 1978–79 revolution attacked the role of citizen, and Jews are struggling to combine traditional and new religious definitions of themselves to fit the idiom of an Islamic regime (Goldstein 1981).

Both Muslim and Jewish women in Yazd are generally veiled. The only exceptions are women from outside Yazd in the upper, official echelons—they ride in cars instead, although they veil when visiting the bazaar. Younger women living in Tehran, where they do not wear the *chador,* put it on when they return to visit Yazd. There is often a concerted donning of *chadors* on the bus when it is within two hours of the city.

Women (like Jews) are employed in the civil sphere and to a limited extent in banks and schools. They also hold the more traditional jobs of seamstress, diviner, religious teacher, and carpet weaver. Poor women work as maids and, increasingly, in textile mills on the city's outskirts. They are never merchants or shop assistants, either in the newer stores on the main street or in the older stalls in the bazaar. (This is true even for stores that specialize in women's intimate apparel.) Men do most of the daily shopping for food and staples; women go to the stores for more specialized purchases such as cloth. The younger the woman, the more education she is likely to have. Women who do continue in school generally quit when they accept a marriage proposal, and the desire to stay in school is often given as an excuse to refuse a suitor.

Within all three official religions in Yazd (the Baha'i case is complicated), women are more involved in interstitial religious practices than are men. They are active in visiting shrines, making vows, combating the evil eye, using traditional healers and healing rituals, and patronizing diviners. These practices are viewed with some suspicion by the official religious leaders and by men in general.

A Story in Three Aspects

In the Jewish community of Yazd, the distinction between male and female loses its primacy to the unequal relation of Jews with the dominant Muslim community. The distinction between Muslim and Jew effectively encompasses the distinction between male and female. In such communities women's stories are not clearly differentiated from men's, but are rather versions and inversions of the community's shared repertoire of stories. Women's stories in Yazd are not told in opposition to men's stories, because both men and women accept the community's key myths. The women's stories are thus well within the larger mode of discourse, although women may tell stories that men do not. Such stories are often clearly derived from those of men, but they undergo a change of tone. Thus, as will be illustrated, a woman's variation of a central miracle tale becomes comic rather than solemn.[2]

The following three sections are oriented around a tale of magical causation. First, I discuss the forms such tales take and provide some examples of how similar stories can be told as general cases of Muslim attempts to convert Jewish women, or can be attributed to particular women. In the next section, I elaborate on my argument that the women's stories take place within a larger framework of well-known community tales. From this perspective, the tale of magical causation is best understood as a version of a miracle tale central to the Jews of Yazd. The third section examines how the stories are told and describes a contemporary event that could provide the material for a further tale of magical causation.

Abstract Categories and Repetition

Particular conversion stories are told about known persons, living or dead. The stories this paper explores concern attempted but unsuccessful conversions. They are told as true stories, but this does not prevent people from realizing that they have an abstractable form. One such telling, from a female informant, is as follows:

> For example, you've heard, someone came and said, "Give me three hairs from your daughter." He comes and takes three hairs, for example, from a sheep and gave it to him. For example, a sheep which had been killed. From under the sheepskin rug, they took three hairs and gave them to him. Then they went and saw that this sheepskin rug, by itself, was going up and down and up and down and went. We understood that they had done sorcery so the girl would go to their house. Hah! It was like that.

Stories about attempts at magical seduction (and conversion, because the two are generally synonymous) take two common forms. In the first, something belonging to a woman, such as the three hairs in this story, is worked on to make her follow what had belonged to her to the house of a Muslim man. In the second type, a Muslim man gives a magically treated gift of food to a Jewish woman, who, if she eats it, returns his love and converts. Both story types work by a metonymic principle (Frazer's principle of contagion). In one case the girl follows a part of herself that has been magically treated; in the other she eats something from the outside that becomes part of her. In both cases she is coerced by something that was or has become part of herself.

The next story, told to me by another woman, shows how the abstract form of a story can become historically precise. It is interesting because it combines the two main forms these stories take.

> My uncle [mother's brother] Daiy Aqajan's mother-in-law, who lives in Castine, always worked with silk. They [her family] had a silk-preparation workshop. They [Muslims] came and bought silk from them. They did piecework for them. They saw this woman [the mother-in-law] and liked her. They went and took a bit of sugar (*nabat*) and brought it and gave it to this woman and said, "*Zan oostad*, take this and eat it." She, thank God, had reason (*aql*), and she did not eat what was in her hand but put it on her sheepskin rug. She threw the rug under the mortar and pounded meat. She

put the sugar on the sheepskin rug and saw that the rug began to go up and down. Because this sugar was put on the rug—they had done magic with the sugar so that the woman would eat it and become impassioned and go to their house. That time, the woman fortunately did not eat it, but put it on the sheepskin rug. At that time, the rug, step by step, made itself go up and down until it got to the door of the house. Then they understood what had happened. They came, took the sugar and threw it out. Yes, in the past they always did a lot of this kind of thing.

This story has the authenticity of personal detail. All the people involved, members of the teller's family, are still living. It also uses legitimating devices found in Islamic/Iranian narratives generally, where *hadith,* or oral traditions, are judged valid if the chain of tellers can be traced: "I heard from so-and-so who heard from so-and-so." The story's lesson is general—"in the past they always did a lot of this kind of thing"—and so its truth is not suspect because it is told in so many forms.

Versions and Inversions

The key myth of Yazdi Jews is about their apical ancestor, the great rabbi Mulla Or, a teacher and scholar. A paraphrase of this myth follows:

Mulla Or often studied far into the night. One evening the governor of Yazd looked over toward the Jewish quarter and saw a shaft of light ascending from the roofs of the quarter to the sky. He sent some of his men to investigate. They went to the quarter and saw that the light extended from Mulla Or's house [or head, in some versions] to the sky. They reported back to the governor, who realized that this was a mark of Mulla Or's holiness. On the following day the governor sent him a finely embroidered sheepskin coat. Mulla Or put it away until Yom Kippur [or Shabbat, in some versions], when he decided to wear it to synagogue. He put it on and then said to himself, "This is too much for me." He cut off the sleeves and then went into the street. The servant of the governor saw him and in a rage raised his hand to strike the mulla for the disrespect he showed by cutting the sleeves. The servant's arm dried in its upright position. Nothing he did could cure it. Some days later the governor asked, "Where is my servant so-and-so?" They brought him to the governor and he finally told the whole story.

The governor told him he had erred in behaving disrespectfully to such a man and suggested he go to Mulla Or and apologize. He did, Mulla Or said a blessing [and in some versions told him not to behave this way again], and the man's arm was cured.

A number of central themes appear in this story.[3] The story concerns Muslims and Jews. It is particularly about the miraculous power of a special Jew, implying a relation between that man—and by extension, the community of Jews—and God. It is also about the recognition that, ideally, Muslims give Jewish miracle workers and (again by extension) Jews as a whole, because of their connection with the divine.

If one talks to Yazdi women long enough, one will hear one of the variations of this tale, the initial telling of which will be preceded by laughter and a comment like, "I bet you haven't heard this before. A lot of people don't know it." Here is one variation:

One day Mulla Or saw a Muslim urinating against the wall of the synagogue [or on a Jewish gravestone]. He told the man that he was urinating in a holy place and he should stop. The man rudely refused. Mulla Or said, "So, pee" (az, be-shosh). The man could not stop, no matter what he did and what cures he tried. Finally his friends asked what he had done and elicited the story. They told him he had insulted a holy man and advised him to apologize. He did, Mulla Or said a prayer, and the problem was solved.

These two stories—key myth and variant—present variations on dry and wet, on holiness of Jewish place and Jewish person, and on the major theme of Muslim/Jewish relations. In both, the culminating success for the Jews comes through Muslims' recognition of the Jewish holy man. The second story is funny—a parody of the first. One thinks of carnivalesque reversals and the focus on what Bakhtin (1968) refers to as grotesque aspects of the body. However, what is important is not reversal—the story is not told to belittle Mulla Or or to deny that he is holy—but the genre switch.

Women say Mulla Or was naive. They separate his home life from his life in the world. He seemed able to get the Muslims to respect him through his miracle working, but he was less successful with his own wife. This does not prevent him from being one of the central figures women call on when they are in trouble, but "the voices of the domestic interior" (Meeker 1979:227) sound subversive.

By telling stories about how his wife treated him, women emphasize Mulla Or's ordinary human qualities. In interviews, women stress that the ideal woman is chaste, obedient, and religious, sometimes illustrating their points with a moral tale about the virtues of a good wife. But when they talk about Mulla Or and his wife, their stories contain something rather different between the lines:

> One night Mulla Or woke his wife up. "Hurry," he told her, "and prepare yourself. The governor's men are coming here." She asked him if he were crazy and told him to go back to bed. "What business do the governor's men have with you in the middle of the night?" He himself got up and lit the lamp and, to their surprise, the men found him waiting for them.

This story is ostensibly told to illustrate Mulla Or's ability to see the future, but I find the skeptical role of the wife intriguing. Not only is she not judged harshly, but women also tell another story of how she tricked her husband on a point of law when he wanted to take another wife. She has, however, no miraculous powers of any kind.

These stories about Mulla Or's wife show how Iranian Jewish women use the corpus of community stories to stress themes of their own choosing. I would not call these "female versions" of the stories, but I would suggest that another story from a different narrative domain—from descriptions of attempted magical seduction, part of the domain of magic rather than miracle—is the female version of the story of Mulla Or and his coat. The story falls into the category of attempts at magical seduction, but it differs from the two main types of stories (abstract and specific) previously described. It has more detail than the abstract summary, but it does not have the *isnad,* or chain of authenticated tellers, of the personalized story. The storyteller prefaced it by saying, "This is from old times, 100 years ago."

> Another Jewish woman, many years ago, gave a velvet coat to a male [Muslim] tailor to sew for her. He, that is, the tailor, made sorcery (*sar o jado*) on the coat of this woman. He sewed it into the coat. For example, he wrote some words, and put them in the middle of the coat and sewed them in, so that when she wore it she would be fired up [with passion] and go to his house. The girl, no, she wasn't a girl, she was a woman, she said it was a shame to wear it. She said she would save it for Yom Kippur eve. The eve of Yom Kippur,

when she wanted to get dressed for synagogue, she put on this velvet coat. When she put on the coat, she was fired up, and she no longer knew that it was the eve of Yom Kippur and she had to go to synagogue. Immediately, she went straight to the tailor's house, the Muslim tailor's house. She went there, and she was warm and went to the roof. She went up to the roof, and he was happy she came. She went, and she became very impassioned and threw her coat down. At the moment she threw the coat on the ground, she looked and realized, "I, on Yom Kippur eve, went to the house of a goy [non-Jew]." She threw the coat on the ground now—she was freed from him. She immediately threw herself down from the roof. When she understood it was Yom Kippur eve and she had gone to his house, she was very upset. She was not hurt. She went to the synagogue and then went home. I don't know who the girl was. I was a little girl when they told me that such a thing happened.

While the story about Mulla Or and his coat is the key myth and the one about urination is a parody, this conversion story is a woman's version that "quotes" the key myth. What distinguishes this story is its complex relations with other aspects of local Yazdi Jewish culture.[4] Both Mulla Or and the woman receive a coat from a Muslim. The coat symbolizes the admiration the Muslim feels for them—the governor realizes the rabbi has a divine connection, the tailor is struck by the woman's beauty. Sacred time is present in both stories—Mulla Or and the woman put on their coats for Yom Kippur, thus setting the frame in which divine intervention is possible. Both the mulla and the woman have special qualities—Mulla Or has merit, or *zechut,* through which he can take certain actions in the world; the woman has reason, or *aql,* which allows her to save herself once she is in a bad situation.

From this point the differences are more significant than the similarities. Mulla Or does something to the coat; he cuts its sleeves. Conversely, the coat does something to the woman; it compels her to go the the tailor's house. She is less active, less effective than Mulla Or. The relation of Mulla Or and the woman to the Muslims, respectively, is also crucially different, although both receive coats from admirers. In Mulla Or's case, the gift implies an acceptance of his holiness. The threat to his status is overcome, leading to the recognition of his autonomy, defined as the recognition of his connection to a divine source of legitimation. In the woman's case, the treated coat, an acknowledgment of her beauty, leads to the threat of incorporation and is overcome by her achievement of separation. The recognition of her autonomy, of her right to her own marriage within her own community, is not at issue (she is already married, as indicated by the narrator's correction, "The girl, no, she wasn't a girl, she was a woman"). Whereas Mulla Or's story ends with his achieving a certain equality within the religious domain, the woman is not "recognized" by the Muslim, but instead escapes through a combination of intelligence, luck, and implied divine protection. She remains subordinate to the Muslim (in the sense that he does not change his attitude toward her), and though she saves herself, her actions do not transfer any benefit to the community, as Mulla Or's do. After all, recognition of the religious legitimacy of their leader symbolically redounds on the Jewish community.

The power relations are also reversed. Mulla Or affects the bodies of his adversaries; he causes the arm of one man to dry up and makes it impossible for another to stop urinating. But Jewish women's bodies are controlled by Muslim magic. Far from causing changes in others, they cannot resist the changes others cause in them.

Some further observations about the women's version will serve as a preliminary summation. Women's stories about attempts at magical seduction are body-oriented. The woman is beautiful, and the magic is worked on parts of her body, or through foods and potions that become part of her body when consumed. The body does things the mind does not know about. When a conversion is avoided it is because of *aql*—best understood in this context as a moral sense, rather than, as usually glossed, an intellectual quality.

These stories belong to what I have referred to as the storyteller's "interpretable" world. Something happens that is "understood" in hindsight. The weaker party is the one on whom the burden of interpretation falls: the man with the dried-up arm is asked to recount his deeds before the governor so the cause of his malady can be ascertained. The urinating man's friends prevail upon him to examine his actions to see why he has been punished. In the case of the women, a rug rises and starts moving out the door, and a whole series of events is abstracted from that fact. A glass of *sharbat* (a sweet drink) is given to a girl smart enough not to drink it; it then starts to move and crawl in revolting ways a few days after it has stood, undrunk, by the window.

The women constructing these tales know what it means when something in their everyday world has gone awry. Reading the signs, they know that what was in the glass did not ferment naturally, but was magically transformed. They understood this, *contra* Ginzburg (1980), by analogy and not just through the reading of signs; the principles of interpretation determine the signs. The scheme of causality is as follows: Inanimate objects that come to life are bewitched. These objects are used for rituals of contagious magic, and this kind of magic is aimed at the destruction of boundaries. The item crosses the threshold in one direction, and the woman crosses in the other. The sixth sense a woman might have lets her see the sign for what it is even *before* it signifies. The concrete interpretation of signs is important, but the knowledge of social processes that identifies something as a sign lies at the heart of interpretation.

The Tale in its Telling

As Sartre writes of storytelling, even the simplest narrative takes something out of the stream of everyday reality and therefore changes it, even if only by telling it backwards.

> But when you tell about a life, everything changes; only it's a change that nobody notices: the proof is that people talk about true stories. As if there could be true stories; events take place in one direction, and we tell about them in the opposite direction. You seem to start at the beginning . . . but in reality you have begun at the end . . . the end is there, transforming everything. (Sartre 1972:58–59)

The operations of what we call history are not unrelated to storytelling; history also takes events out of an unmarked sequence. What is important here is not only that women's magical narratives are thought to be true, but that they are not fully differentiated in the telling from events outsiders would see as more properly historical, events that are recent and unmarked by magical causation.

To illustrate, I present a particular narrative sequence in which tales of magical causation were told. The sequence begins with a description of events that took place in Yazd in 1979. Just after Ayatollah Khomeini's return to Iran, a young Jewish girl in Yazd did not turn up at school. The school informed her parents, who went to all the Jewish homes, inquired at the hospitals, and asked about her at the municipal centers. They eventually learned that she had been seen going off in a car with two young Muslims. She was said to be at the home of the Muslim religious head of Yazd, about to convert and marry one of the two boys. She came from a poor family and had worked after school at the boy's house, weaving rugs. At this point in the narrative, I asked the woman who was recounting the events whether the girl had wanted to marry the boy. She replied:

No, no. She didn't want to marry. See, they deceived her. They said they'd give her gold, money. She was a child and left. She saw she had to work, go to much trouble, there was poverty. It didn't reach her *aql* [reason] that there were things even more unfortunate. Yes, she herself didn't understand what it meant to become Muslim.

The girl was also compromised because her picture had been taken with the boy and the picture was found with them. The narrator said, "It seems as if their neighbors quietly, secretly, talked to her. They stole her heart." But she did not talk of magic and trickery.

The girl's parents were very upset, and through a complicated series of events her case came before the Komiteh. It was decided that because of her youth, the girl's decision to convert was invalid. I was told, "God helped. If it were in the time of the Shah, things wouldn't have worked out this way. Some other girls who, in the time of the Shah, left home never came back again. But she, thank God, came back healthy." Again, "Until now there were no cases like this, that a Jewish girl went to a Muslim's house and came back whole, with her religion, to her father's house. This kind of thing hadn't happened until then. From what I remember, some people became Muslims and not one of them, like this, turned out well." The woman then told the story of the woman and the coat, follow by that about the sugar and the sheepskin rug.

The set of events to which the girl's unsuccessful conversion belonged was the set of near-conversions. This was so in spite of the fact that the other cases involved magical seduction, while the current case involved persuasion, hope, and naiveté. Certain implicit cultural associations made the smooth transition between these stories possible. As this paper documents, attempts at conversion are aimed at those culturally defined as vulnerable; magic is employed most effectively against those who are powerless. This particular girl's youth and corresponding lack of *aql* made the use of magic unnecessary. In her case, sweet words could replace adulterated sugar. The boundaries of the community are threatened from the inside by the weak and from the outside by the strong. Often those who are strong use magic against those who are weak, but they do not always need to do so.

The Social Context of Conversion: The Stories as Myth

Yazdi Jews offer four paradigmatic explanations for conversion to Islam: forced conversion, revenge, pragmatic conversion, and tricked conversion.[5] Forced conversion is the overwhelming image of what conversion to Islam means and is based on particular episodes in Iranian history—for example, the forced conversions of the seventeenth and eighteenth centuries commemorated by the poets Babai b. Lotf and Babai b. Farhad.

Conversion for revenge is a rarer form. The typical case, often told throughout Iran, involves a butcher who slaughtered (in the Yazdi example) ninety sheep in preparation for a Jewish holiday. The rabbi inspected them and found one was *trefe,* unfit to eat. The butcher did not remove the animal from the group sold, and the rabbi declared all the meat not kosher. The butcher, in a fury at the economic loss he had incurred, converted and turned against his former community.

Pragmatic conversion denotes individual cases and does not function, as does tricked conversion, as a general interpretive frame. One type of pragmatic conversion is caused by poverty: one converts for material benefits. The other type is to avoid punishment. For example, the treasurer of the Jewish school was caught adjusting accounts and was to be confronted when he returned to the school from the bank. He suddenly disengaged himself from the one or two Jews walking with him, hopped up on a car, and declared, soapbox style, that he was converting to Islam. A huge crowd gathered, and he and the other Jews with him were swept off to a nearby mosque. One of these men recounted the story, telling how afraid he had been, especially when the rabbi, who was one of those who had been gathered up in the flow of people, lost patience with the jubilation around him and asked a particularly triumphant individual at his side, "What are you so happy about? You've got yourselves a thief."[6]

These three types—forced conversions, revenge, and pragmatic conversions—form the larger context into which cases of tricked conversion are set. The stories examined here concern tricked conversion, which is the explanation most often used and most often applied to women. The frequent application of this type to women raises an interpretive problem: if both men and women have converted to Islam, why are the magical narratives told exclusively about women? There are two possible answers, the first of which is simple: Muslim men can marry

Jewish women, even if they do not convert to Islam, but Jewish men cannot marry Muslim women and Muslim women cannot marry Jewish men. Thus, from the perspective of the Jewish community, women are vulnerable in a culturally specific way.

The second answer I offer is more complex. In a universe of exclusively defined groups in which one group is clearly dominated, and in which crossing between groups, generally from the minority to the majority group, takes place, there must be an ideological explanation for the possibility of such shifts. Minority groups in Yazd have generated a schema in which crossing between groups is undesirable but can be accounted for ideologically. They tell stories about conversion and thereby account for historical facts. But why in the vast majority of stories is it a woman who crosses group boundaries? I suggest that because of the Iranian cultural construction of woman's nature that considers her reason comparatively weak, a woman's decision to convert is perceived as less threatening than a man's. This weakness makes women more susceptible to trickery, and, as the stories have shown, their resistance is interpreted as the triumph of their reason: "Thank God she had *aql.*"

Another cultural idea about women also makes them appropriate figures in conversion stories. Yazdi Jewish women often claim that women who have converted to Islam have somehow remained Jewish "in their hearts." One woman, for example, is said to fast every year on Yom Kippur, although she has been Muslim for at least twenty-five years. I suggest that this idea is related to the emphasis on the body in the stories. The convert's body, born Jewish and raised Jewish, somehow stays Jewish, beyond her rational control. These ideas about women's nature make it possible to tell such stories. Because these stories do not allow for the possibility of choice, they do not provide an example for others (both men and women) and thus can be told safely.

Narrative as a Socially Significant Act: The Stories as History

Conversion narratives suggest a permeability between personal stories about identifiable people and "mythic" stories. In *Anatomy of Criticism,* Frye (1973) draws a distinction between the two. He argues that histories "describe specific and particular actions" and that *mythos* "is a secondary imitation of an action, which means, not that it is at two removes from reality, but that it describes typical actions, being more philosophical than history" (Frye 1973:82–83). This distinction is not unrelated to that Ginzburg draws between thought based on the particular and that based on generalization. Ginzburg writes, "a fine common thread connected [the conjectural disciplines]: they were all born of experience, of the concrete and individual. That concrete quality was both the strength of this kind of knowledge, and its limit—it could not make use of the powerful and terrible tool of abstraction". (Ginzburg 1980:21). I believe that Iranian Jewish women's tales of magical causation can be understood as *both* myth and history, and that these stories therefore offer evidence that Frye's and Ginzburg's oppositions are not as universally apt as they might seem to be. I present here some speculations on why women's magical and historical narratives are not distinct genres.

The Yazd Jewish community is a remnant community, whose numbers have been radically reduced through emigration. Whereas only a generation ago it was not uncommon for five or six families to live together in one house, each family taking a room, today the nuclear family is the norm, and even that unit may have missing parts, because grown children often leave Yazd. In this context, stories about people take the place of the people themselves. Stories keep alive names and relatives, recreating them almost as if they still lived around the corner. But the stories also become more communal and less personal. One shares the ancestors of others.

The anonymization of a woman in a story does not merely reflect the status of Iranian women and their comparative lack of named public identity. She does not represent the loss of collective memory. Neither is she proof of the inability of Iranian women to distinguish between myth and history. Instead, her nonspecific identity and her repetitious behavior mean that many people can talk about her. In small, bounded communities people *know* each other's stories. But in a remnant community with pressure on its boundaries—in a cultural situation in which people must constantly reproduce a sense of the whole community—people *tell* each other's stories. It is not unusual to hear the same stories over and over again in a small community, but the collective nature of these stories is worth noting. Family stories are like family property—but there the analogy with private ownership breaks down. The woman who told the abstract story about the affected sheepskin rug began, "For example, you've heard [this kind of story]." She then told a story about no one in particular. Another woman related a similar tale about someone quite particular—her uncle's mother-in-law—and used phrases almost identical to the former rendition, which had no named character.

The move between the particular and the general can also be observed in a story about *gilgul*, or the rebirth of souls:

> In a dream a man was visited by his brother, who had died before being married. The brother asked him to go to Nosratabad, a village near Yazd, and wait until some sheep came along and to buy a certain sheep, regardless of the price, because, he said, "That sheep—it should not happen to you (*na shma*)—is me." The man doubted the dream but decided to obey it anyway and went to Nosratabad, where he saw the very sheep his brother described, of a certain color and a certain fatness. After some difficulty, he bought it, then brought it back to Yazd to the home of Hajji Hillel, the leader of the community and a ritual slaughterer. He told Hajji Hillel the dream, and Hajji Hillel read something for the sheep and ritually slaughtered it, freeing the soul of the man's brother, who had been reborn in the sheep's form and could only be freed if Jewish prayers were said over him.

The narrator of this story was interrupted twice by her daughter-in-law. The woman began the story by saying, "A boy had a brother who died. He hadn't yet become a groom. One night he came to his brother in a dream . . . ," and went on until the man's arrival in Nosratabad. At that point her daughter-in-law said, "He himself told this story. You know who it is, it was the husband of Taos Xanom from Isfahan who just came. . . . It was his brother." The storyteller agreed that he was the original teller of the tale; the events had happened to him. But she told the story without recourse to this "proof," without certifying it in a way that an ethnographer might interpret as adding to its "authenticity" or to its value as history.

The storyteller continued after the interruption, reaching the part of the story in which the main character went to see Hajji Hillel (a real historical figure, with the position described in the story) and said he had seen a dream in which his brother appeared. At this point the daughter-in-law broke in and said, "He saw the dream twice. The first time he said, 'It means nothing.' The second time the brother said, 'No, this is true. I'm your brother.'" The daughter-in-law's second comment reversed the direction of the first. Whereas the first comment attached the story to a particular person, this second point enhanced its formulaic quality.

Classically, in Jewish and Persian-Jewish folktales, a dream is doubted when it first occurs and is proven to be sent from good rather than from evil sources only when it is seen two or three times. In another story from Yazd, a man's father appears to him in a dream with rather shocking instructions for him. The man rejects the dream the first time as the work of Satan but accepts it the second time when his father threatens him (saying, "Do you want me to suffocate you now?") and orders him to obey. In her second commentary, the daughter-in-law sacrificed a certain particularity for the legitimation the story would acquire by conforming to the standards of miracle tales.

Magical narratives and miracle stories have both a personal or particular and religious or general level. By and large they concern a particular individual (named or unnamed, remembered or talked about) who has an experience that becomes narratable (and here magic, miracle, and history together determine what is passed on) because it involves that individual with the next world. The individual receives a significant dream, for example, or escapes at the last minute through providential help. The connection between Jews on earth and the divine in heaven is made possible through individuals and their experiences or virtues. These connections take place through concrete historical individuals, but they all support a notion of the Jewish relation to God, to their social environment, and to their history. If the experiences did not have both personal and otherworldly aspects, they would not be "storyable."

Thus the telling of these stories operates on two levels. People in immediate contact with the person in the story, usually kin, tell the story to illustrate the merit of their family member or ancestor. These stories are those in which particular people see Eliahu Hanavi and Sara bat Asher, and save brothers' souls. In these tellings, the stories resemble what we consider history. Other people may tell virtually the same story to make general points about the presence of the holy in their midst. For instance, Taos Xanom from Isfahan might tell the story of the redemption of the brother's soul as a story about her husband. The woman I heard it from, however, told it as a story about the rebirth of souls. The family with whom I lived told a story in which the father's father studies one night with Eliahu Hanavi in the synagogue; other Yazdi Jews relate a story about the sighting of Eliahu Hanavi in a Yazdi synagogue, thus conferring the miracle on the whole community and generalizing what was a story about someone's ancestor. These stories, then, are truly community property; anyone can tell them, and everyone does. In some cases, they stress history, in others myth.

Conclusion

The dialectic between individualized stories and anonymized stories characterizes a collectivity in which units other than the individual alone are valorized, in which persons are not only seen as constituting worlds in themselves, but are also parts of worlds. A study such as this one can enrich our understanding of the complexity of conceptualizations of social realities like "community" and "individual," but we should be wary of reducing the richness of these conceptualizations in favor of a master code generalized beyond its power to illuminate. Returning to Jameson's comment that "only the emergence of a post-individualistic world, only the reinvention of the collective as the associative, can concretely achieve the 'decentering' of the individual subject," I suggest that what I have presented here are contemporary examples of decentered individuals, that it is through a dialectic relation with their community that they are decentered in narrative and that "the reinvention of the collective" occurs all the time, especially in remnant and immigrant communities.

In Iranian Jewish women's tales of magical causation, people are often most memorable when they illustrate cultural truths that have little to do with them as individuals. Except for extraordinary persons such as Mulla Or (and even he is a limited exception), people's life histories are not reflected in the stories told about them. Characters do not develop over time, but instead make one significant appearance in which they are the loci of larger forces that act through them at given moments in time. They are not worlds in themselves, but point to the connection between worlds. They point to the world of the dead, but also the world of the living, in which they have a definite role. The individual is not "dissolved" (these are not pre-individualistic narratives), but rather becomes visible as he or she separates from and then returns to the ordinary world. Personalized or anonymized, the individuals in these stories simultaneously illustrate the enduring nature of certain relationships—living and dead, Jewish and Muslim, female and male, powerless and powerful—and their periodic concretization in social life.

Notes

1. This paper was read, in somewhat differing versions, as "Women's Magical Narratives: Popular Concepts of History and Causality in Iran," Women's Studies, Princeton University, March 23, 1983, and as "Iranian Women's Magical Narratives," Institute for Advanced Study, Princeton, N.J., March 31, 1983. I am grateful to both audiences for their comments and to Janet Dolgin, Deborah Dash Moore, and Kay Warren for their critical readings of the paper. This paper was also read for me in my absence at the Anthropological Society of Washington's seminar on religion, January 21, 1984, and I thank Phyllis Chock and June Wyman for their excellent editorial suggestions. The paper is based on fieldwork in Iran, 1973–75, and in Israel, 1978–79 and the summers of 1980 and 1981. I thank the Fulbright Committee and the National Institute of Mental Health for supporting the fieldwork in Iran, and Vassar College for research and Mellon grants for the summer fieldwork in Israel.

2. The Yazdi do not have a very specific or large nomenclature for different types of narratives. They do, however, distinguish between domains and regard miracle stories as Jewish and appropriate for delivery in sermons, while secular folklore such as jokes, tall tales, rhyming songs, and verbal games are told in informal social settings. In addition to content and form, storyteller and context also determine a story's domain. Miracle stories are referred to by the Hebrew term, *ma'aseh*, and Persian terms for story—*geiseh, dastan*—would not be used for a story with Jewish content. Men tell the miracle stories when they are told in sermons. Women tell secular Iranian stories, but also relate Jewish stories, both magical and miraculous, in conversational modes. The women's tales of magical causation are a sliding genre, belonging to more than one domain. While they need to be seen as a genre different from men's stories and the miracle stories told in sermons, they must also be understood as directly related to the miracle tales of community discourse.

3. For an examination of this central tale in the modern context of foreign occupation and the Islamic Revolution, see Goldstein 1981.

4. A folklore note: a collection of "wonder stories" (*maasim niflaim*) compiled in Baghdad and published there in 1890 contains a similar story. It has been republished in Bin Gorion 1976, pp. 1104–1105.

5. It is interesting to compare the four reasons for conversion to Islam current in the Yazdi community with those in the following passage by Ibn Kammuna, who wrote an essay on Judaism, Christianity, and Islam in Baghdad in 1280: "There is no proof that Muhammed attained perfection and the ability to perfect others as claimed. . . . That is why, to this day we never see anyone converting to Islam unless in terror, or in quest of power, or to avoid heavy taxation, or to escape humiliation, or if taken prisoner, or because of infatuation with a Muslim woman, or for some similar reason. Nor do we see a respected, wealthy, and pious non-Muslim well versed in both his faith and that of Islam, going over to the Islamic faith without some of the aforementioned or similar motives" (Perlmann 1971:149). (I am grateful to Bernard Lewis for reminding me of this passage.)

6. Conversion to the Baha'i religion (the other religion to which Jews have converted) is also explained pragmatically by Jews. Baha'is are thought to take care of other Baha'is, and some poorer Jews are said to have converted because they needed

financial help. Neither force nor trickery are felt to be motivations for converts. Baha'is describe themselves as having converted through intellectual conviction, and many non-Baha'is accept this explanation. However, it is also said by some non-Baha'is that people who converted in fact lacked intellect. If asked why someone converted, many (Jews and Muslims) respond "Marz-esh charab eh" ("His brain is ruined").

References Cited

Bakhtin, Mikhail
1968   Rabelais and His World. H. Iswolsky, transl. Cambridge, Mass.: MIT Press.

Benjamin, Walter
1969   The Storyteller. In Illuminations. Hannah Arendt, ed. pp. 83–109. New York: Schocken Books.

Bin Gorion, Micha Joseph
1976   Mimekor Yisrael. Vol. 3. Bloomington: Indiana University Press.

Bonine, Michael
1981   Shops and Shopkeepers: Dynamics of an Iranian Provincial Bazaar. In Continuity and Change in Modern Iran. Michael Bonine and Nikki Keddie, eds. pp. 203–228. Albany: State University of New York Press.

Dumont, Louis
1970   Homo Hierarchicus. Chicago: University of Chicago Press.

Frye, Northrop
1973   Anatomy of Criticism. Princeton, N.J.: Princeton University Press.

Ginzburg, Carlo
1980   Morelli, Freud and Sherlock Holmes: Clues and Scientific Method. History Workshop 9:5–36.

Goldstein, Judith L.
1981   The Paradigm of Protection: Minority "Big Men" in Iran. Social Analysis 9:89–102.

Issawi, Charles, ed.
1971   The Economic History of Iran 1800–1914. Chicago: University of Chicago Press.

Jameson, Fredric
1981   The Political Unconscious. Ithaca, N.Y.: Cornell University Press.

Meeker, Michael
1979   Literature and Violence in North Africa. New York: Cambridge University Press.

Perlmann, Moshe, transl.
1971   Ibn Kammuna's Examination of the Three Faiths. Berkeley: University of California Press.

Sartre, Jean-Paul
1972   Storytelling. *In* The Philosophy of Jean-Paul Sartre. Robert Cumming, ed. pp. 58–59. New York: Vintage Books.

Popular Mythologies and Subtle Theologies: The Phenomenology of Muslim Identity in Afghanistan

Jon W. Anderson
Catholic University of America

To describe ideological analysis phenomenologically, in terms of the mental and textual operations it involves, rather than in the framework of any of the specific historical conceptions of ideology available to us . . . does not mean that history itself is a text, only that it is inaccessible to us except in textual form or, in other words, that we approach it only by way of its prior textualization.
—Fredric Jameson (1982:73)

Durkheim's dictum that in simple, relatively undifferentiated societies "every mind being drawn into the same eddy, the individual type confounds itself with that of the race" (1915:181) has enabled an anthropology of "primitive" religions that has produced some formidable results. But tying theories of religion to such a data base has made them poorly translatable to complex societies. Complex societies with literate traditions and manifold specialist views impose "a vast scheme of interpretations" that Durkheim viewed as a "psychological gap between the cause and the effect . . . [that] has become more difficult for the mind to leap," and dismissed as intermediate forms "popular mythologies and subtile [sic] theologies . . . which, though holding to the first [causes of belief], of which they are an elaborated form, only allow their true nature to appear very imperfectly" (ibid.:20). Not fitting into Durkheim's search for "ever present causes upon which the most essential forms of religious thought and practice depend," these intermediate transformations were left as elective rather than necessary affinities in which Weber (1949) identified a play of interests that constitute history and consciousness.

Reconciling such views is problematic. Abstraction from different data bases to limited case theories (and, occasionally, misplaced concreteness [cf. Wrong 1961, Giddens 1977]) underwrites conceptions of societies on the one hand without history and on the other with too much (Pletsch 1981). The insights of Durkheim and Weber become privileged points of reference either in the society that is the vehicle or in the interest articulated by an ideological symbol; the sharedness of beliefs, values, and ideas is analytically accounted for by broadly psychological or existential referents, of which culture is taken as an approximation. Much of the history of anthropology consists of arguments over whether culture represents some version of Mind (human or psychological "nature") or some metacontext (a political or economic "nature") by which it is situated and which draws on, draws out, reflects, or otherwise conveys in some skewed fashion a reality prior to its own. This consequentialism amounts methodologically to assimilating culture to a figure on various precultural or metacultural grounds that are taken to enable or to limit it. Meanwhile, lived-in dimensions of other modes of thought on which Durkheim and Weber focused so subtlely, if pessimistically, are left begging and their textures flattened to intermediate moments within a longer *durée*.

It can be argued that the intermediate moments comprise if not what Schutz (1967, 1971) called the "paramount reality" of everyday life, then at least its paramount continuity. This continuity is not so much said, and still less routinely spoken of, as it is experienced (cf. Tyler 1978; Stoller, this volume) or, from a more epistemological point of view, stipulated and hence problematic in its own settings. In this paper, I aim to bring these intermediating moments into a more unified perspective by examining a set of origin stories in which Afghans identify themselves with Islam and Islam with themselves. Rather than studying a historiographic sensibility (e.g., Packard 1981), or moral imagination (e.g., Beidelman 1981, Geertz 1983), or using any number of other conventions for problematizing cultural constructs, I focus on formal properties of the more immediate associations in constructions that are at once derivative and *sui generis,* and examine the discursive qualities of popular mythologies and subtle theologies that are valued so differently when problematized primarily in terms of provenance.

In Islamic studies, provenance is every bit the issue that reference is in theories of culture. Said (1978) has drawn out the critical presumptions in philologically minded Orientalist disciplines that owe as much to a view that, as Brown (1981:19) put it in another context, "'popular religion' exhibits modes of thinking that are best intelligible in terms of a failure to be something else" as to fraternity with the medieval scholars who provide the texts. Such views do not withstand ethnographic scrutiny. Yet something very like Orientalism appears in treatments of popular beliefs from the ethnographic side. Using Geertz's (1969) interpretation of how Moroccan and Javanese Islam(s) are profoundly infused with immediate local and personal significances as a central example, el-Zein (1977) has argued that anthropological methods converge with those of Muslim theologians in presenting Islam as skewed particularizations of something more general, though a different generality. Insofar as Geertz employs a theory of interpretive traffic between "experience-near" and "experience-distant" conceptions (Geertz 1976), his analysis, like those cast in terms he otherwise opposes, appeals to some extra-ideational setting for the configuration of ideas.[1] This observation is no less true of el-Zein's own adumbration (1974) of Islam as encompassing (from the viewpoint of a Muslim scholar) the role that Lévi-Strauss assigns to the human mind. The result in each case is an ambivalent constitution, partly by analytical attention and partly independent of it, rather like Berkeley's trees falling silently in a forest of symbols until noticed by some "public relations officer of the mind."[2]

Such essentialist methods are not so dissimilar to Durkheim's pursuit of final causation, and obscure more immediate associations in this sort of data. Among the more immediate associations are priorities that Muslims assign to Quranic learning and to approximating it within their own discourse, which assure its presence in the same settings as local traditions (e.g., Antoun 1979). Those settings include a strong textualism in which the Quran provides the model text, including the model of what a text is, and a tendency for Quranic exegesis to become the most solemn form of interpretation, to which all others are assimilated as more narrowly contextualized mundane versions (Eickelman 1978). Inviolability of the Quranic text as a radical fusion of word and deed in revelation sanctions interpretation in just such terms. So tensions identified as being between "great" and "little" traditions occur not between different communities of discourse, but within communities over differences articulated in this interpretive tension (Anderson 1984).

It is to retrieve such immediate associations that Jameson turns to the proximal environment of an ideological discourse in its subtext, "to describe ideological analysis phenomenologically, in terms of the mental and textual operations it involves, rather than in the framework of any of the specific historical conceptions of ideology available to us" (Jameson 1982:73). This kind of analysis aims to specify a context of the same order of phenomena, instead of a context in which phenomena of different orders are related to each other by assimilating a local discourse to another brought by the analyst. This spare usage, adapted from Kenneth Burke, implies no *actus purus,* such as Durkheim sought in society, or such as the philologically minded seek in the genetic properties of language, or as are claimed in post-cartesian existentialisms. An analytical focus on text/subtext rather than on text/context relations amounts to taking ideas to be first about other ideas, rather than about something extra-ideational, and questions about the priority or privilege of one or another class of facts to belong not to the analyst but to participation in ideological analysis.

Bringing this setting into focus requires tracing connections between conceptions in their reproduction and transmission. This cannot be a completely realizable goal because of its fundamentally reconstructive nature (Weber 1949). But ethnographers have an access to the ongoing analogizing by which production (and reproduction) proceeds that is denied to historians and literary analysts. In such metonymic inscription of the tracks of metaphors, changes are rung on a theme that is not itself accessible except through their concrete operations. These comprise the sort of popular mythologies and subtle theologies that Durkheim saw as derivative but which, in their own context, inscribe the paramount continuity of culturally constructed realities as—to borrow another phrase from Durkheim—a "solid frame which encloses all thought."

Afghans are known in an extensive literature as Pashtun, Pakhtun, and Pathan from an Anglo-Indian corruption of the plural *pakhtana* but call themselves *avghaan* and, despite attempts by governments of Afghanistan to extend the name to all citizens, are the only ones locally so called. They extend across southern Afghanistan and western Pakistan in continually segmenting, named patrilineages that are identified with portions of this territory in the same nominal fashion as Afghans as a whole are identified with the overall "homeland" (*wataan*). This identification of nominal lineage segments with their *wataan* is presumed to be primordial, whether rooted in conquest or in peaceful expansion and sub-segmentation, or "lost" to memory. By this identification, territorial and genealogical space are mapped as aspects of the same process of succession of sons to fathers and division among brothers over time. The mapping is not perfect. Land can be acquired through purchase (or lost to the heirs through sale), and relatives can be acquired through marriage (and similarly "lost"); but both contingent transactions are subordinated to patrilineal succession and to rights to acquire land and brides, set by the same rule of codescent (Anderson 1975:590–591; 1982a:413–414). Among the pressures toward keeping particular social fields congruent with a patrilineal scheme, succession both measures time and links the most solemn versions of Afghan presence and the more mundane versions of sons succeeding fathers by dividing their patrimony into replicas of it.

Afghans' most solemn link to Islam is articulated as part of that heritage—indeed, as its frame. Afghans conceive of themselves as hereditary Muslims and to exist *as* Afghan wholly within the temporal-spatial realm of Islam (*dar al-Islam*) in a social and cultural as well as territorial sense. As they tell it, there were no Afghans as such in the *Jahiliyya*, a time of chaos and misbelief before God's revelation to Muhammed. Genealogies drawn back to this Noachian period by court chroniclers (Dorn 1829) belong more to dynastic legitimations than to popular belief. In popular belief, all genealogies terminate in Qais, who is held to have lived at the time of Muhammed and to have gone to Mecca, where he received Islam directly from God's final prophet. Afghans thus hold themselves as Qais's descendants to have emerged with and wholly within the *dar al-Islam*, which is in turn the *a priori* of their existence as a body. They have no equivocal histories of conversion that would place some Afghans before others as Muslims, and because apostasy would be a stage in the loss of Afghan identity, there are no non-Muslim *avghaan*. By the same measure, they admit to no one's being "more" Muslim than they, save, and then not unequivocally, Muhammed's own descendants (*sayyids*). Instead, there is an implied claim, and sometimes an explicit one, that Afghans are equal as Muslims to the Arabs who accepted Islam directly from God's chosen messenger.

These are strong words, and, Barth (1969) has noted, strongly contrast conceptions that no Afghan "submitted" (the meaning of "Islam") before any other to all their neighbors' having been converted by other converts. Afghans' conceptions of themselves resonate deeply with this identity as not only among the original Muslims but as among the unconverted converters; their role in bringing Islam to India, as they

conceive of that to have happened by conquest and the force of their exemplary devotion, is a source of pride and self-esteem. The resonances
are more thoroughgoing than claims made throughout Southwest Asia
to contact with a limpid stream of submission unmediated by lesser humans than the Prophet of God. For Afghans, an uncompromising
monotheism and their own integrity include not only rejection of
Shiism, with its apostolic-like succession of Imams (a Muslim "perfect"
enough to lead others in prayer) back, not to Muhammed, but to his son-
in-law. These ideas also involve notions of themselves as primordial
actors, among the determiners rather than the determined of history and
equally superior to non-Muslim neighbors, to converts of all stripe, and
to all others who are in some measure incompletely Muslim.

This identity as Muslims extends beyond adherence to Islam to a
notion of virtual unity with patrilineal succession and standards of behavior that together situate an overall identity in the most radical sense
of an irreducible integrity. Barth (1969) has described Islam, patrilineal
descent, and *pakhtunwali* (the "code" of the Afghans as it is known on
the Northwest Frontier of Pakistan and in eastern Afghanistan) as the
elements of their identity. The superficial ethnographic reality is that
Afghans themselves feel no need to account for that conjunction. They
take the matter for granted—and literally as a matter of fact—but in no
sense unreflectively. It is continually explored in concretizations placing that conjunction against some action as its background or setting.
What analytically can appear as a tissue of distinct ideas is played out in
metaphorizations and more or less explicit analogies that connect Qais
and Afghans, on the one hand, to Qais's action and God's revelation, on
the other, as parts of a continuous process.

Qais is a model ancestor as well as an original Muslim. He himself
has no ancestry that is considered realistically knowable, or interesting
to know. It is lost in the *Jahiliyya,* escaped by his submission to revelation. His action, like the revelation it complements, goes unration-
alized, save in the most perfunctory manner. It may be glossed as
fortuitous, serendipitous, even gratuitous, but generally requires no explanation. Its characteristic is lack of any mundane motivation. What
counts is that "he just knew to go to Mecca." Such self-interest as that
action bespeaks is in the most solemn version of the self known as ^{c}aql,
or the ability to know God's will. That "he just knew to go to
Muhammed" contains no sense of Qais's participating in revelation.

Qais is not represented as a prophet or as comparable to Muhammed in this respect, any more than Muhammed is considered divine or comparable to God. Instead, the point of the comparison is that Qais acted to receive God's revelation from the one chosen by Him to deliver it to other humans. Quais's relationship mirrors Muhammed's as the human completion of revelation; by his literally self-defining act, Qais stands to Afghans as Muhammed does to all humans—as the mediator of their most embracive identity.

A similar ambiguity is central to conceptions of both Qais and Muhammed as simultaneously mediators and initiators. As points of origin for moral communities, their actions merge contiguity and likeness. Each defines a community: Muhammed an eschatological one of believers and Qais an existential community of Afghans within it. Muhammed is the human who received the final revelation of God's will for humans. Qais, having accepted Islam in the most direct form available to humans and without ulterior motive, or indeed any specific motive, in turn transmits his self-creating action, which defines his existence in the world, to his descendants, whose own orderly existence depends wholly on his.

Self-creating acts are routinized in what Barth identified as the third component of Afghan identity, *pakhtunwali* or, as it is more commonly put, "doing Pakhtu" (*pakhtu kewul*). Afghans contrast "doing Pakhtu" to "talking [in] Pakhtu" (*pakhtu wayul*). Speaking Pakhtu is an acquirable characteristic, although Afghans hold it to be difficult for others to learn their language and that they never speak it properly, because the language itself is part, albeit a superficial part, of *pakhtana*. Within that frame, the contrast between the merely acquired and the emergent characteristic of "doing Pakhtu" is strongly marked: as Barth (1969) noted, failure to "do" Pakhtu leads to loss of Afghan identity. Such failures are represented as diluting or dissipating the *huy* or "character" of Afghan-ness, because the latter is made manifest through actions of self-assertion and values of being self-actuating rather than being dependent upon others. This ambiguity resolves both ways; just as it is possible to lose identity by lack of action, as Barth noted, so is it possible to gain it by creative action relative to the present. Afghans routinely reject the imputation of contradiction as uninformed and, indeed, as evidence of what transcendent acts transcend by, in effect, uniting. The archetypical case, but by no means the only one, is Qais's "creation" of *avghaan,* the ultimately abstracted model for all subsequent foundations that link the present with the (post-*jahiliyya*) past that provides the present's frame, origin, and point of comparison.

Afghans conceive of their integrity from the beginning of the present to the directly experienced present as a process of successions in which a patrimony is shared by division into replicas of the former unity. The process is explicitly conceived as division into equal parts that have the characteristics of the whole save its precedence over them in time, and is recorded genealogically as father-to-sons links that theoretically unite all Afghans. In practice, genealogies rarely extend farther back than euphonious tribal ancestors who are variously said to have divided or enlarged the heritage of Qais, and so are memorialized as founders. Each such successor repeats, in progressively more immediate terms, the self-defining acts of Qais within a frame set by all previous acts, beginning with Qais's most sublime of human acts and extending down to the most immediate present, where sons emerge from the social and personal identities of their fathers.

At the level distinguished from all others by its immediacy and vitality, Afghans vividly conceive of succession as an effort by those who are most alike to distinguish themselves from each other. In the normal course of events, sons have no separate political-economic identities from their father during his lifetime. In his command over their possessions and his accountability for their actions, sons remain extensions of their father's relations to others, which began when his own father arranged his marriage. Sons' brides are added to their father's household as daughters-in-law, gradually becoming practically daughters as they bear sons for his sons (Anderson 1982a:411-412; 1982b), who will succeed to that household. The process is a drawn-out one of growing up under, and then out from under, the tutelage of the father through increasingly self-initiated action. Before the father's death, subhouseholds of married sons with their children emerge marginally as domestic units, primarily of consumption. After his death, though not immediately after it, the process of division accelerates to encompass more and more of the physical, especially the productive, heritage of the father's household.

Division proceeds outward from the household. Beginning with separate domestic quarters, established sometime between the sons' marriages and the births of their first children, division continues with dedications of certain portions of the father's property to the care of a married son *cum* father, and on to testamentary dispositions in which fathers anticipate the division of their total property. Brothers may temporarily keep their less intensively used property together, in something like the form they knew as sons, but division is inevitable as their identity as sons is supplanted by their becoming fathers themselves (see Anderson 1975:587–588). In the best case, division continues throughout the sons' maturity and may not be complete at their deaths. In any case, each household sits within a series of concentric circles of increasingly shared property to which wider ranges of collaterals have access by right and not just by invitation. Each of these circles, in turn, is defined by some progressively remoter ancestor in whom they are united in some progressively more abstract or limited respect.

Ancestors are memorialized as conquerors of a territory, as colonizers, or by some other definitive act of establishment that frames the present. That is, their personae are routinely retrospectively modeled from self-imagery entertained or promoted by and about a group. The equivalence is worked both from the vital to the abstract and vice versa through their continuous merger. It may be said that household processes are thus globalized by a process of abstraction; but it can equally be said that the mundane and immediate are concretizations of abstract qualities of a series of increasingly one-dimensional ancestors.

Afghans argue both ways, as if from different ends of the same proposition to commentaries on self-creating acts that constitute and distinguish the shape of time. Each act frames those subsequent to it and is framed by those prior to it. Ancestors punctuate history insofar as they were sufficiently outstanding in relation to their own contemporaries to transcend them and the subsequent time. Correlatively, as each superior ancestor corresponds to less (because more widely shared) identity in the present, the personae of ancestors become thinner, as do genealogies, as one moves back in time from representations of recent generations by sets of brothers to ancestors with no known (that is, relationally insignificant) siblings. Between mundane, multidimensional fathers in the present and Qais, the most solemn but also most abstract father, falls a continuum of fathers who were also sons. Each is framed as consequent to prior actions and is memorialized for some action that remains present in proportion to the extent it is shared in the present. Groups so identified are said to have a common character manifest as personality traits (*huy*), a composite territory that is a portion of the homeland, and specific propensities for actions uniting the two.

When discussing such schemes, Afghans make clear that the significance of an ancestor for the immediate present depends on his predecessors, descendants, and contemporaries. Each is defined by contexts set by earlier ancestors; some stand out from contemporaries in ways that define only their own successors, others in ways that also affect collateral descendants by restoring some previously diminished unity. All living leaders, in turn, attempt to transcend the mundane decline that is marked by the division of residual unities. Each self-creating act that survives as a marginally corporative identity among descendants, along with the ambiguity that it is somehow less than previous acts, signifies a re-creation, a redirection, or a dead end, down to sons' dividing their father's estate with all the mixture of momentary greed and transcendent power that this process entails. So an inventory of self-creating acts that constitute Afghan histories concretizes the abstracted properties of the frame itself.

The same residue of irresolution characterizes the texture of existence as well as the measure of time. And it is in such terms that founders of the component Afghan tribes and component lineages tend to be diminished versions of Qais, more densely contextualized within the frame established by previous actions already transmitted into a state of being. Every tribe has such personalized foundation stories that account for its establishment and that project its characteristics temporally into the present, where reputations are cultivated in such terms. The seven Ghilzai tribes of eastern Afghanistan, for instance, are said to stem from the union of a renegade prince with a Pakhtun woman, whom he seduced or abducted, and who had the "strength," relative to her kin, to merit "adoption" as an Afghan. Against versions offered by Ghilzai themselves in greater or lesser detail, non-Ghilzai emphasize that Ghilzai are "sons of a thief" (ghal-zi) and that this origin accounts for a thieving, or at least an opportunistic, character. Ghilzai in turn play to a reputation as "wild" or "unfettered" (yaghi) Afghans, by placing a more positive gloss on their origin as the quintessence of pakhtana, while disparaging other Afghans as near anarchists or as merely people "of work" rather than "of fight." Similar double-sided comparisons are drawn down the line among subordinate subtribal groupings. As a type, such comparisons are open-ended accounts of similarities and differences that represent the ambivalent character of relationships at once vital and arbitrary. Pastoral and agricultural components of these tribes represent relationships between and within their ways of life through double-edged portraits. In one such example, brothers who found a donkey loaded with grain, one taking the donkey, another the load, thus committed their respective descendants to different ways of life.

These representations become more explicitly and densely comparative the nearer they are to the present. They incorporate in comparisons a continuum from the most immediate and mundane to the most abstract and solemn self-creations, constituted by a framework of overlapping accounts and reformulations marshaled in arguments that recall or appeal to other arguments with the same structure. The ambivalence of comparison assures their continuity as a series of resolutions, each of which reposes its problem at a higher or lower level. Terminating at one end in short-term self-interest, this continuum terminates at the other in the most solemn terms of comprehensive submission to God's interest. This is also the continuum Afghans imagine for the individual human life-course, from the passion of bodily drives to the moral repose of salvation as a complete Muslim whose activity in the world has been stripped down to the essential calmness of doing no work other than God's. This lifelong process is known theologically and popularly as *jihad al-ᶜaql*, the "struggle" to know God's will. Like Qais's act of will to accept God's will, human actions emerge against an encompassing frame that sets the human parameters of existence in the actions of Adam and Bibi Hawa (Eve), who, as the ancestors of all humans, set those mundane parameters by subordinating sensibility (ᶜaql) to momentary desires and appetites (*nafsh*). It is against this frame that submission to God's will and the establishment of peace (both meanings of "Islam") amount to recreating what was originally created in Paradise. Afghan claims to priority as Muslims evoke this priority of creator over creations.

The self-confirmation in this framework of interpretation marks a radical or, in Durkheim's terms, solid enclosure, which Afghans themselves explore in such mutually constitutive implications as these. Not all do explore them, or explore them all the time. But this frame encloses common attitudes that what counts as Islamic is what Afghans *do*, including customs and institutions they often pass on in proselytizing capacities as essential to a Muslim life (Jettmar 1961). It similarly encloses even less examined attitudes that everything they do "must" be Islamic "because" they are wholly encompassed by the presence of Islam in this world. It is present in judgments, often ironic, they make of themselves, such as "there are things which are required which are not done and things done which are forbidden," which refers to the explicit

Islamic classification of acts (as required, recommended, neutral, disapproved, and forbidden) implicit in the previous judgments. Above all, the frame enters argumentatively into narrative accounts, rationalizations, assessments, and programs by which Afghans seek to cut through paradoxes by shifting issues toward more sublime or more mundane versions, only to face the same paradox of self-actuation in another guise.

This sample of conceptions about the Islamic quality of identities differs, of course, both from Geertz's descriptions of Moroccan and Javanese Muslims and from theologians' (and their exegetes') depictions of Muslim identities (from whom Orientalists have drawn their depictions of Islam). But neither generic similarities nor local differentiations necessarily provide the best vantage on a structure of interpretation. In fact, they preempt it. Weber's demonstration of elective affinities makes it clear that more immediate configurations are parts of the same data, and that appropriation to a larger frame only restratifies information to reflect not the subjects' inquiry but their subjection to analytical inquiry. A transformation by appropriation might suit a historical frame removed from one the authors of the text themselves take, but at that point analysis becomes not merely a critique. It becomes, as Sahlins (1976:95) put it, a "derivation of ontology from methodology." To query how Afghans might have made over Islam in their own image or as an approximation of something else—whether historical tradition, social necessity, or psychological exigency—is both to waste data and to preempt interpretation of subordinations that are the part of the data which account for their integrity. The ethnographic fact about this accounting is not that Afghans fit Islam to their measure, or that some fit those measures around Islam, but that what is most unambiguously Islamic for them provides the most solemn versions and model versions of a vast scheme of mutually subordinating interpretations that is "about" the terms of its own engagement. If the local integrity of such interpretations is first of all local (before it is something else), their subordinations account for that integrity.

There is more than merely additional data in the stratifications of text and subtext. Popular mythologies and subtle theologies are the currency of ongoing interpretation and assessment. They are indeed derivative, but their derivations have another significance for the study of culture than to provide a shortcut, or a problem of translation, to some other, more essential analysis. Focusing on text/subtext relations retrieves the metonymic paths of metaphors that provide the paramount continuity of account which itself conveys the experience of a meaning-filled, if not always coherent, world. Necessarily elective, metaphors draw attention to the effort they exemplify. Arguably, their more outstanding quality is not to resolve but to state paradox and, in relocating it, to embrace paradox and make it the very shape of existence. In their derivation from each other, popular mythologies and subtle theologies are not a substitute or mechanical displacement of knowledge better stated in other terms (the "true names of things"), but the very effortfulness that, phenomenologically viewed, is the meaning of meaning. Better than claims made for modes of thought as representation, shifting emphasis from classification to communication opens analysis of immediate affinities in which modes of thought are framed and advanced.

What this paper has outlined could be described as a historiographic sensibility or as a moral imagination, but not, I think, as a "model" of the form of something else. What I would like to suggest is how attention to discursive properties opens a kind of analysis as different from those as from analysis as charter. I have focused here on continuities within and between representations that are linked in and as origin stories that specify and make them known through contingencies that are their subtext. An imagery of history and morality as problematic in the same ways, as sharing the same contingency (which they are, in a sense, about), unites them in the same discursive explorations. Each story of Qais, of tribes, and of lesser groupings is not so much a text in a corpus of transformed forms—although they are that, too—but, more intensively, each presents a point of view in relation to the others. Such stories give and take meaning not only to and from their subjects, but also to and from other stories. To capture these relations, what I have in mind is less a mentalist ontology of redaction than the continuity of differences within frames that unite them as part of the same data.

If necessary, I would call attending to the formal properties of immediate associations in a scheme of interpretations a phenomenological structuralism and single out Dumont's treatment in Homo Hierarchicus (1970) as its "type site" (Anderson 1982a:408). In ethnography, both phenomenology and structuralism could be, and are, employed ontologically, like charter, to identify a privileged class or aspect of data about cultural constructs by adding information that the mind, as in Lévi-Strauss's structuralist phenomenology, or that situation, as in existentialist ones, is immediate in these constructions. But there is in fact no choosing between a nature inside and a nature outside of experience to account for the tracks of metaphors that confer its accessible shape.

The value of phenomenology to such analysis is, as in Jameson's spare implementation, to direct attention to how representations are collected in the first place. Where hermeneutics emphasizes part-whole relations—hence, "larger" contexts that are epistemologically problematic—a phenomenology approaches what such contexts may be in relations of texts to the subtexts they gather, address, reflect, and reflect upon. If Durkheim's most troublesome insight was to dissolve the distinction between symbol and referent by dissolving its antecedent mind-body distinction between intension (in value) and extension (in action), it was Weber's even more troublesome insight that ideas are first about other ideas whose contingency is problematic. When taken into account as the primary setting of representations, these associations are no longer miscellaneous adumbrations or reconstructions of some other kind of interest, but rather something more like the central tendency in both that unites them in activities to social processes far less elusive as intertextual than as intersubjective. This appreciation of how representations are collective is subordinated in low estimations of popular mythologies and subtle theologies as false sociology, psychology, economics, or some fancy, just as the kind of continuity they do present is underappreciated when made to depend on extrinsic continuities of experience.

Notes

Acknowledgments. This paper is based on fieldwork in Afghanistan, 1971–74, supported by U.S. National Science Foundation grant no. GS-30275, and was prepared on facilities of the Catholic University of America Computing Center. I am grateful to Phyllis Chock for her careful reading and comments.

1. Asad (1983:230) makes the similar point that a "paradox results from Geertz's adherence to a confused phenomenology in which 'reality' is at once the distance of an agent's social perspective from the Truth, measured only by the privileged observer, and also the substantive knowledge of a socially constructed world available to both agent and observer, but only to the latter through the former."

2. The characterization is Beidelman's (1971) description of Lévi-Strauss's project.

References Cited

Anderson, Jon W.
1975 Tribe and Community among Ghilzai Pashtun. Anthropos 70:575–601.
1982a Social Structure and the Veil: Comportment and the Composition of Interaction in Afghanistan. Anthropos 77:397–420.
1982b Cousin Marriage in Context: Constructing Social Relations in Afghanistan. Folk 24:7–28.
1984 How Afghans Define Themselves in Relation to Islam. In Revolutions and Rebellions in Afghanistan. M. Nazif Shahrani and Robert L. Canfield, eds. pp. 266–287. Berkeley, Calif.: Institute for International Studies.

Antoun, Richard T.
1979 Low-Key Politics: Local-Level Leadership and Change in the Middle East. Albany: State University of New York Press.

Asad, Talal
1983 Anthropological Conceptions of Religion: Reflections on Geertz. Man, n.s., 18:237–259.

Barth, Fredrik
1969 Pathan Identity and Its Maintenance. In Ethnic Groups and Boundaries. F. Barth, ed. pp. 117–134. Oslo: Universitetsforlaget.

Beidelman, T. O.
1971 Public Relations Officer of the Mind. A Review of Lévi-Strauss by E. R. Leach. Anthropos 66:217–222.
1981 The Moral Imagination of the Kaguru. American Ethnologist 7:27–42.

Brown, Peter
1981 The Cult of Saints: Its Rise and Function in Latin Christianity. Chicago: University of Chicago Press.

Dorn, Bernard, transl.
1829 History of the Afghans. London: Oriental Translation Committee.

Durkheim, Emile
1915 The Elementary Forms of the Religious Life. New York: Allen & Unwin.

Eickelman, Dale F.
1978 The Art of Memory: Islamic Education and Its Social Reproduction. Comparative Studies in Society and History 20:485–515.

el-Zein, Abdul Hamid M.
1974 The Sacred Meadows. Evanston, Ill.: Northwestern University Press.
1977 Beyond Ideology and Theology: The Search for the Anthropology of Islam. Annual Review of Anthropology 6:227–254.

Geertz, Clifford
1969 Islam Observed. New Haven, Conn.: Yale University Press.
1976 "From the Native's Point of View": On the Nature of Anthropological

Understanding. *In* Meaning in Anthropology. K. H. Basso and H. A. Selby, eds. pp. 221–237. Albuquerque: University of New Mexico Press.
1983   Local Knowledge. New York: Basic Books.

Giddens, Anthony
1977   New Rules of Sociological Method. London: Hutchinson.

Jameson, Fredric R.
1982   The Symbolic Inference; Or, Kenneth Burke and Ideological Analysis. *In* Representing Kenneth Burke. Hayden White and Margaret Brose, eds. pp. 68–91. Baltimore: Johns Hopkins University Press.

Jettmar, Karl
1961   Ethnological Research in Dardistan 1958. Proceedings of the American Philosophical Society 105:79–96.

Packard, Randall M.
1981   Chiefship and Cosmology: An Historical Study of Political Competition. Bloomington: Indiana University Press.

Pletsch, Carl E.
1981   The Three Worlds, Or the Division of Social Scientific Labor, Circa 1950–1975. Comparative Studies in Society and History 23:565–590.

Sahlins, Marshall
1976   Culture and Practical Reason. Chicago: University of Chicago Press.

Said, Edward
1978   Orientalism. New York: Basic Books.

Schutz, Alfred
1967   The Phenomenology of the Social World. George Walsh and Frederick Lehnert, transl. Evanston, Ill.: Northwestern University Press.
1971   The Problem of Social Reality. Collected Papers, Vol. 1. Maurice Natanson, ed. The Hague: Martinus Nijhoff.

Tyler, Stephen A.
1978   The Said and the Unsaid. New York: Academic Press.

Weber, Max
1949   "Objectivity" in Social Science and Social Policy. *In* The Methodology of the Social Sciences. E. A. Shils and H. A. Finch, transl. pp. 50–112. New York: Free Press.

Wrong, Dennis
1961   The Oversocialized Conception of Man in Modern Sociology. American Sociological Review 26:183–193.

The Outsider Wife and the Divided Self: The Genesis of Ethnic Identities

Phyllis Pease Chock
Catholic University of America

> Intertextuality is the family archive. . . .
> —Jonathan Culler (1981:108)

In the course of long interviews with Greek Americans[1] about their families, I was sometimes offered a parenthetical remark or story about a remarkable relative, nearly always a woman who, though not Greek, had married into the family and so transformed her life that she "became a Greek," in fact "a better Greek than most all the rest of us."[2] These stories were volunteered without my probing to elicit them. There are ten in all from my interviews; later I found two more in an article (Moskos 1977) and a book (Petrakis 1970) by Greek-American authors, for a total of twelve. The stories were told by both men and women, all of whom belong to the first generation of their families born in the United States. Eleven concern women and one is about a man. They range in length from a single sentence to a short narrative. Taken together, they are distinctive texts-within-texts. This paper presents an interpretation of these stories in an attempt to understand what the informants were saying, both to me and to themselves.

The interviews that produced these texts aimed in part to explore what it means to be a Greek American to an American-born person more than fifty years after his or her parents arrived in the United States. The American-born generation is generally prosperous, ensconced in predominantly white-collar occupations, and imbued with a middle-class outlook. The texts collected here come from three teachers and a school professional, a family business head, a lawyer's wife, a city employee, a secretary, a hairdresser, a writer, and a professor. Most lived in the Chicago metropolitan area in 1967–68, when the interviews were conducted. They lived in different middle- and upper-middle-income neighborhoods throughout the city and suburbs, as is characteristic of this generation. (Moskos and Petrakis have also lived in Chicago and its suburbs.)

Most of these informants were well-educated, some with college degrees. Most were Greek Orthodox, though their involvement in church communities varied. Some were participants in Greek-American civic, political, or fraternal affairs. Many had more non-Greeks than Greek Americans in their networks of friends and acquaintances, so that most of their "Greek" relationships were with kin. All lived most of their everyday lives through American institutions and in American English. Some were proud of the bits of Greek they remembered from their childhoods, while others maintained some degree of fluency in the language. Most knew Greece principally through family connections (such as remarks and anecdotes told by the immigrant generation or visits to relatives there), sightseeing and vacations, and the myths of its classical past. A minority of this generation had active business, professional, or other ties to Greece.

This generation seeks to understand that part of their "identity" that is Greek and its relation to the American part. Because they are "true" Americans (that, they never doubt), the Greek part, they presume, is tied up with themselves as "persons" (Schneider 1980). The texts thus represent attempts to puzzle out answers to the question: What am I as a Greek American? These are stories in search of an indigenous understanding of ethnic identity. To probe how such stories build an ideology of ethnic identity requires an analytical strategy that reconstructs a "family archive": the stories must be read in conjunction with other texts that enlarge their meaning, overriding differences of form, source, and occasion.

The texts and their uses of tropes also suggest that a theoretical understanding of Greek-American ethnicity—and other American ethnicities—must appreciate how social worlds are built by discourses. If anthropology learns any lesson from the program of the ethnography of speaking (Hymes 1974 [1962]), it must learn that speaking constructs the very settings in which people talk. People enunciate, argue, assert, and perform their worlds with speech; sometimes they reduce them with ironies (Chock 1985). Ethnicity is one construction of some of the settings of the social world. My analysis of the texts here rests on the assumption that ethnicity in indigenous American forms is conceived and acted as "ethnic identities." Each identity is the particular work of tropes in talk about the world. I begin my analysis with one trope that I call the "outsider wife."

The Texts

The texts presented here are the "best" ones of the set. They most explicitly discuss the ethnic identity of the subject of the text and, implicitly, as I argue below, the ethnic identity of the speaker.[3]

(A) My mother, who was a Catholic, became a Greek Orthodox, and worked for the Greek church all her life, and finally became a Greek Orthodox when my brother was out from the service. Why, I don't know, because when you are an outsider—especially that generation, marrying a Greek, you are an outsider, unless. . . . She left her family completely and became a Greek. My mother spoke seven languages, spoke Greek very fluently, and hardly anyone knew she wasn't Greek. Most people thought she was.

(B) I can't even say just customs alone, but I'm talking about food. Once you're used to Greek food, you cannot go on out. . . . My sister-in-law Jane [BW] is an example. She came from . . . she calls them shanty-town Irishmen. And she mixed with the Pappases, and married one, and started to develop their way of cooking. So when her parents' home was demolished in that . . . tornado, they moved in with her, and her mother was doing the cooking for her, assuming to be helping her. But my brother-in-law and Jane herself couldn't stand it. She went up to the baby's godfather, who was an adjuster for All-State, and she said, please give them their money, so they can move out of my home, I can't take the Irish cooking. Her husband lost twenty pounds. They were incompatible, they wouldn't speak to each other. It was that she had grown; her tastes had differed also. And I said, it's your family. You've lived with them for twenty years, Jane. She said, I know, but then I met a Greek and learned how to cook. And I can't do elsewise anymore.

(C) And then—oh, dear . . . George [FBS] just got married two years ago. Sharon [FBSW]. This girl is of Jewish religion, but she became a

Greek Orthodox. She was baptized. Probably a better Greek than most all the rest of us. Knows more about it and everything.

(D) Then Frank [MBS] is married to Mary [MBSW]. That family's still in existence. We keep contact with them. Mary is Bohemian, but she speaks Greek very well. They remained Greek and Orthodox, where the others sort of drifted away.

(E) And my husband is very proud of Mark's [DH] knowledge of Greek; he brags about it. He even has his letters xeroxed and showed it to the Greeks, and said our son-in-law knows about Greek. They didn't believe he was that good, because he never makes any mistakes. He knows it grammatically. And this [cousin] couldn't believe that my son-in-law. . . . So he says, okay, I'll make a copy for you. He says, not even I could do this well. He'd gone to high school. So my husband's quite proud about what Mark knows and what he's able to do. He doesn't stress the Jewish angle. . . .

Analysis of Texts

There are a number of similarities among the twelve texts. All are told by speakers who are part of the first American-born generation. All but one are about women, and they all concern relatives. The subjects of the texts are almost evenly distributed between the speaker's parents' generation and the speaker's own; the exception is about the son-in-law. All the texts describe someone who has an unclear claim to a Greek identity. Eleven involve non-Greek individuals who, either by marrying a Greek American or by establishing a relationship with a Greek-American family (as a nursemaid, for instance), make their ethnic identities ambiguous: in what sense, if any, are they Greek? The final case concerns a woman whose father was Greek American but whose mother was not; her already uncertain identity was further complicated, not clarified, by her marrying a "Greek from Greece."

Each text quoted above is a comment about a person's biography. All are about a single person. They establish points about the person's previous identity—Catholic (A), Irish (B), Jewish (C, E), and Bohemian (D). Each text then relates a change in identity to a transition in the person's life. The mother in A "became a Greek Orthodox"; she "left her family completely and became a Greek." In B the sister-in-law "had grown." She "met a Greek," "learned how to cook," and "can't do elsewise anymore." In C the woman was baptized and became a Greek Orthodox. In D the woman learned to speak Greek and, with her family, became "Greek and Orthodox." The son-in-law in E mastered the Greek language as a scholar. But he writes his Greek-American in-laws letters in Greek and consequently they downplay his Jewish identity. The transitions, then, in all the texts are associated with a person's bringing Greek qualities to a relationship with a Greek family.

Each person is credited with a superlative accomplishment. She or he speaks or writes Greek "fluently," "very well," or "grammatically." The three women who became Greek Orthodox "worked for the Greek church all her life," kept her family Greek, or became a "better Greek than most all the rest of us." The Irish sister-in-law learned to cook Greek food so well that the disruption caused by her mother's cooking made her and her husband "incompatible." Each person thus not only meets Greek Americans' expectations for non-Greeks, but overshadows Greek Americans themselves.

The "better Greek than us" identity bestowed on these spouses signals admiration for the person and, when the subject is one's mother (three texts), a good bit of sentiment. At the same time it is awarded with no little irony to these outsiders by the very people who, if there is any measure of Greekness to be found among the American-born, ought to be that measure. Self-deprecatory humor tends to accompany these remarks, followed by a smile or chuckle of self-recognition.

"Mixed" marriages between Greeks and non-Greeks[4] generally occasion questions about Greek identity by introducing a spouse who is nearly always accorded his or her own ethnic identity. Mixed marriages call attention to the "ethnic" identity of the non-Greek partners, and except for a few cases, they are designated by a non-Greek identity. Sometimes an unmarked, residual category, "non-Greek," is sufficient. A specific ethnic or religious descriptor, such as Irish, Polish, Italian (none with the "American" tag), Catholic, Jewish, or combined ethnic and religious categories (Irish Catholic), is usual. A mixed marriage is a "marked" marriage requiring a comment about the non-Greek spouse. In contrast, informants simply generalized about all other marriages, colorfully summed up as "one hundred percent olive oil" or "true to the blue and white."

Greek Americans thus use stories about the outsider wife to gain an understanding of themselves. They situate themselves in relation to their immigrant parents on the one hand and to Americans on the other. The problem set by Greek Americans for themselves is how to resolve what is Greek and what is American so as to make it possible to "go one way or the other" as they create an ideology of ethnic identity. To learn how these texts address this problem, I use an analytic strategy that treats them as texts within a constellation of texts.

The Family Archive

"Intertextuality is the family archive" (Culler 1981) is a superb image that I have used as a guide in looking for family resemblances (Needham 1975) among the texts. The archive houses my data as texts that constitute individual identities from an ideology of group identity. The question all the texts address is: What am I as a Greek American? Like a totemic operator (Lévi-Strauss 1966:152), this ideology assembles an individual out of disassembled species; here, individual identities are assembled out of ethnic practices the stories ascribe to outsider wives. These assemblages of practices, however, impart no defining attribute to either wives or individuals; the classifying project, generating ethnic identities, proceeds on partial similarities among texts (Tyler 1978:281).

I have taken the set of texts about non-Greek wives and considered them in relation to three other sets. One set bears a formal resemblance to the first set about non-Greek wives, in that its texts are spontaneous, parenthetical comments, with some narrative elements, about particular persons. This second set, to be introduced much later, concerns the "good bride." These first two sets generate a range of alternative ways of conceptualizing wives (and occasionally husbands) as outsiders in Greek families and thereby of conceptualizing the boundary between Greek and non-Greek. The third set of texts differs from the first two in containing autobiographical remarks in which the speakers analyze their own marginality. This group of texts initiates a dialectic with the outsider-wife stories by posing the "I" as subject against the "rest of us," who are compared with the wives, and suggests why the wives may be better Greeks than "us." The fourth set of texts is autobiographical, like the third, but these are first-person accounts from children of "mixed" marriages. They explore how differences between ethnic identities are generated and canceled. They also complete the family archive by returning to Mother, a symbol that condenses thought about differences between generations and among ethnic identities, Greek and non-Greek.

Taken together, the four sets of texts constitute a complex ideology of ethnic identity that none reveals when read alone. They enable me to use the resemblances each bears to the others to make this reading. None by itself reveals much, except perhaps the matter-of-fact observation that non-Greek spouses sometimes change identities. What each story means is the first problem to treat. How these stories constitute meaning is the second problem. Their membership in the four sets of texts—not a homology between any two or more stories or sets of stories—provides a key to both problems. This archive, of course, does not exhaust the outsider-wife stories of all possible readings—another family, other meanings. I have assembled only one family.

The Divided Self

Let us consider some autobiographical remarks in which individuals whose parents were both Greek immigrants mull over the reasons for the marginality or dividedness they perceive in themselves. These remarks linked the stories about non-Greek wives to reflections on the self. A comment from one man in its entirety was this:

> Living, in the past, as we did in the Greek environment, though we were clannish, now that I look back, but there was this important thing to consider: if one of our relatives would marry a non-Greek, so to speak, if that person were halfway accommodating or reasonable, we would accept him immediately in the environment. But many of my aunts who speak good Greek today were non-Greeks. It seems we adopt them quickly to the Greek. . . . We don't force, we're more democratic. But once they're in the Greek environment, it seems that we accept them much more readily. However, even though we were clannish, now that I look back again, when I went to school, I was able to adapt to the American environment without, at least outwardly speaking. . . . Unless they knew me intimately . . . they wouldn't know how marginal I was.

In this comment the speaker presents the experiences of his non-Greek aunts as commentaries on his own marginality. The non-Greek aunts faced the problem of being accepted into the "Greek environment," and he, being from a "Greek" background, had to find his way in the "American environment." Each was foreign, accepted for being "accommodating." The speaker makes his aunts' experiences a mirror image of his own, but they fit only imperfectly. His final remark is telling: "they wouldn't know how marginal I was." He questions how well his transformation from Greek to American has gone, and elsewhere he made these remarks about his marginality:

I grew up sort of divided, sometimes I wondered who I was. . . . I wasn't completely satisfied with the Greek environment and I wasn't completely satisfied with the American environment.

To which his wife added:

We were a unique generation, because we were half new and half old. We were the generation who bridged the gap between the old world and the new world. We grew up with our parents, knowing only the old-world customs, and when we were old enough to go to school, we'd have to adopt the new. . . . It was a very unique position to be in, and it's something our children won't have to go through.

Nor was this couple alone in their views; other people volunteered similar reflections. For example, another man described his marginality in these terms:

[My wife's] brother-in-law . . . has often said, "let's face it, our generation are very much schizoids." I kind of think that may be true.

A woman reported much the same thing:

[The Greek is] sort of in two worlds, you might say. The Greek world and the world he lives in. Although some kids I've talked to (kids, I mean people my age) say they feel like they're psychotic— you know, living in two worlds.

Both comments share the ironic tone of the honorific stories about non-Greek wives, but they indicate that at least for some people of this generation their position between their immigrant parents and the

American "world" is problematic. Since they find themselves caught in the middle, they are required to build "a bridge" between the two worlds. How are bridges to be built? How is an authentic personal ethnic identity to be constituted?

Some informants cast the problem in terms of "choosing." It was untenable, their reasoning went, for a person to be neither of his parents' generation, that is, unable to practice the "old ways," nor of the American world, "the new." Further, despite the ideological prescription that it is better to be "one thing or another," it was impossible for a divided self to be exclusively old or new. Each world already had claims on the individual. What was left was for him or her to "choose" and "adapt."

Choosing and adapting are not simply pragmatic adjustments, nor do they provide self-evident solutions to this problem. They are elements of an ideology that makes use of models at hand, in this case the outsider in the Greek family, the wife who is a stranger and who is taken in. If she is able to do more than simply resolve her dilemma, a solution must also await the marginal man or woman. The outsider starting from nothing becomes more than a marginal or divided Greek; she becomes an exemplary Greek. The model suggests that the divided Greek American may also be transformable.

The Mixed Child

What does the transformed outsider offer to the Greek American torn between two worlds? One clue comes from the daughter of such an outsider. Her comments about herself and her Polish mother linked the status of outsider wives to the texts of self-reflection. It is the first of a third group of texts, those about mixed children:

> I'm half-and-half. My mother's Polish and my dad was Greek. And my mother speaks Greek fluently, and she taught us Greek. And I'm very proud of the fact that—taking a person from the outside and coming in and wanting to learn and making you a complete Orthodox. . . .

This daughter used "half-and-half" to describe herself, an image that resonates with the dividedness of the immigrants' children. In this third group of texts the outsider effects the transformation of her children.

She makes them "complete." The outcome for such children, however, is not certain, as another child of marriage with an outsider attested:

Like my mother and father—my father is a Greek and my mother is an American, and there are so many others who are the same way—it seems like the children of families that are already mixed either go one way or the other. They either become part of the Greek community or they become part of the American community.

Each story describes possible valued outcomes. An outsider wife may become a better Greek than the rest of us; a mixed child may become a complete Greek. Each suggests that the divided self may also be a "better" or "complete" Greek, a conclusion that appears in a number of texts from individuals who place themselves in the predicament of being divided. One reads:

I feel I've reconciled the two worlds, and that in some ways I'm very Greek and that in some ways I'm very American. I hope that I've taken the better part of the two worlds and combined them. I don't think that anyone would have to be psychotic about it. Wherever there is a conflict between the two ways of thinking, I can't say that the Greek has always won out.

The superlative implied by "very" is underscored by the implication that combining the "better" parts of two things results in a "better" outcome. As a matter of fact, most of the "choosing" is done on the Greek side of the conjunction. A variant text pursues the choosing from a shopping list of "things Greek," eliminating, for example:

superstitions . . . family pictures all over the house, and . . . the house filled with furniture and flowers. . . . My children have icons in each of their rooms, but I don't like candles. I think of it as a fire hazard.

The transformation is accomplished for the divided self, this text suggests, by eliminating Greek things that are incompatible with American tastes and practices, much as learning and accommodating transform the outsider wife.

The transformation is a perpetually unsettled one, however. The question the child of immigrants asks—what am I?—is begged by this paradigm. Where the question ought to have a unity as its answer, the conjunction of Greek and American belies resolution. The tales of outsider wives and half-Greek children both entail transformations into a single entity, a better Greek or a complete one. But the conjoined, yet still divided, self suggests that modeling the self after the outsider wife is full of pitfalls. Instead of confirming their promise of transformation, the outsider wife stories simply recycle or bury the question. We must return to that question, Who am I?, and reconstruct its proxy: Who is the outsider wife? Why is she, and not some other figure, the model?

Identity, Practices, and Choices

Resemblances between the outsider wife and the Greek-American self that are not self-evident can be found in the transforming choices by which the self constructs its identity. Wives are cited in these stories for having constructed an identity out of practices. A wife's identity is embedded within routines of everyday life—speech, cooking, and rituals. She allows whatever questions may have arisen from her husband's introducing an outsider into the family to be laid to rest. Such a wife also outwardly attests to the superiority of the Greek world in a manner in which one born into it is never called upon to do, and thus she is acclaimed a "better" Greek than most. She confirms what every Greek should know.

In contrast to the outsider wife, the divided Greek-American self is placed in the dilemma of having to choose among and ultimately renounce some Greek things. This suggests the different direction of the wife's and the divided self's problems: coming from the outside and going to the outside, respectively. For the divided self, the daily practices of family life are thrown into relief by the operations of the outsider wife. A Greek-American person, regardless of gender, is required to choose and, like the woman quoted above, to choose the "better" part.

The question, Why the wife?, is answered in her mastery of daily practices, thus holding out hope for the divided self's mastering of choice. But for the divided self, choice represents the ultimate Americanization. The divided self thus turns the act of choosing from among many possibilities, each marked as distinctively Greek, into an affirmation of being American. Who else but an American would be required to build one's own identity? The divided self in choosing becomes the quintessential American, modeled ironically after the quintessential Greek—the outsider wife.

The Good Bride

Before a final resolution can be offered, yet another kind of wife, a figure from the fourth and final set of stories in the family archive, requires attention. She is the "good *nifi*," the "good bride."

The *nifi* texts suggest why the son-in-law in Text E is a problematic case. Two accounts of these women are pertinent, because in form they roughly parallel the comments about the outsider wives but are combined into a single text. A third text describes a self-examination by a woman who finds herself being called upon to be a good *nifi*. The three stories, like the outsider wife texts, span the immigrant and American-born generations. The combined stories are these:

> It's common among Greek families for a woman to go to her husband's people. We usually think of the opposite here, don't we? Like Panayiota [HZ]—they make it a point to please the husband's people more than their own. . . . So my husband and I have sometimes felt neglected in Panayiota's attitude toward us. We're always here. We won't go against her. But she has to be especially careful of her husband's people. And they have caused her some unhappiness. But she holds her tongue, and she wants only good relations with them. My aunt Eleni [MZ] in Gary did the same thing. Very careful of her husband's people, neglect of her own. It's so common. I resent it. I don't like it at all. My aunt Eleni took care of her mother-in-law, who was bedridden, for ten years. When she'd come here, she'd visit her husband's cousins, and not us. This used to bother us a good deal. This importance of being the good wife, the good bride.

This is about half the entire text, which at this point begins the story anew, in the same form, with more details about Panayiota.

The American-born young woman who married a Greek immigrant provides this analysis of her situation:

> I'm not sure how I feel. But I think that the way I'm supposed to feel is that I've become a part of their family and have become ab-

sorbed in them. I'm the one whose name has changed, so that I therefore belong to the Pappas clan. . . . Which means that I am available to provide any services that the family may need. If there's a celebration, that I will not only attend, but help with the cooking and whatever other preparation may be necessary. And that I will remember everyone on name day and special celebrations. And that I will prefer to be with them rather than other people. Other friends or acquaintances. . . .

After providing some details about her husband's family, she concludes:

I don't feel the loyalty that I think I'm supposed to feel. That I feel is expected of me. I feel typically American, in that I married George and I didn't marry his family. And this is a little hard for everyone concerned. Not for George, but the rest of them.

In all three accounts the *nifi* is a token for a devalued, old-world way of life. The judgments the stories contain about norms and feelings distance the good bride from the good outsider wife. Though both are women, only the outsider wife mediates between the old world and the new for the divided self.

The good bride, however, does suggest why the son-in-law in Text E is a relatively weak figure in the company of the outsider wives. The good bride provides the model for the outsider wife, as both are women and outsiders in their husbands' families. The son-in-law resembles the outsider wife because his actions permit his Greek-American in-laws to suppress his Jewish identity. But he cannot be a paragon of Greek identity because his gender intrudes. His nearest model, the *eso-ghambros*, who is beholden to his father-in-law, is an object of "slight social stigma" (Friedl 1962:65) in village life and of derision among Sarakatsani shepherds (Campbell 1964:145). He is devalued because he falls short of the superior masculine status called for by the "ideology of male dominance" (Herzfeld 1983:162). In the United States recent immigrants from Greece continue to use the term to tease men whose wives are better off than they, but, unlike the *nifi*, the *eso-ghambros* does not figure in stories among the American-born. The son-in-law in Text E is rewarded for his excellent Greek, but at the risk of losing status because he earns it from a feminine source.

Finally, behind the outsider wife lurks still another question. Why should a person—whether the wife or the divided self—carry the burden of the identity of a generation? The problem with which this paper began—how can I be one thing or another?—is posed by a person. The proposed resolution juxtaposes a person against a person and seeks a remedy in choices made by a person.

Genesis of Ethnic Identities

The question of the outsider wife entails not one but two questions. The first concerns ethnic identity, a problem for the Greek American. The second involves the genesis of ethnic identities, a problem for the cultural analyst. The two are not really separable because they are both products of an ideology by which the Greek American and the analyst are equally caught. This ideology generates the individual[5] as the locus of ethnic identity and gives him or her the responsibility for manufacturing that identity. I will address each question in turn.

For Greek Americans, the stories of outsider wives and divided selves attempt to wrench an individual identity from the lived experience of another generation. The stories do so by "objectivating" (Berger and Luckman 1966) domestic practices through the medium of the outsider wife, in order to convert them into an identity constituted by and for a person. The wife concretizes a social process—intermarriage between Greeks and non-Greeks. The wife as trope offers the medium through which a generation searches intermarriage for insights into individual identity. The wife as ideological operator works by objectivating practice—transforming practice into isolable accomplishments—and converting these accomplishments into markers of identity. The "choosing" that the ideology thrusts upon a person depends on a group life (domestic practice) being made manipulable; the outsider wife stories do just that by converting practice to individual accomplishment, as though each practice were a discrete part of family life. Practice is transformed and limited to speaking the language, cooking the food, serving the church. Ideology makes these stories instruments for achieving immediate ends.

Individuals then make them tools. The outsider wife's accomplishments in the stories are not exclusively in aid of family life. They also single her out. She stands apart from her family, unlike the good *nifi*, who is imagined inside the family, merging with it. The outsider wife is, in effect, more of a good American, less of a "better Greek"; she is an individual defined by her achievements (an apt model for an American identity). The divided self aspires to her achievements. The proper choices, fitting an individual's proclivities, enhance the possibility of one's success in manufacturing this ethnic identity to be claimed as a person, not as a social being. The outsider wife stories thus devalue community in favor of individualism.

The outsider wife also exemplifies how intermarriage as a social process places the individual at the center of Greek-American life in other ways. For the American-born, the choice of a spouse, for instance, is shifted out of the realm of family, where it was lodged in the days of "fixed" marriages, into the realm of personal preference. My informants explicitly contrasted stories they knew from their parents' generation with what they understood of their own. As they would say, "it depends on the person." "My son's [or daughter's] happiness comes first." Relinquishing parental, family, and community settings for the selection of mates, the American-born placed "happiness" of a person ahead of other considerations. At the same time they relinquished the expectation that the spouse chosen would necessarily be "Greek." "Whatever makes him happy" entailed ethnic identity choices as well as marriage choices.

Analysts of ethnicity in the United States have by and large not taken the question of an individual ethnic identity to be problematic (Gans 1979; Parsons 1975). Their analytical error is to construe the cultural within the frame of the social or psychological. They take the individual as given and not as a constructed category until they face the "third generation" phenomenon, where people appear to be constantly assuming and shedding "ethnic" impedimenta. "Symbolic ethnicity" (Gans 1979), for example, captures the analysts' puzzlement over "expressive behaviors" that are not functional. In this kind of analysis, ethnic identity is treated exclusively as a matter of "sociopsychological elements that accompany role behavior" (ibid.:202). Individuals, free to choose to be ethnic or not in the absence of real social costs, elect for "personal" reasons—nostalgia, socialization of children, or voluntary group membership—to adopt an ethnic identity.

Schneider (1980) and Yanagisako (1978), on the other hand, have posed the individual as a problem for cultural analysis. In Schneider's argument, the "person" is an American cultural "unit" assembled out of symbols drawn from many domains that contextualize each other. Kinship, nationality, and religion, inextricably fused domains of American culture (Schneider 1969), are only imperfectly pulled apart, whether by the native or by the analyst. For example, Yanagisako (1978:23) found

Japanese Americans building a dual ideology by pairing exemplars (decontextualized symbols) from the American and Japanese cultural orders. Similarly, the outsider wife stories enable Greek Americans to extract exemplars of a "person" from Greek contexts, bestowing two identities—personal and ethnic—and legitimacy at once. For the analyst to appreciate the constructedness of "the individual" requires attention to the ideological devices operating in the cultural order.

Finally, the outsider wife must be understood as a peculiar type of ideological device. The outsider wife and divided self stories mutually reflect a sense of irony and self-parody. They remind Greek Americans not to take themselves too seriously. For Greek Americans, marginality is only a memory, erased by their successes at being American. The stories and self-examination distance Greek Americans from their childhoods and their parents' generation. While the American-born may fail to extract a separation of themselves from their immigrant parents (metonymically they are bound together), the outsider wife stories accomplish the separation metaphorically by mediating between the American-born and the *nifi,* who is made a token of the old ways of the immigrants. The *nifi* without the outsider wife is powerless to speak for or to the American-born; she is as distant as she is odd. The outsider wife frees the American-born of her and leaves them with their own "Greek" identity, however individual, incomplete, and ironic.

The outsider wife stories, though few, are thus not individual musings but collective representations. They are a social currency, told and retold—although they may be first-person accounts and contain elements of both the teller's and the subject's biographies. Their exemplars—language, religion, food—are motivated by the story as much as by biography. The stories encapsulate a generation's thought about itself. Each telling creates anew the ethnic identity that the outsider wife offers.

Among the media of ethnogenesis, however, these stories are an impoverished form compared to alternatives outside the modern world (see Drummond 1981; Whitten 1976). Myths of cultural origin in other parts of the world are resplendent with multi-vocal symbols, like the self-generative serpent of Arawak myth (Drummond 1981), that conjure powerful images as both physiological and theoretical devices. The outsider wife stories are domesticated versions of this "wild" thought. The people who tell them do not seem to be reflecting on ethnic identities so much as tossing out half-formed questions. The stories resemble the stuff of common sense (Geertz 1975). They proceed only a step beyond the social classifications of ethnic identities. They divert this classifying project away from the ethnic boundaries (Barth 1969) set by intermarriages (where the question concerns what other ethnic categories exist), to individuals asking themselves who they are, as persons.

At this point, this particular Greek-American family archive has probably yielded whatever secrets it holds. Its one ideological operator, simple as it is, by no means exhausts the tropes of Greek-American ethnicity. There are other, richer ones, even in this modern setting. Greek descent, Pericles and Athens, and Greek Orthodoxy all have to be reckoned with, and they are only a few of the more powerful operators, each constituting identities with their own problematics. The particular operator this paper has dealt with is neither unique among nor identical to any of the others, but it enables us to imagine the variety of ethnic identities. It offers one exploration of the social landscape of everyday life.

Notes

Acknowledgments. The fieldwork on which this article is based was supported in part by a National Institute of Mental Health Predoctoral Fellowship (5-F1-MH-29, 915), the University of Chicago, and Catholic University of America. Jon Anderson, Marjorie Balzer, Ruth Fredman, and June Wyman generously provided many critical comments on the manuscript, for which I am very grateful.

1. Terms for "American of Greek descent," the expression preferred by some American-born Greek Americans, also include "Greek American," "Hellenic American," and "Greek." "Greek" is also used for "Greeks from Greece." In the interest of economy, I use "Greek American" for the first category and "Greek" for the second, except where the context makes the meaning clear.

2. Michael Herzfeld informs me that "a better Greek than us" is a stock phrase in communities in which he has worked in Greece. There the phrase has the semiotic function of shifting categories of local and national Greek identities.

3. All the names are fictitious. The texts are verbatim transcripts. Some identifying details are omitted.

4. The rate of intermarriage between Greeks and non-Greeks has increased steadily in each generation since the immigrants arrived. (See Table 1.) Because men outnumbered women among the first immigrants and what women there were were more sheltered than their brothers, outsider wives were more frequent in this generation than outsider husbands. In the first American-born generation, however, women began to catch up with men in marrying out, and in the next generation the sexes have equal rates of intermarriage. All told, among the immigrants roughly

Table 1 Intermarriages of Greek-American Men and Women
by Generation

Generation	Marriage	Men N	% Out	Women N	% Out	Sex Unknown N
IMM	In	39		20		1
	Out	13	25%	2	9%	
AB1	In	36		61		7
	Out	41	53%	26	28%	
AB2	In	4		9		
	Out	6	60%	9	50%	

Key:
IMM = Immigrant generation
AB1 = First American-born generation
AB2 = Second American-born generation

one-fifth of all marriages were with non-Greeks; in the second American-born generation more than half are. These proportions derive from my analysis of genealogical data and should not be taken to do more than suggest the scope of inter-marriage.

5. My analysis of the individual has been influenced by Dumont (1965, 1970).

References Cited

Barth, Fredrik
    1969   Ethnic Groups and Boundaries. Boston: Little, Brown & Co.

Berger, Peter, and Thomas Luckman
    1966   The Social Construction of Reality: A Treatise in the Sociology of Knowledge. Garden City, N.Y.: Doubleday & Co., Anchor Books.

Campbell, J. K.
    1964   Honour, Family and Patronage. Oxford: Clarendon Press.

Chock, Phyllis Pease
    1985   The Irony of Stereotypes. Manuscript in the files of the author.

Culler, Jonathan
    1981   The Pursuit of Signs: Semiotics, Literature, Deconstruction. Ithaca, N.Y.: Cornell University Press.

Drummond, Lee
    1981   The Serpent's Children: Semiotics of Cultural Genesis in Arawak and Trobriand Myth. American Ethnologist 8:633–660.

Dumont, Louis
1965   The Modern Conception of the Individual: Notes on Its Genesis. Contributions to Indian Sociology 8:13–61.
1970   [1966]Homo Hierarchicus: The Caste System and Its Implications. Mark Sainsbury, transl. London: Weidenfeld & Nicholson.

Friedl, Ernestine
1962   Vasilika: A Village in Modern Greece. New York: Holt, Rinehart & Winston.

Gans, Herbert J.
1979   Symbolic Ethnicity: The Future of Ethnic Groups and Cultures in America. In On the Making of Americans: Essays in Honor of David Riesman. Herbert J. Gans et al., eds. pp. 193–220. Philadelphia: University of Pennsylvania Press.

Geertz, Clifford
1975   Common Sense as a Cultural System. Antioch Review 33:5–26.

Herzfeld, Michael
1983   Interpreting Kinship Terminology: The Problem of Patriliny in Rural Greece. Anthropological Quarterly 56:157–166.

Hymes, Dell
1974   [1962] Sociolinguistics and the Ethnography of Speaking. In Language, Culture, and Society: A Book of Readings. Ben G. Blount, ed. pp. 335–372. Cambridge Mass.: Winthrop Publishers, Inc. Reprinted from Anthropology and Human Behavior. Thomas Gladwin and William C. Sturtevant, eds. Washington, D.C.: Anthropological Society of Washington.

Lévi-Strauss, Claude
1966   The Savage Mind. London: Weidenfeld & Nicholson.

Moskos, Charles C., Jr.
1977   Growing Up Greek American. Society 14:64–71.

Needham, Rodney
1975   Polythetic Classification: Convergence and Consequences. Man 10:349–369.

Parsons, Talcott
1975   Some Theoretical Considerations on the Nature and Trends of Change of Ethnicity. In Ethnicity: Theory and Experience. Nathan Glazer and Daniel P. Moynihan, eds. pp. 53–83. Cambridge, Mass.: Harvard University Press.

Petrakis, Harry Mark
1970   Stelmark: A Family Recollection. New York: David McKay Co.

Schneider, David M.
1969   Kinship, Nationality and Religion in American Culture: Toward a Definition of Kinship. In Forms of Symbolic Action: Proceedings of the 1969 Annual Spring Meeting of the American Ethnological Society. Victor Turner, ed. pp. 116–125. Seattle: University of Washington Press.
1980   American Kinship: A Cultural Account. 2nd ed. Chicago: University of Chicago Press.

Tyler, Stephen A.
1978 The Said and the Unsaid: Mind, Meaning, and Culture. New York: Academic Press.

Whitten, Norman E., Jr. (with the assistance of Marcelo F. Naranjo, Marcelo Sante Simbaña, and Dorothea S. Whitten)
1976 Sacha Runa: Ethnicity and Adaptation of Ecuadorian Jungle Quichua. Urbana: University of Illinois Press.

Yanagisako, Sylvia
1978 Variance in American Kinship: Implications for Cultural Analysis. American Ethnologist 5:15–29.

Ideology and Everyday Life in Sami (Lapp) History

Sharon Stephens
Johns Hopkins University

In recent years anthropologists representing theoretical schools as different as sociobiology, cultural ecology, and French structuralism have been unwittingly united in their underlying argument that forms of social life or systems of belief can be explained as diverse reflections of an immutable physical reality lying outside the meaningful order of culture itself. In different theories, this fixed, external reality has been variously conceived as "selfish" strands of DNA, individual biological needs, the dictates of material production, or even the neural structure of the human brain. In contrast to such "naturalistic" explanations, proponents of what we might call a "radical culture theory" have argued that each culture must be understood in terms of its own system of thought and action (see, for example, Sahlins 1976; Geertz 1973; Schneider 1968).

Cultural explanations need not deny that humans have biological needs or that general physical laws can be formulated to describe regular occurrences in a material world. The point is that for "material realities" to provide specific limits and possibilities for human societies, these realities must operate as parts of an already symbolically constituted social whole, rather than from a fixed position "outside" of culture. As Sahlins (1976:viii) has argued, the decisive quality of any culture is not that it "must conform to material constraints, but that it does so according to a definite symbolic scheme, which is never the only one possible."

"Culture" from such a perspective is the mediating structure ordering both practice within a material world and beliefs about the world. It may therefore seem remarkable that some symbolic anthropologists, espousing what they see as fundamentally cultural explanations, have been criticized for ignoring "history, event, action, the world." (See Sahlins's discussion [1981:6] of widespread criticism of an apparently ahistorical "structuralist perspective.") However, symbolic anthropologists have often left themselves vulnerable to such criticisms by paying only lip service to cultural constructions of material reality, while focusing on myths, religious beliefs, and other conceptual systems whose symbolic content seems less distorted by material contingencies.

Such narrowly symbolic studies may be possible within complexly differentiated societies, where distinctions can be made between formal ideologies and everyday practice; but even the most persistent seeker of abstract symbolic structures might be driven to despair by a society like the Sami of northern Scandinavia.[1] The apparent lack of a formal, internally consistent system of religious beliefs led one early observer of the Sami to claim that they simply viewed as their gods whatever they saw in the morning as they emerged from their tents, whether this was stone, stump, or other natural formation (Itkonen 1946:2). Another student of Sami religion (Christiansen 1953:50) finally concluded, in only thinly veiled exasperation, that in regard to Sami gods, "the emotional aspect predominates, there is hardly any intellectual activity, e.g., hardly any speculation upon the nature and existence of these spirits when not in action." Even Pehrson (1954:14), one of the first anthropologists to try to see a coherent structure in Sami "optative" bilateral kinship, asserts:

> The Lapps are highly pragmatic and relativistic in their approach to life. . . . Certainly they have little ritual or ceremonialism and are ever ready to shift techniques and approaches in response to the changing problems of a variable and difficult environment.

As Pehrson's statement indicates, the Sami, with their apparent lack of abstractly formalizable ideologies, have been particularly subject to "naturalistic explanations" that identify Sami beliefs and social forms as reflections of a harsh and variable Arctic environment. The loose structures and objective pragmatism identified in the constantly shifting membership of Sami hunting bands and reindeer herding units have been seen as affording selective advantages in changing ecological situations (see, for example, Ingold 1976:123). Insofar as fragmented and context-bound ideologies can be identified, they have been seen as transparently reflecting the variable material circumstances of Arctic life.

Some of these claims about the Sami are certainly exaggerated. We have quite detailed sources describing complex rituals among seventeenth- and eighteenth-century Sami (for example, descriptions of the ancient bear ceremony by Schefferus [1971, originally 1673] and by Reuterskiöld [1912], who summarizes the most important early accounts). Other sources indicate that the social alliances and territorial connections of Sami hunters and fishermen varied considerably less than has often been claimed (Itkonen 1948 II:246–251; Vilkuna 1971:233).

Nevertheless, it is true that in many small-scale societies like that of the Sami, particular material circumstances seem to dictate the kinds of cultural symbols and meanings that are foregrounded at any given time. Bear ceremonies and other hunting rituals occur only within particular productive contexts, while more complexly differentiated societies may have "religious domains" of far more permanence and independence from everyday material contingencies. I have heard early Sami hunters and fishers described as lacking the ability for fully abstract thought, and as incapable of conceiving of consistent systems of gods or kinship structures that are not associated with concrete circumstances.

In contrast, the more I have worked with the early Sami material, the more convinced I am that the study of such small-scale, seemingly "loosely structured" societies challenges anthropologists to develop new conceptions of the relations between symbolic structures and pragmatic action in material environments. An explicitly cultural approach to such societies must confront the apparent structural flexibility and concrete logic that leave such societies so open to materially reductionistic explanations. At the same time, these societies also force symbolic anthropologists to grapple with problems of action and everyday life that are too often simply "bracketed out" in the analysis of complex "ideological systems" of binary oppositions and proportional structural relations.

To set the stage for this discussion of "ideology and everyday life in Sami history," I will begin by outlining some important aspects of that history, and by briefly mentioning my own long-term research objectives.[2] Sami history can be divided into three periods: a so-called "traditional period," in which seminomadic Sami lived primarily by hunting and fishing; a "pastoral period," beginning in the sixteenth century, when some groups of Sami in northwestern Scandinavia began to make extensive migrations with large herds of domesticated reindeer; and a "modern period," dating from World War II, when many formerly nomadic Sami began to live in fixed residences and to practice a kind of "reindeer ranching" within a Western market economy.

This periodization simplifies the complexity of historical development in various Sami culture areas in order to present more clearly what I see as three quite different cultural orders. One aim of my own research has been to understand Sami history not just in terms of narrowly defined "economic transformations" from hunting to pastoralism to reindeer ranching, but in terms of total cultural systems of thought and action. Changes within each period can then be seen as changes still within the bounds of a coherent cultural whole, while transitions between historical periods can be associated with fundamental cultural transformations.

I argue that each period has been organized by its own primary relations and categories, constructions of the self and of the social whole, ecological patterns, and mode of historical reproduction. Most relevant to this discussion, each period has also been organized by its own way of relating consciously articulated beliefs about the world (or "ideologies") to action in "everyday life," characterized by objects and relations that often seem to possess the quality of "given realities" existing outside culturally variable symbolic systems. Although every culture has areas where divisions between things, people, and events are taken for granted and areas where classificatory divisions can be more consciously manipulated and transformed, cultures differ in their modes of relating these realms of thought and action. How responsive are conscious ideologies to changes in the practice of everyday life? How open is the everyday order to changes generated on more consciously creative, transparently symbolic levels? Answers to such questions can be approached only within the context of total, culturally variable systems of meaning and action.

This paper discusses in detail the systematically distinctive relations between ideology and everyday life in the traditional and pastoral Sami cultural orders. (A more extended comparison of traditional, pastoral, and modern Sami systems is developed in Stephens 1984.) It then concludes with a brief discussion of how such systematic understandings help us to move beyond contemporary theoretical debates about the roles played by ideology and material practice in the formation and reproduction of societies, and to see that such questions should be logically subordinate to considerations of the different *kinds* of cultural orders with which we are dealing.

The Traditional Sami Cultural System

Turning now to the traditional system of early Sami hunters and fishers, I aim to suggest the outlines of a cultural order in which the boundaries of concrete actors and objects were more temporally provisional and transparently symbolic than they are within Western culture, while native ideologies were also more concretely grounded and context-bound than our own conceptual models of the world. I will discuss the traditional Sami seasonal division of material production, the formalized "maps of the cosmos" painted upon ceremonial drums, and the traditional construction of the individual Sami actor, who brought material practice and ideology together as an indissoluble whole.

Obviously I do not want to begin by dividing the traditional Sami world into Western domains of economy, kinship, or religion, or even by looking for abstract native models of the world to compare to outsiders' observations of how the natives "really" behaved. After I spent a long period puzzling over disparate source materials, the one relation that emerged as underlying every other traditional Sami categorization of objects and actions was that of male and female. Virtually every aspect of traditional Sami life was perceived in terms of how it brought together basic male and female powers and properties. Rocks or tree stumps might be classified as either male or female, depending upon their shape, the time of year, and the goals of human action in relation to them. Men were usually associated with male powers and activities and women with female, but there were also times when men and women performed tasks associated with the opposite sex. I then tried to understand what these central categories of male and female were "about" in traditional Sami society, and to explore why in some contexts male powers were regarded as dominant over female, while in other situations female powers took precedence.

In general, I discovered, male powers made divisions in the world or maintained established divisions. For example, men were the hunters whose killing of game was regarded as breaking the continuum of human and animal souls. Men were associated with the working of hard materials like wood or bone with sharp cutting instruments such as axes and knives. Male heads of households "stood for" their separate domestic groups in trade relations with other households, when completed exchanges of goods were aimed at leaving both parties as separate as they had been before the trade. Further, separate male-headed households were associated with summer divisions of the band territory, giving each household virtually exclusive rights to the resources within its own territory.

In contrast, female powers brought together separate units and transformed given relations. It was by means of women's participation in the hunting ceremonies that male-created divisions between humans and animals (considered a prerequisite to the human slaughter of animals) were transformed once again into a human/animal unity, without which, the Sami believed, animals could not be used as human food. Women generally worked soft materials like furs or skins with noncutting instruments like scrapers or needles. Women's instruments thus operated on whole objects or brought different pieces together into a new whole. During the winter period of common residence in a central village, separate households were seen as united through the ties afforded by women's dual roles as wives to some men and sisters to others.

In certain situations (described later in this paper), Sami ritual actions aimed at tapping more encompassing male or female powers of the universe by temporarily bringing into being various male or female gods. The important point here is that, as we might expect, male gods of hunting, weather, and death had the power to make divisions in the world—for example, between humans and animals, men and gods, or the living and the dead. In contrast, female gods were associated with the power to unify such divisions and create new wholes. The all-encompassing female god *Maddarakka* ("Stem- or Foundation-Mother") represented a level of cosmic unity in which formal differentiations between gods and humans, men and animals, and humans and the land disappeared in favor of a general identity of female integrating substance. It was from this female foundation that all differentiated human, animal, and land forms were believed to emerge and enter into relations or exchange among themselves until their deaths, when they once again returned to their undifferentiated foundations.

This brief look at what male and female were "about" in traditional Sami culture yields a basis for interpreting seasonal divisions in the traditional year, split between a winter period of common village residence and a summer period of dispersed household residence within territories radiating outward from the central village. Summer was considered a time when a female material world was subject to predominantly male actions. It was a period of intense hunting and fishing, considered male activities because they divided the continuum of human and animal worlds. The summer material world embodied female powers within its melting waters, lush vegetation, and profusion of fish and small game animals. Humans created male boundaries within this female unity in order to allocate separate summer territories to separate households. In the summer period, separate households varied widely in their techniques and strategies of hunting and fishing. What little explicitly ceremonial activity occurred was also highly variable in terms of which gods received sacrifices and how sacrifices were performed. Commonly, however, summer gods were male, and sacrifices to them aimed at ensuring important male divisions in the summer world. For example, sacrifices to the most important hunting god, the "Alder Man," were associated with the separation of the external world of male hunters from a Sami women's sphere within the tents, and with the separation of human hunters from their animal prey.

In contrast, winter was considered a time when a male material world—embodied in the frozen landscape and large, distinctive game animals such as wild elk and deer—was subject to the integrating (female) actions of humans. Winter was a period of intense social and ritual activity. The winter community saw itself as associated with the entire band territory. Elaborate, standardized ceremonies periodically brought together the worlds of the living, the dead, and the gods.

It was through such ceremonies that humans believed they could tap higher-level female powers in the universe and acquire the power to dissolve, temporarily, lower-level male divisions in human society itself. Only the winter assembly could approve proposed marriages, adoptions, or other changes that would redistribute people among summer territories. Only the winter assembly could create new summer territorial boundaries and redistribute land among existing households.

This arrangement of the traditional year has been explained as a social adaptation, allowing a delicate responsiveness to environmental pressures like fluctuating game abundances and human demographic variations. The point I wish to make is that winter assembly decisions were not merely reflections of particular external events. Rather, these events were perceived by the Sami as at least partly the results of prior human actions and conscious orderings of the world. Game abundances within summer territories, for example, were influenced by the size of household groups and the number of adult male hunters within given territories. Births and deaths within households were clearly influenced by previous communal decisions about marriages and household memberships.

Traditional Sami had no category for an external nature providing ready-made material objects and forces that existed independently of human actions. Winter assembly decisions had to accommodate everyday particular events of summer life; but, just as significantly, summer productive activities took place within objective frameworks laid down by winter assemblies according to transparently symbolic beliefs about a balanced world order.

I have described traditional seasonal dispersal and aggregation in terms of a Western notion of fixed individual persons, who retain their separate identities whether they live in villages or isolated territories. At this point, however, I turn to the Samis' own interpretations of the yearly cycle and of the shifting boundaries of the active Sami "self." Rather than assuming that the basic unit of traditional social action is always the individual, I have drawn upon anthropological understandings that culture in its broadest sense gives form to both categories of the active self and the "objective environment" (Mauss 1968; Fogelson 1982).

The traditional Sami order makes clear the culturally provisional nature of an active self in the contextually shifting references of the crucial native term *siida*. In every situation, from the most "everyday" organizations of domestic life and productive activities to the most "extraordinary" occasions of ritual sacrifice, the term *siida* refers to a diffuse unity of humans, animals, and the land. Traditional Sami believed that at the birth of a child, a new *siida* unit was created. This unit consisted of the human child, its particular "animal guardian spirit," and a particular "land spirit" (represented by the "birth stick" that marked the spot where the placenta was buried). A higher-level *siida* unit, foregrounded in the summer months of intense productive activity, included the separate domestic household (usually all those living in one tent), its summer territory, and the animals within that territory. Still more generalized was the winter *siida* assembly, including the entire human community, the total band territory, and all its animals. This range of *siida* individuality emerged in contexts of intense winter ritual activity. Finally, the most general *siida* unit—operative only in the most important and carefully controlled ritual contexts—consisted of both this world and the other world of the gods, the dead, and the generalized animal guardians. At this level, the *siida* was identical to the all-encompassing female earth god, the Stem-Mother mentioned above.

An intimate connection was postulated between this cosmic female god and the most particularized female realms of human women, animal mothers, and female land forms. By means of cosmic female powers, differentiated forms of this world—the concrete subjects and objects of everyday life—were created in the physical bodies of particular female beings. All human beings, for example, were thought to be originally female. In the case of a boy, special cosmic powers created the male form shortly before birth.

This order of the traditional world, which returns upon itself from any direction, is strikingly depicted in the map of the cosmos painted on the traditional ritual drum (Figure 1). A central rhombic form represents the most generalized female god or *siida*. From this figure emanate separate "god lines" carrying male gods of hunting and weather. Around the drum boundary are painted lesser divinities and figures associated with everyday life in the material world—from hunting and fishing to human birth and death. Sami interpreted the outer ovoid form as female, and saw it as leading back into the most generalized inner sphere.

This traditional map of the world, with the all-encompassing female god at its center and particularized *siida* forms along the periphery, corresponds to a model of the annual cycle with the winter *siida* assembly at the center and differentiated *siida* households radiating outward from the hub to separate summer territories (Figure 2). In both cases, we can interpret the differentiated forms as aspects of a higher-level unity.

If instead we take the most particularized *siida* individual as the center, we can observe a kind of inversion of the generalized cosmic scheme (Figure 2). As a Sami became older, he or she became associated with capacities for existing at the center of increasingly generalized *siida* units. A young Sami male, for example, generally had only limited powers to expand the boundaries of his *siida* self. Therefore, his actions were primarily important in productive activities such as hunting, in which divisions between hunter and prey were essential. In contrast, elderly Sami had developed capacities to expand the boundaries of their *siida* selves to include the entire winter village, its territory, and all its ani-

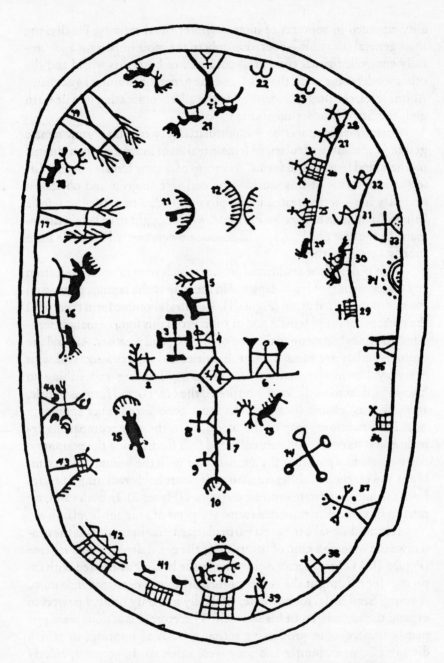

Figure 1 Åsele Drum Design (after Manker 1950:219, Drum #1)

Figure 2 Schematic Comparison of Traditional Sami Cosmic Map, Annual Migration Pattern, and *Siida* Organization

Traditional Sami Map of the Cosmos
(peripheral representations of differentiated gods seen as returning to undifferentiated unity at center; schematic focus on most generalized *siida* level)

Traditional Sami Annual Migration Pattern
(differentiated households migrate to separate summer territories and return to undifferentiated winter village site; schematic focus on generalized *siida* level)

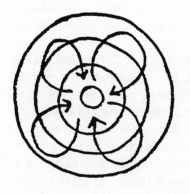

Traditional Sami "Ego-Centered" View of the Siida
(in various contexts of action, differentiated *siida* individual expands the boundaries of the active self to the most generalized *siida* range and returns to transformed lower-level *siida* units; schematic focus on particularized *siida* level)

mals. The actions of such Sami elders were therefore primarily important in winter *siida* assembly decision-making and in winter rituals of unification with the other world.

It is difficult not to sound as though describing a primitive Sami mysticism. Expansions of *siida* capacities generally occurred with age, but they might also be effected by creative visions or by ritual drumming. Some Sami were believed to possess special powers that allowed them to shift the focus of their vision and to "see" the boundaries of their selves expand. In so doing, these visionaries created a focus for a higher-level *siida* unit capable of transforming provisional lower-level units. Traditional shamans or *noaidis* were believed to have the power to call animals to particular hunting territories and to correct imbalances in temporary game abundances, because at the highest level of ritual unity animals and *noaidis* existed as one. Subsequent redifferentiations of lower-level units were believed to bring the world back to its proper balance of hunters and prey within separate hunting tracts. In the traditional period, the sacred drum was important primarily for its world-transforming sounds. Powerful Sami might expand their self-centered *siida* boundaries along the field of sound radiating outward from a beaten drum.

Such seemingly mystical acts were associated with the creation of *siida* units that had different capacities to effect what a Westerner would characterize as "real" changes in the material world. Only a higher-level *siida* unit had the power to change the boundaries and contents of its component parts. Thus, only a *siida* household unit could make decisions to change the customary hunting or trapping areas of adult males within that household and summer territory. Only the winter assembly had the power to change summer *siida* unities of humans, land, and animals by redistributing people among territories or territories among households.

Western observers, assuming that the effective cultural actor is always the body-bounded human being, might interpret the winter assembly as a collection of separate individuals whose behavior conformed to a shared code of conduct. In contrast, a variety of individual strategic choices and pragmatic adaptations to environmental fluctuations seemed to characterize the summer season, in which the primary *siida* units were the domestic households and not the *siida* village as a whole. If we neglect the Samis' own notions of the acting self and its relation to the social whole, we will surely be puzzled over why Sami behavior seems at times to conform so closely to "collective representations" and at other times seems merely to reflect disparate material realities.

I would argue instead that it is the symbolic construction of the shifting *siida* actor that orders the most "abstract" traditional world view, while also giving shape and direction to the most "concrete" forces in the material world. How do we then identify separate realms of everyday life and ideology among traditional Sami? We might see the drum's cosmic map as an abstracted ideological inversion of the particular Sami individual interacting with concrete objects in his or her environment. But what I hope is clear from even this abbreviated account is that individual actors and concrete objects were themselves symbolically constituted, changing their boundaries over time until actor and object merged within the most generalized conception of a *siida* unit. On the other hand, the drum's cosmic map was not simply a picture of the universe as it existed at any given time. Rather, drumming could effect transformations in *siida* levels and corresponding changes in *siida* actors and their objects. In such a system, abstract conceptual structures and concrete material practices were more transparently connected than they are in Western culture, which continues to generate volume after self-reflective volume exploring the problematic relations between structure and event, thought and action.

The Pastoral Sami System

In turning now to the pastoral Sami, my aim is to sketch the outlines of a cultural system in which separate levels of ideology and everyday life *are* more identifiable. However, I argue that it is still not valid to interpret ideology as a symbolic reflection of everyday material practice; in fact, in many ways everyday life itself appears to have been a metaphor of the fixed pastoral world order organizing the pastoral drum's map of the cosmos, the ideal pattern of annual migration, and the ideal model of the basic pastoral herding unit.

Space limitations preclude a detailed explanation of the transformation from a traditional to a pastoral Sami order. Clearly, this topic is central to understanding the relations of thought and action in Sami history. I believe, however, that general understandings of the cultural systems organizing Sami life *within* each major historical period should be logically prior to the understandings of transformations *between* these systems, which occurred at particular historical points of contact between Sami and Scandinavian cultural orders.

I will mention only a few factors specific to the original development of a pastoral Sami culture in the sixteenth century within an initially small area of northwestern Scandinavia. Early standardized Sami/Scandinavian trade relations in this area made Sami accumulations of domesticated animal wealth a culturally conceivable goal, while particular conditions of the northern mountain tundra made large-scale reindeer domestication a practical possibility. Scandinavian colonial incursions associated with the sixteenth-century emergence of northern nation-states depleted wild game and limited Sami territories, and traditional interpretations of these events were important triggers in the transformation of traditional culture itself.

That this transformation was not simply a response to external material events is clearly shown by the fact that in other traditional Sami areas, such as northern Finland, the same objective causes produced quite different social effects. Traditional Finnish Sami bands that could not move into more isolated territories farther north often dispersed into groups of itinerant beggars, were assimilated into Finnish peasant society, or simply died out (Tegengren 1952). In Finnish Sami areas, where previous Sami/Scandinavian interactions had been much more irregular, a less internally differentiated traditional order reached its limits in confrontation with sixteenth- and seventeenth-century Scandinavian culture. Nevertheless, this same traditional order had remained remarkably stable for many centuries, despite its supposedly loose structure, the vicissitudes of the Arctic environment, and numerous contacts with other cultures from Balto-Finnic to Siberian Samoyed.

In the western Scandinavian pastoral system, we can observe a breakup of the totalizing male/female logic that had maintained the traditional world as an integral whole. Instead of the traditional balance between a stable male order and periodic female transformations of this order, the pastoral period was characterized by permanent divisions within the world, and by a corresponding de-emphasis of female powers of integration and transformation.

The most basic pastoral division was between the spirit world of the gods and the physical world inhabited by humans and their deer. Fixed divisions were maintained between objects and actors within the physical world (although they all shared a common physical substance), because each unit had its own separate guardian spirit in the world of the gods. These guardian spirits protected the boundaries of objects and made sure that these boundaries were not subject to periodic female transformations, as they had been in the traditional period. Pastoral Sami constructed elaborate hierarchies of such guardian spirits, ranging from lower-level spirits of each rock, tree, animal, or human being to the supreme male god *Radien Ačče* (the "ruling father"), whose primary responsibility was upholding the fixed division between the spirit and physical worlds.

Throughout this fixed hierarchy of deities, male gods were seen as controlling the powers and actions of their female consorts in order to prevent any far-reaching female transformations of the existing order. The traditional all-encompassing female god or Stem-Mother— originally representing the undifferentiated unity of gods and humans, men and animals—was relegated in the pastoral period to the status of a minor women's deity, concerned mainly with activities (primarily menstruation and childbirth) that occurred within women's circumscribed sphere of the pastoral tent.

Just as male pastoral gods were permanently ascendant over female, so also were human male powers associated with the permanent control and regulation of human female powers. Pastoral women were still associated with the creation of a diffuse household unity within the tent, but they were forbidden to participate in ceremonies connected with the sacred world of the gods. In regard to the sacred, pastoral women were considered polluting or impure, because they threatened the maintenance of the fixed pastoral order.

Within human society as well, social ties through women were deemphasized in favor of ties between male siblings or cousins. The basic pastoral herding unit consisted of a single household and its domesticated deer. Occasionally, external conditions—such as pasture depletions or large numbers of predators—were seen as calling for temporary aggregations of herding partners, their households, and their herds. Such alliances tended to be transitory, however, with herding groups returning to their ideal household-based dimensions as soon as external conditions allowed. Pastoralists preferred to base herding partnerships on ties between male relatives, because these were perceived as more easily broken than integrating ties through women.

The relation between gods and men was one of symmetrical exchange between fundamentally separate parties. Humans made sacrificial offerings of animal souls to feed the gods. In return, gods maintained fixed divisions within the material world or reaffirmed these male divisions when female powers threatened to transgress their given boundaries.

This relation between gods and men was replicated in the relation between separate herding units. Such units might exchange services and women, but these exchanges did not fundamentally alter the separate identities of household-based herding groups. Even the relation between humans and their deer was organized as a symmetrical exchange. Humans gave deer new pasturelands and protection from predators, while deer provided humans with their principal food and raw materials for clothes and handicrafts.

We can characterize the pastoral Sami system as a series of separate levels of action, such as the domestic household, the realm of *siida* herding activities, and the spirit world. Each level was bounded by fixed male divisions. Within each level existed the same subordination of female to male powers. Male gods controlled and regulated their female consorts. Human males guarded against women's polluting influences in sacred ceremonies, while temporary herding partnerships were based on male rather than female bonds. Connections between these similarly structured levels were understood as symmetrical exchanges, which left both parties to the exchange as separate as before.

We can see a striking visual illustration of this order in the pastoral drum picture (Figure 3). Separate levels represent the underworld, the human realm, and the upper world of the heavenly gods. The drum border no longer functions as a meaningful design element, as it did in the traditional drum painting, where a female design border integrated everyday activities depicted along the periphery and formally connected them to an undifferentiated cosmic center.

Only ritual specialists, the shamans, could travel from level to level of the pastoral universe, and such movements could occur only as ecstatic "soul journeys" that left the shaman's body in the physical world. Movements between levels were restricted, to prevent any major transformations of the boundaries separating gods and men, or the worlds of the living and the dead.

At times the pastoral drum was beaten to induce the ecstatic trance journeys of pastoral shamans, but its most important function was visual divination. A ring was placed on the drum face, and its movements from figure to figure were interpreted as the drum was lightly beaten. Divina-

Figure 3 Finnmark Drum Design (after Manker 1950:431, Drum #71)

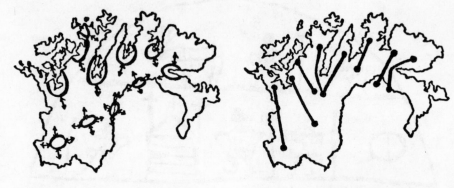

Traditional Sami Migration Patterns
(800–1600)

Nomadic Sami Migration Patterns
(1717, as recorded by von Westen)

Figure 4 (adapted from Vorren 1968:6, 10)

tion aimed to understand an imperfectly known cosmic order, so that humans might better adapt themselves to the cosmic design. Note that the pastoral drum cosmic map represented a *picture* of the differentiated cosmic order, which was believed to exist prior to any particular human actions in the world. In contrast, the traditional drum had been an *instrument* by which traditional Sami changed *siida* levels and participated in the ongoing creation of the universe.[3]

The pastoral drum's representation of the world as a series of separate, structurally equivalent levels was also the pattern organizing annual migrations of pastoral herding units. Figure 4 shows changes in migration patterns in northern Finnmark that were associated with the move from a traditional to a pastoral order. At least ideally, a single pastoral household-based herding group migrated in a straight line between summer and winter camps located either in the mountains and forest, or on the coast and inland.

The pastoral Sami Johan Turi explained the extensive migrations of pastoral Sami nomads as the result of a shared Sami and reindeer "nature":

Really the Lapps have almost the same nature as the reindeer. Both of them migrate north and south, in the way they are used to migrating, and both of them are a little shy, and because of this shyness they have been driven from everywhere, and so the Lapps must now stop where there are no other folk than Lapps, that is on the naked high fells, although in olden times the Lapps spent the winter in the forests and lived in peace, each on his own mountain. (Turi 1966:65)

Anthropologists have also explained pastoral migration patterns as reflections of nature—in this case, the nature of tundra reindeer, which migrate over long distances from winter forest areas to fawning grounds and summer ranges in the open coastal or mountain regions. When Scandinavian colonial penetration reduced hunting territories and wild reindeer stocks, the argument goes, Sami were pushed into isolated tundra regions and began to accumulate ever larger herds of domesticated tundra deer. Pastoralists were then forced to follow these herds along their customary annual routes. However, there is increasing evidence (Manker 1953:46) that wild tundra deer did not originally migrate to the forests but stayed in the mountains or on the coast over winter. Thus, the long migrations of pastoral Sami deer were a consequence and not a cause of their incorporation into the nomads' herds.

I would suggest that this change in the nature of reindeer nature itself was part of a broader change in Sami culture that predisposed pastoralists to think in terms of bounded units moving linearly between fixed and symmetrical poles. The emergence of symmetrical exchange as the dominant relation in pastoral Sami culture was associated with intense, standardized contacts with a predominantly differentiating western Scandinavian culture (characterized, for example, by a mercantile emphasis on symmetrical trade between essentially separate parties, and by religious doctrines of an otherworldly God dispensing salvation to human beings in return for their worship). Pastoralists' everyday lives, including their annual migration patterns, can then be interpreted as reflecting Sami notions of a generalized cosmic order, rather than simply mirroring natural dictates existing outside the pastoral cultural system.

Ideally, while the territories of pastoral migrations frequently changed, the basic form remained the same. Differentiated household-based herding units migrated annually between winter and summer camps. In practice, however, the formation of temporary herding coalitions frequently violated this ideal pattern. Particular conditions of pasture quality, predator numbers, or the number of adult male herders in each household might call for temporary alliances between herding partners, who then migrated together (along with their herds and families) for all or part of the year.

Observers of pastoral Sami have disagreed about the primary "on-the-ground" structure of the pastoral herding band. Pehrson (1957:5) observed bands in northern Sweden consisting of from one to four households that migrated together all year long. He also noted seasonal population shifts within some local bands, which came together during the summer into groups of up to twelve households and then dispersed during the winter into three or four smaller groups. Gjessing (1954:56) notes that among northern Norwegian Sami pastoralists the time for larger band units was during the winter, while these groups dispersed into household-based groups during the summer months. A single household might change group affiliation four or five times within a single year. There were no hard and fast rules for the coming together and dispersal of pastoral bands. The Sami themselves saw group affiliations as reflections of external conditions existing outside human knowledge or control.

For the traditional Sami, yearly cycles of migration between common winter village and differentiated summer territories were the culturally recognized basis for periodic transformations of lower-level *siida* units by the higher-level winter *siida* assembly. However, the pastoral Sami ideology of annual migrations undertaken by autonomous herding units afforded no such basis for communal transformations of existing relations between humans, deer, and pasturelands. This was true no matter how many pastoral bands were brought together. As I suggest later in this paper, the pastoral loss of traditional capacities for transforming everyday relations between humans and animals had profound consequences for pastoral ecology and periodic natural crises.

If we now turn to the cultural construction of the basic pastoral herding unit itself, we can see the same pattern of fixed divisions and symmetrical (and therefore basically untransformable) relations between separate units that we observed in the pastoral drum picture (Figure 3) and in the map of pastoral migrations (Figure 5). Among pastoral Sami, the term *siida* was given a more restricted meaning: the herding unit, consisting primarily of an autonomous human household and its deer, and secondarily—by extensional reference—a temporary aggregate of such basic units.

Among traditional Sami, *siida* referred to various ranges of human, animal, and land unity, with the most generalized *siida* unit having the

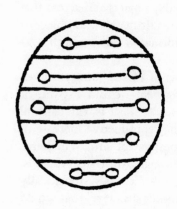

Figure 5 Schematic Comparison of Pastoral Sami Cosmic Map, Annual Migration Pattern, and *Siida* Organization

Pastoral Sami Map of the Cosmos
(movement primarily within each level, with only restricted shamanic movements between levels)

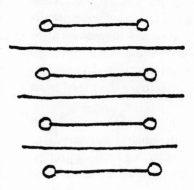

Pastoral Sami Annual Migration Pattern
(linear migrations by separate households between summer and winter camps; households come together only temporarily and under restricted external conditions)

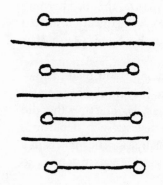

Pastoral Sami Siida *Herding Units*
(expansion of pastoral self possible only upon a "single plane"—through reproduction of a separate household or of its herd; pastoral *siida* coalitions formed only under restricted external conditions lack traditional *siida* powers to transform lower-level human/animal/land relations)

power to transform the boundaries of everyday objects and actors that were differentiated within lower-level *siidas*. Ultimately, no object or event was considered to lie outside the transformative powers of the traditional *siida* organization.

In contrast, the pastoral *siida*—consisting of a fixed connection between formally distinct humans and their deer—could expand or contract its boundaries only upon a single plane. That is, the pastoral *siida* could expand its boundaries only by the reproductive increase of human households or by the growth of domesticated herds. The herds of single pastoral households sometimes numbered in the thousands. But no matter how large the pastoral *siida* grew, it was systematically prohibited from moving to a qualitatively higher *siida* level that would have allowed transformations of ostensibly given relations among humans and animals—for example, by calling for the periodic redistribution of large herds among human beings. Pastoralists were notoriously reluctant to sell their deer to others, to give deer to impoverished kin, or even to slaughter their deer for their own household's consumption, claiming that such losses of deer diminished the pastoral owner. An understanding of the pastoral *siida* self enables us to see the literal truth of such statements.

Throughout this discussion, I have referred to various external conditions of the environment, such as pasture quality and predator numbers, that called for shifting social alliances among herding groups. Such a reference to external conditions does not, however, undermine my argument that material forces represented specific limits and possibilities for social life only as parts of an already constituted cultural whole. The pastoral order itself—with its fixed divisions among herding units, between gods and men, and between the *siida* and its variable pasture territories—constituted certain objects and conditions as permanently external to the primary pastoral unit of action, the *siida* herding unit. In this way, a fixed pastoral order became systematically insulated from periodic transformations of that order by Sami pastoralists themselves.

Among pastoralists—much more than among traditional Sami—we can identify disjunctions between formalized ideologies of the way the everyday world should be organized and everyday practices that did not always conform to ideal patterns. Nevertheless, such departures from pastoral ideals—no matter how "statistically significant" from a Western point of view—did not transform ideological structures to bring them more readily into line with material practice. Rather, departures from the ideal were perceived as only temporary aberrations, explained by the inability of pastoral Sami to fully divine the existing world order and to fit their actions to it. As soon as external conditions again permitted, everyday practice resumed a closer correspondence with ideal structure. *Siida* units reverted to their fixed household boundaries and to their autonomous linear migrations, at least until the next externally produced crisis.

Such disjunctions between ideology and everyday life and periodic natural crises were, I would argue, an inevitable product of the pastoral Sami system itself. This was so not because of a universal logic that counterposes changing material realities against the superstructural epiphenomena of ideologies that lag behind changes in production. Rather, pastoral crises were themselves generated *within* a culturally specific organization of material reality and productive action.

Let us consider very briefly the characteristics of the pastoral Sami ecology. As previously noted, pastoral Sami, unlike their traditional ancestors, had no culturally recognized means for transforming everyday relations between humans, animals, and the land. Pastoralists accumulated ever larger herds as a cushion against minor fluctuations in deer numbers; ironically, however, the larger the herd size, the more pastoral herds were subject to major crises that might decimate a herd almost overnight. Protected from animal predators and subject to human predation that killed off only the nonreproductive portions of the herd, domesticated deer could multiply to the point of depleting—and in some cases destroying—their pasturelands. Herds might then be decimated by starvation; by epidemics that swept through large, weakened herds; or by packs of predators, whose numbers may actually have risen with the move to pastoralism, because it is easy to attack domesticated deer on the peripheries of large herds. Ingold (1980:53) has characterized the Sami pastoralists as presiding over a looming ecological catastrophe—the destruction of both herds and pastures.

Pastoralist folklore abounds with tales of fabulously wealthy herders who became paupers overnight. We have considerable evidence that many impoverished pastoralists were indeed forced to leave for the coast to take up the despised life of "fish-slime eating" fishermen. We might imagine a pastoral order in which externally produced crises called for reallocating deer among various households, or for redistributing destitute Sami among the households of more fortunate relatives.

But in that case such ecological crises would not be endemic to a cultural system in which fundamental social changes were accepted alternatives to poverty and migration to the coast.

Among the pastoral Sami, constant shifts in migration routes, territories, and alliances among herders were not so much adaptive responses to the natural conditions of a variable Arctic environment as they were de facto responses to ecological crises generated largely by the pastoral order itself. With its fixed divisions and untransformable relations, this order was in many respects accurately reflected in pastoralist ideologies of the cosmic order, ideal migration patterns, and ideal composition of the basic herding unit. Everyday life within such a system seems to have been acted out as a metaphor of culturally more primary ideological realities.

It is not until the modern Sami period that we encounter a relation between ideology and everyday life more familiar to Western culture. Here everyday practice is no longer prefigured as the imperfect reflection of formalized ideological structures, as among pastoral Sami. Rather, modern Sami changes in material practices and objects—for example, the introduction of snowmobiles into reindeer herding and the consequently increasing "wildness" of domesticated deer (Pelto 1973) —have become the rationales for changing social relations among kin, between men and women, and between young and old, just as they are the motivations for changing Sami understandings of this rapidly developing world. The apparent correspondence between the historical dynamic of modern Sami life and Western notions that world views and social relations reflect more fundamental natural realities should not be surprising, when we recall that a defining characteristic of the modern period is the postwar absorption of a reindeer ranching economy into the Western market system. Although modern Sami notions of ethnic identity, kinship relations, or religion reveal continuities with traditional and pastoral Sami beliefs, these noneconomic realms are increasingly subject to radical reorganizations to accommodate shifting market pressures in the contemporary world.

Conclusion

In this discussion of the traditional and pastoral Sami cultural orders, I have aimed to suggest some problems of analytic strategies that begin by tracing connections between preconceived domains of material practice and ideological structure. The totalizing male/female logic of the traditional Sami order and the predominantly differentiating order of Sami pastoralists both reflect relations between ideology and everyday practice that confound Western common sense. As Barnett and Silverman (1979:3) have argued, by setting out instead to look for "fundamentally different approaches to cultural categorization itself, towards what is prior to the understanding and existence of any concrete category," we can open the way for conceiving of modes of conception, social practice, and material production truly different from our own.

In thus recognizing the fundamental differences separating total cultural systems, anthropologists are not forfeiting the possibility to make legitimate and illuminating cultural comparisons. Rather, we are placing such comparisons on the only justifiable foundation—on understanding total systems of cultural meaning, rather than on theories of how different cultures supposedly reflect material realities independent of human consciousness and action.

Notes

The study resulting in this paper was made under grants from the Social Science Research Council, the American-Scandinavian Foundation, and the Fulbright-Hays Foundation in Finland. The conclusions, opinions, and statements presented are, however, those of the author and not necessarily of the funding agencies.

1. In the eighteenth century, Swedish writers adopted the term "Lapp" as a designation for the aboriginal population of northern Scandinavia, although the people referred to themselves as "Samek" (singular, "Sapmelaš"). In recent times the term "Sami" (the English form preferred by the Nordic Sami Council to designate Sami language and people, both singular and plural) has acquired connotations of ethnic pride and political solidarity, while the majority population's use of "Lapp" is associated with derogatory connotations of "backward" and "unenlightened." "Sami" is used throughout this paper, except in direct quotations from other sources.

2. The issues dealt with in this paper are aspects of a long-term, much broader study which formed the basis of my dissertation on "Cultural Transformations in Sami (Lapp) History" (Stephens 1984). The study included three years of archival and library research at the University of Chicago, Indiana University, and the Library of Congress in the United States and at Helsinki University, Oulu University's Sami Institute, and Rovaniemi Library in Finland. Source materials on the Sami are abundant. (See the two-volume Sami bibliographic survey compiled by O'Leary and Steffens 1975, and Stephens 1984 for an evaluation of various sources relating to the different Sami cultural systems.) Source materials for my own research included seventeenth- and eighteenth-century accounts of the Sami by travelers and

missionaries, wide-ranging scholarly works by the late nineteenth- and early twentieth-century Scandinavian "Lappologists," and current archeological, linguistic, and ethnographic studies. In Finland, parish documents, Sami newspapers, the journals of the reindeer herding association, and Nordic Sami Council reports also provided valuable materials relating to the modern period. In addition, I did fieldwork in northern Finland for nine months in 1980. Most of my time was spent in Angeli, a small reindeer-herding village on the Finnish-Norwegian border. I also lived for one month at the Utsjoki old people's home, where conversations with elderly Sami residents provided additional insights into old Sami ways. In this paper, analysis of the traditional order is based on written source materials, while information about the pastoral period comes from written sources and interviews with elderly informants. Analysis of the modern Sami period (receiving only a suggestive peripheral treatment here) is based upon written materials, interviews, and my own "participant observation."

3. Detailed discussions of the classification of drum designs, the areal distribution of design types, native interpretations of cosmic map paintings, and the contexts of drum creation and use can be found in Manker's masterly two-volume study of Sami drums (Manker 1938, 1950). The argument that different design types represent native understandings of qualitatively different cultural orders is developed in Stephens 1984. Discussion of the complex problems involved in interpreting Sami drum iconography lies far beyond the scope of this paper, in which drum pictures have been introduced mainly to show in a visual mode how my proposed schemes of Sami cultural organization (and their graphic representations) are supported by native Sami constructions of the cosmos.

As a brief background for interpreting the drum pictures included here, I merely note the principal differences between drum creation and use among traditional and pastoral Sami. I have argued that in the traditional order drums were constructed and cosmic maps painted by "family shamans" (that is, male heads of households), each of whom had a drum and could act as a center for *siida* expansion. During winter assemblies, individual village elders might beat the drum on behalf of the entire community to effect a generalized ritual unity of humans, gods, land, and animals. However, reports of the most archaic bear-hunting ceremonies make no mention of specialized *noaidi* drummers. In the pastoral period, drums became more exclusively associated with shamanic religious specialists, who used drums as aids in making ecstatic trance journeys to the spirit world or to divine temporarily active constellations of supernatural forces affecting human herders and their deer. Pastoral *noaidis* fashioned their drums under extremely circumscribed ritual conditions aimed at protecting everyday life from dangerous otherworldly transformative powers.

References Cited

Barnett, Steve, and Martin G. Silverman
    1979 Ideology and Everyday Life: Anthropology, Neomarxist Thought, and the Problem of Ideology and the Social Whole. Ann Arbor: University of Michigan Press.

Christiansen, Reider Th.
1953   Ecstasy and Arctic Religion. Studia Septentrionalia 4.

Collinder, Björn
1949   The Lapps. Princeton, N.J.: Princeton University Press.

Düben, Gustaf von
1873   Om Lappland och Lapparne. Stockholm: P. A. Norstedt och Sönersförlag.

Fogelson, Raymond D.
1982   Person, Self, and Identity: Some Anthropological Retrospects, Circumspects, and Prospects. In New Approaches to the Self. B. Lee, ed. pp. 67–109. New York: Plenum Press.

Geertz, Clifford
1973   The Interpretation of Cultures. New York: Basic Books.

Gjessing, Gutorm
1954   Changing Lapps: A Study in Culture Relations in Northernmost Norway. Monographs on Social Anthropology 13. London: London School of Economics and Political Science.

Ingold, Timothy
1976   The Skolt Lapps Today. Cambridge, England: Cambridge University Press.
1980   Hunters, Pastoralists and Ranchers: Reindeer Economies and their Transformations. Cambridge Studies in Social Anthropology. Cambridge, England: Cambridge University Press.

Itkonen, Toivo Immanuel
1948   Suomen Lappalaiset Vuoteen 1945. Vol. 1 and 2. Porvoo, Finland: W. Söderström.

Manker, Ernst
1938   Die lappische Zaubertrommel: Eine ethnologische Monographie. I. Die Trommel als Denkmal materieller Kultur. Acta Lapponica 1.
1950   Die lappische Zaubertrommel: Eine ethnologische Monographie. II. Die Trommel als Urkunde geistigen Lebens. Acta Lapponica 6.
1953   Swedish Contributions to Lapp Ethnography. Journal of the Royal Anthropological Institute 82:39–55.
1963   People of Eight Seasons: The Story of the Lapps. New York: Viking Press.

Mauss, Marcel
1968   (1950) A Category of the Human Spirit. Psychoanalytic Review 55:457–481.

Nickul, Karl
1977   The Lappish Nation: Citizens of 4 Countries. Bloomington: Indiana University Publications.

O'Leary, Timothy J., and Joan Steffens (compilers)
1975   Lapps' Ethnographic Bibliography, Vol. 1 and 2. New Haven, Conn.: Human Relations Area Files, Inc.

Pehrson, Robert N.
1957   The Bilateral Network of Social Relations in Konkämä. Slavic and European Series 5. Bloomington: Indiana University Publications.

Pelto, Pertti J.
1973   The Snowmobile Revolution: Technology and Social Change in the Arctic. Menlo Park, Calif.: Cummings Publishing Co.

Reuterskiöld, E.
1912   De Nordiska Lapparnas Religion. Stockholm: Populäre Etnologiske Skrifter 8.

Sahlins, Marshall
1976   Culture and Practical Reason. Chicago: University of Chicago Press.
1981   Historical Metaphors and Mythical Realities: Structure in the Early History of the Sandwich Islands Kingdom. Ann Arbor: University of Michigan Press.

Schefferus, Johannes
1971   (1673) The History of Lappland. Stockholm: Rediviva.

Schneider, David M.
1968   American Kinship: A Cultural Account. Englewood Cliffs, N.J.: Prentice-Hall.

Stephens, Sharon
1983   Changes in Sami (Lapp) Conceptions of Male and Female as a Key to Cultural Transformations in Sami History. Michigan State University. Working Papers on Women in International Development 36.
1984   Cultural Transformations in Sami (Lapp) History. Ph.D. dissertation, Anthropology Department, University of Chicago.

Tegengren, Helmer
1952   En Utdöd Lappkultur i Kemi Lappmark: Studier i Nordfinlands Kolonisationshistoria. Acta Academiae Aboensis.

Turi, Johan
1966   Turi's Book of Lapland. The Netherlands: Oosterhout N.B. Anthropological Publications.

Vilkuna, Kustaa
1971   Mikä oli lapinkylä ja sen funktio? Kalevalaseuran Vuosikirja 51:201–238.

Vorren, Ørnulv
1968   Den Samiske Bosetning. Ottar–Tromsø Museum 58 (December).

Wagner, Roy
1981   The Invention of Culture. Chicago: University of Chicago Press.